THE GIFTED
AND THE CREATIVE

Volumes based on the annual Hyman Blumberg Symposia
on Research in Early Childhood Education
Julian C. Stanley, general series editor

THE GIFTED AND THE CREATIVE: A FIFTY-YEAR PERSPECTIVE

Revised and Expanded Proceedings of the Seventh Annual
Hyman Blumberg Symposium
on Research in Early Childhood Education

EDITED BY JULIAN C. STANLEY,
WILLIAM C. GEORGE, AND CECILIA H. SOLANO

THE JOHNS HOPKINS UNIVERSITY PRESS
BALTIMORE AND LONDON

The Johns Hopkins University Press, Baltimore, Maryland 21218
The Johns Hopkins Press Ltd., London

Library of Congress Catalog Card Number 77-4790
ISBN 0–8018–1974–1
ISBN 0–8018–1975–X (pbk.)

Library of Congress Cataloging in Publication data will be found on the last printed page of this book.

To the memory of Francis Galton, Alfred Binet, Lewis M. Terman, Leta S. Hollingworth, and other pioneers in the area of intellectual talent whose ideas live on.

ACKNOWLEDGMENT

Table 7.1 was adapted and Figure 7.2 was reproduced by special permission from McGraw-Hill, Hightstown, New Jersey 08520.

CONTENTS

TABLES

FIGURES

CONTRIBUTORS

Ann H. Barbee is a research assistant for the Terman Study of the Gifted at Stanford University, Stanford, California 94305.

Lynn H. Fox is the coordinator of the Intellectually Gifted Child Study Group and an assistant professor of education in the Evening College and Summer Session of The Johns Hopkins University, Baltimore, Maryland 21218.

William C. George is the associate director of the Study of Mathematically Precocious Youth and instructor for the Evening College at The Johns Hopkins University, Baltimore, Maryland 21218.

J. W. Getzels is the R. Wendell Harrison Distinguished Service Professor in the departments of education and of behavioral sciences at the University of Chicago, Chicago, Illinois 60637.

John Curtis Gowan is the executive director of the National Association for Gifted Children, editor of the *Gifted Child Quarterly*, and Professor *Emeritus* of Education at the California State University, Northridge, California 91324.

William B. Michael is a professor of education and psychology at the University of Southern California, Los Angeles, California 90007.

Phyllis Brown Ohanian is the librarian at Staples High School in Westport, Connecticut 06880.

Pauline S. Sears is Professor *Emerita* of Education at Stanford University, Stanford, California 94305.

Cecilia H. Solano is an assistant professor of psychology at Wake Forest University, Winston-Salem, North Carolina 27109.

Julian C. Stanley is the director of the Study of Mathematically Precocious Youth and a professor of psychology at The Johns Hopkins University, Baltimore, Maryland 21218.

E. Paul Torrance is a professor of educational psychology at the University of Georgia, Athens, Georgia 30602.

George S. Welsh is a professor of psychology at the University of North Carolina, Chapel Hill, North Carolina 27514.

PREFACE

This is the seventh volume in the Blumberg series and the third one concerned with intellectual talent. It is based substantially on revised versions of papers presented at the Seventh Annual Hyman Blumberg Symposium on Research in Early Childhood Education, which was held on November 6–7, 1975, in Shriver Hall on the Homewood Campus of The Johns Hopkins University. The symposium was organized by us and chaired ably by J. W. Getzels.

This is No. 3 in the *Studies of Intellectual Precocity* series. Nos. 1 and 2 were, respectively, *Mathematical Talent: Discovery, Description, and Development*, 1974, and *Intellectual Talent: Research and Development*, 1976.

We are greatly indebted to the Amalgamated Clothing Workers of America (ACWA) for a sizable endowment to Johns Hopkins, the income from which helped finance this symposium. (The late Hyman Blumberg was the executive vice president of ACWA.) Funds from a grant by the Spencer Foundation of Chicago that started the Study of Mathematically Precocious Youth (SMPY) at Johns Hopkins were also used for this purpose. These combined resources enabled us to hold a two-day symposium that for at least one of its sessions attracted some 600 persons from all over this country and several foreign lands, including India, Ireland, New Zealand, and South Africa. The audience consisted of the following groups: specialists in the education of gifted children; child development specialists; schoolteachers, counselors, and administrators; parents, grandparents, and friends of the gifted; college students, faculty, and administration; gifted children; and other interested individuals.

We are grateful to many individuals who made this symposium and the ensuing volume possible, even though it is not feasible to list their names here. Especially, we are indebted to two administrators at The Johns Hopkins University for their continual support over the years: President Steven Muller and former Vice President for the Homewood Campus George S. Benton. Scarvia B. Anderson, James J. Gallagher, and Rogert R. Sears provided valuable editorial counsel, but of course they should not be held accountable for any imperfections that persisted into the published version.

Without the utter dedication to this project that two secretaries, Virginia S. Grim and Lois S. Sandhofer, exhibited throughout, the project would have been completed much later and less well.

Most of all, perhaps, we are indebted to the 3,000 mathematically talented, bright boys and girls whom SMPY has tried to help since 1969. Without our continuing contact with them personally, by telephone, by correspondence, and by newsletter (our *Intellectually Talented Youth Bulletin*) we would not have learned enough about intellectually talented youths to warrant our conducting a symposium concerning them and publishing a volume based on its proceedings. Splendid mathematical reasoners, we salute you!

THE GIFTED AND THE CREATIVE

1
INTRODUCTION

Julian C. Stanley

The gifted-child movement may be considered—in modern times, at least—to have begun around 1869 with the work of Francis Galton on "hereditary genius." Essentially, though, it is a product of the twentieth century. Lewis Madison Terman used Alfred Binet's intelligence test to develop his own and inaugurate during 1921–22 the first major longitudinal study of intellectually talented boys and girls. Though Terman died in 1956, systematic follow-ups of his gifted group of some 1,000 high-IQ persons born during the first score of years of this century continue. A major study based on the 1972 follow-up is reported in this volume.

The first study of Terman's group (originally, 1528 children) was a book published in 1925. To commemorate the fiftieth anniversary of the appearance of this first volume in his *Genetic Studies of Genius* series (five volumes thus far, 1925–59), I organized at The Johns Hopkins University in Baltimore, Maryland, the Lewis M. Terman Memorial Symposium on Intellectual Talent. It was held on November 6–7, 1975. The program consisted of five major papers, four reports of special programs, a two-hour panel discussion by sixteen bright youths with an adult audience, and a three-hour general discussion among specialists. This volume includes the five major papers, the general discussion, and specially commissioned papers by Phyllis B. Ohanian, E. Paul Torrance, and George S. Welsh.

The text that follows is divided into four major sections. The first, entitled "The Gifted-Child Movement," contains the keynote paper by John C. Gowan. In it he discusses trends within the movement from the latter part of the nineteenth century to the present and provides a distinctive interpretation of them. Pauline S. Sears and Ann H. Barbee examine rather thoroughly the satisfaction of the women in Terman's group with their work and personal lives. Their expert use of data gathered at several points in time over a fifty-year period for the same cohort is unparalleled in all the gifted-child literature. This is the first publication based on the 1972 follow-up of the group. Other reports

1

about that are being prepared by Lee J. Cronbach and Robert R. Sears, both of Stanford University, for publication elsewhere (e.g., see Sears 1977). Part I concludes with a sequel by Phyllis B. Ohanian regarding the attention that Terman in his 1930 volume had given to her as an infant and later to her sister and her as adolescents. It is fascinating to learn how well she and her family have achieved, both academically and in the performing arts.

The second section, entitled "Two Longitudinal Studies at The Johns Hopkins University: The Study of Mathematically Precocious Youth and the Intellectually Gifted Child Study Group," consists of two papers. The first of these is my detailed explanation of the assumptions and hypotheses underlying the large longitudinal study that my associates and I are conducting. Next, Lynn H. Fox reports on her work in the perplexing area of sex differences in mathematical aptitude and achievement. Dr. Fox, who helped start SMPY, has devised procedures that improve girls' performance in mathematics.

The third major section consists of three papers on creativity. William B. Michael's mainly concerns mathematical and scientific giftedness, especially as viewed in the light of J. P. Guilford's structure-of-intellect model. E. Paul Torrance reports findings from his distinctive and widely used approach to creativity, including his longitudinal study of creative potential. Creativity and its relationship to the disadvantaged gifted are discussed. George S. Welsh explains his "origence–intellectence" two-way classification and shows some consequences of studying creativity in this manner. These three major reports by outstanding scholars bring together somewhat different points of view that are rarely juxtaposed.

The fourth main section concludes the book with J. W. Getzels' expert editing of the long discussion among thirty-one professionals in various areas related to giftedness that followed the symposium. In it, many of the difficulties and concerns of the movement are well represented. Several basic disagreements among the discussants are evident.

In this introduction it would have been easy to discuss each paper at much greater length. That would be superfluous, however, because each of the papers speaks for itself. Together they form an ensemble that should be of considerable value to almost anyone interested in the gifted.

REFERENCE

Sears, R. R. 1977. Sources of life satisfactions of the Terman gifted men. *American Psychologist* 32(2): 119–28.

I
THE
GIFTED-CHILD
MOVEMENT

2

BACKGROUND AND HISTORY OF THE GIFTED-CHILD MOVEMENT

John Curtis Gowan

ABSTRACT

The gifted-child movement is seen as a part of humanistic psychology. Humanistic psychology, the legacy of William James, embraces first a broad humanism; second, the measurement of individual differences; third, intelligence and gifted children; fourth, creativity; fifth, development; and last, possibly parapsychology. These areas are connected by a sense of the dignity of man, by development, by measurement, and by concern for the unusual.

The first phase of Terman's Genetic Studies of Genius *(1925–59) was epoch-making in its importance for developmental psychology. This five-volume series vindicated longitudinal research and established a case for genetic influences, dispelled myths about gifted children, and laid the basis for later extensions by Oden, Sears, and others. The precision of the Stanford–Binet Intelligence Scale and the statistical procedures used afforded a strong foundation. Minor flaws included consideration of intelligence as one-dimensional and neglect of socioeconomic status, creativity, and ethnic aspects.*

Since Terman's day much attention has shifted to creativity as a major variable and gifted children as the most likely potential pool. Recent developments along these lines hold promise for increasing creative production. [For example, see the contributions to this volume by Michael, Torrance, and Welsh.]

INTRODUCTION: HUMANISTIC PSYCHOLOGY

We meet today [November 6, 1975] under auspicious circumstances. One does not realize *how* auspicious until one probes into history. In the

5

first instance, Johns Hopkins is celebrating its centennial. This university started in 1876 under the brilliant leadership of President Daniel Coit Gilman, who determined to hire only the top professors available in the world. During the next decade with their help he made this institution, at a time when Harvard and other Ivy League schools were mainly undergraduate colleges, the pacemaker in graduate education in this country. One of his first recruits was the British mathematician Dr. James Joseph Sylvester, a genius who coauthored the theory of invariance and who at this university founded the *American Journal of Mathematics* in 1878 (Bell 1937, p. 394). Sylvester's brilliant tenure at Johns Hopkins established this university's preeminence in mathematics, a tradition that has continued to this day and is seen in our host's directorship of the Study of Mathematically Precocious Youth.

A second centennial is the anniversary of the establishment of the first psychological laboratory in 1875 at Harvard University by the legendary William James.[1] One of his early students was Granville Stanley Hall, who took the first doctorate in psychology in 1878. In 1881, Hall went to The Johns Hopkins University. There he taught such students as John Dewey, J. McKeen Cattell, and Joseph Jastrow, as well as founding the *American Journal of Psychology*.[2] In 1888 Hall became president of Clark University in Worcester, Massachusetts, as well as its professor of psychology. Taking a leaf from Gilman, Hall engaged in a heroic one-man effort to upgrade the place. Besides founding the *Pedagogical Seminary* (now the *Journal of Genetic Psychology*) he brought in as speakers psychologists Burnham and Titchener, and later Freud himself, and others equally prominent later, so that under his leadership for a brief time Clark University became the fountainhead for psychological study in the United States. During this golden age, one of Clark's doctoral students was none other than the man we honor at these meetings, Lewis Madison Terman, the father of the gifted-child movement and the author of the *Genetic Studies of Genius* series (Terman 1925; Cox 1926; Terman, Burks, and Jensen 1930; Terman and Oden 1947, 1959), which started just fifty years ago.[3]

[1] William James himself lectured at Johns Hopkins in 1888–89, since President Gilman was trying to get him to join the Hopkins faculty (Allen 1967, p. 219). A similar situation occurred with C. S. Peirce, the founder of pragmatism and James' friend, in 1880–81 (Malone 1934, p. 401).

[2] Wherever he went, Hall attracted pupils who later became distinguished. It is doubtful if any other man had so much direct influence on American psychology. For Hall's delightful reminiscences of his six years at Johns Hopkins, see Hall (1923, chap. 6).

Jastrow says of his teacher, Hall: "The child study movement, the proper appreciation of the genetic principle, the inclusion of the abnormal as an integral illumination of normal phenomena, remain as evidence of his pioneering insight" (Jastrow 1930, p. 139).

[3] Hereafter the five volumes of the *Genetic Studies of Genius* will be indicated simply by their Roman numerals.

But we are not done with coincidences and anniversaries. In Terman's tenure at Stanford were many persons, either as students, laboratory workers, or gifted children. We shall mention only five: Truman L. Kelley, May V. Seagoe, Phillip J. Rulon, Robert R. Sears, and Pauline Snedden, three of whom are still alive. Kelley, who is mentioned prominently in the first volume of *Genetic Studies of Genius* as the main statistical consultant, got his doctorate at Columbia in guidance under the influence of Dewey, E. L. Thorndike, and Kilpatrick and eventually went to Harvard, where he taught, among many others, Frederick B. Davis, John C. Flanagan, John W. M. Rothney, Julian C. Stanley, and your speaker, all of whom have been involved in some phase of the gifted-child movement. Who should turn up at Harvard to help him but Phillip J. Rulon from Stanford, after taking his Ph.D. degree at the University of Minnesota. Rulon became a professor and later acting dean of the Harvard Graduate School of Education. Some of Rulon's many pupils included the host (Stanley) and the keynote speaker of this symposium. Seagoe became a professor at UCLA, where she sponsored the doctorate of your speaker. Robert Sears is a renowned professor *emeritus* of psychology at Stanford University and the chairman of the American Psychological Foundation's Committee on Gifted Children. His wife, Pauline Snedden Sears, a professor *emerita* at Stanford, is one of the speakers at these meetings. So now we come full circle and see the appropriateness of holding the convention at *this* time with *this* host, *this* chairman, and *this* speaker at *this* university. Truly, it is altogether fitting and proper that we should do this. Let us in a larger sense, then, attempt to evaluate what has happened.

The century since the founding of Johns Hopkins, since James' establishment of the first psychological lab at Harvard, and since the pioneer work of G. Stanley Hall, and the fifty years since the inception of Terman's *Genetic Studies of Genius* series have given us enough perspective to see that the movement and process about which we are talking here is something much bigger than merely the education of the gifted. It is indeed a *structure d'ensemble* of which the gifted-child movement is but one part, and perhaps it can be subsumed well under the heading of humanistic psychology. Briefly, this view finds intrinsic value in the individual, who is considered as an end and not as a behavioristic means. He/she has potential for good, for development, and for process that is much more important and much more germane than merely dealing with his quirks and ills. In short, psychology is defined by the humanists as the science of the mind or soul (from its Greek roots), and not the science of the rat. In this process, high intelligence and genius represent the earnest of the future.

This broad humanism embraced a change from indifference and prejudice to respect for the rights of all men and women, from a science of nature to a science of man, from looking without to looking within. Much innovation in educational practice has come from this area.

Concern for the qualities of exceptional human beings arises out of an exceptional concern for the qualities of all human beings, and thus it is that we find humanistic psychologists of all types interested in the rights of man and woman. John Dewey was an early exponent of these individual rights, as was Carl R. Rogers a later one. Leta S. Hollingworth, besides her eminence in the gifted-child movement, was an early champion of women's rights (Shields 1975). E. Paul Torrance has been diligent and effective in championing the rights of the uncommon student to be different, and in his concern for the creative disadvantaged student. This valuing of individual differences, this prizing of the idiosyncratic talents of the uncommon man, is the essence of guidance of gifted and creative persons.

If people have individual differences, and if we prize and value those differences, then why not measure them? This is the creed of a group of high-level, mathematically oriented measurement specialists to which many of us are proud to give our allegiance.

C. S. Peirce is the godfather of this group in the United States (as was Francis Galton in England). It includes Joseph Jastrow,[4] Frederick Kuhlmann, J. McKeen Cattell, Lewis M. Terman, Truman L. Kelley, John C. Flanagan, Phillip J. Rulon, Edward L. and Robert L. Thorndike (father and son), Louis L. Thurstone, and J. P. Guilford in this country, Charles Spearman, Cyril Burt, Godfrey H. Thomson, and Phillip E. Vernon in England, Alfred Binet in France, and many others. Always clear-headed, sometimes monomanical and waspish, seldom the *bons vivants* of our profession, these men helped bring academic respectability to behavioral science, and have set the stage for much solid advance.

Indeed, the adjacent area of intelligence and gifted children can be regarded as no more than the applied aspect of this field. Terman is typical of this group.

Measurement of individual differences involves the belief that human beings have differential talents and that these can be measured, are valuable to society, and should be cultivated. There is a very mathematical flavor to this study, but its ethic was perhaps best enunciated by Terman when he said: "The stage is set for one of the most important educational reforms of this century: a reform that would have for its end the discovery, conservation, and intensive cultivation of every kind of exceptional talent" (III, p. 474).

---

[4]Jastrow shows his membership in this group by upholding the human rights of professors and by joining with Cattell to found the American Association of University Professors (AAUP).

The next section, high intelligence and gifted children, is characterized by a change from unifactor to multifactor views of intelligence, from seeing the gifted child as having a supernormal IQ to seeing the gifted as a pool for potential creativity, and from a concept of intelligence as mechanistic and consisting of cognition and memory to a concept of intellect as emphasized by transformations, implications, and a more creative consciousness. The most typical researcher in this section was Cyril Burt.

The next section, creativity, has gone from a religious to a psychological concept, from an unknown to a turn-on variable, from connectedness to psychological openness, from a neurotic trait to an early dividend of mental health, and from a curiosity to an end in itself or a correlate of self-actualization. No one person completely typifies this new field, but it owes much to Guilford and Thurstone.

The next section, development, is also quite new. It shows change from continuous growth concepts to discontinuous developmental concepts, from separate views of development to fused views of concurrent development of psychomotor, affective, and cognitive processes, and from tests that do not measure developmental process to those that do. Jean Piaget and Erik H. Erikson are typical here.

A final section, still not well defined, still controversial, but still traceable from William James onward (though definitely not supported by Terman himself), is parapsychology. It has gone from quacks, spooks, and psychics to a more scientific investigation of the unknown that has been legitimatized by being admitted to the American Association for the Advancement of Science as a field of study. Finally, it has progressed from a belief in superstitious folklore to an emerging feeling by some psychologists that all phenomena of whatever kind are natural and can be accounted for, though we may not at present be in possession of all knowledge. William MacDougall, the British scientist who headed the psychology department at Harvard and then went to Duke, is typical here.[5]

Common to all these areas are the following overriding characteristics:

1. A sense of the innate dignity, uniqueness, and worth of human individuality, which is seen as something transcending social groups, laws, restrictions, and generalities. The human being is not merely a reactive creature, but is an end in himself or herself.

---

[5]Another very prominent figure was none other than Cyril Burt, probably the leading British educational psychologist of the twentieth century and a leader in his interest in gifted children in that country, and also on record as affirming the reality of parapsychological phenomena. On this matter he said (1967): "I am convinced that there is only one basic Order—which appears as logical or mathematical to our cognitive intuition, aesthetic to our emotional intuition, and moral to the volitional or conative. And it is essentially numinous."

2. A sense of development, of process, of growth, of change, and of becoming or unfoldment. Evolution and man's life are seen as twin aspects of the debut of new powers, an expanding concept of intellect.

3. A mode of mathematical measurement that seeks to quantify data wherever possible but not to reject data which appear unquantified. A scientific rather than a superstitious approach to the unknown that views the universe as subject to natural law but has the modesty to believe that we may not yet understand all there is to know.

4. Concern for the unusual in persons, things, and events, particularly for an understanding and appreciation and valuing of the unusual, because of the possibility that it is through the examination of the unusual that we have the best chance of gaining greater knowledge about things, events, and ourselves.

Having now set the state of the gifted-child movement as a related component of humanistic psychology, and having stated that a great many researchers in the gifted-child area owe their background and training to humanistic psychology in general and James and Hall in particular, let us turn to the second part of this presentation, a detailed examination of the work of the leader of the gifted-child movement, Lewis M. Terman.

THE WORK OF TERMAN

Although intelligence had been recognized since the time of the Romans as the first aspect of character, no one up to the beginning of the twentieth century had been able to solve the puzzle of measuring it. Even the English statistical genius, Galton, the forerunner of interest in the able, had failed to conquer this problem, despite the fact that his book entitled *Hereditary Genius* (1869) contained an ingenious method of getting around the problem in the case of eminent men, so that he was able to predict accurately the regression toward the mean which occurs in their offspring.[6]

It was the genius of Binet, a French psychologist assigned to produce a test which would screen out mentally retarded children from the Parisian school system, that produced the first effective developmental scale. For Binet and Simon (1905) solved this problem by finding out at which ages ordinary children complete certain tasks, such as tying a shoelace or telling the cardinal point of the compass. They then arranged

---

[6]In their autobiographies both Spearman (1930, p. 331) and Terman (1932, p. 331) independently pay tribute to Galton as their most important influence, although for Terman the influence of Binet was also great.

these in serial order by age. Then by measuring a given child on this scale one could tell the child's "mental age," a concept introduced three years later by Binet and Simon (1908) in their revised scale.

This breakthrough advance in developmental psychology was hailed around the world. Some, like Henry H. Goddard, were willing merely to translate the scale into English and use it for testing many children. But here is where the outstanding genius of Lewis M. Terman showed itself. He perceived the following extremely important extensions:

1. What Binet and Simon had discovered was really a method of measuring intellectual developmental progress in *all* children, not just the feebleminded; hence the scale could be modified to all children, and particularly adapted for the measurement of gifted children.[7]

2. The rate of intellectual developmental progress with respect to chronological age represents a ratio less than 1 in the case of the below-average child but greater than 1 in the case of the above-average child. This ratio is the rate of intellectual developmental progress.[8]

Terman multiplied this rate by 100 (to avoid decimals) and named it the *intelligence quotient* (abbreviated as IQ). The phrase quickly passed into the vernacular and became one of the most popular psychological inventions ever made. In this gigantic advance Terman set the stage for developmental psychology and earned for himself lasting fame. The rest of his life was to be spent in little else than the application, measurement, verification, and publication of these principles in his *Genetic Studies of Genius* and elsewhere.

Lewis Madison Terman, the twelfth of fourteen children, was born a few miles southeast of Indianapolis, Indiana, in Johnson County, January 15, 1877, to a farming family of old American stock (Terman 1932, p. 297). Though bright and bookish, he speaks in his autobiography of having feelings of inferiority and introversion (p. 303). Straight from a one-room school, he began attending Central Normal College at Danville, Indiana, in 1892, eventually getting his certificate there in 1898 after several intermittent stints as a rural teacher to gain funds to continue (p. 305). After serving as a high school principal for three years, during which time he married another teacher, Anna Minton, he entered the junior year at Indiana University in 1901 with a wife and child and got his M.A. there in 1903 under Professor Lindley, writing his thesis on leadership (Terman 1904). He went to Clark University that fall (p. 312).

---

[7]See Thorndike (1975) for a careful statistical analysis of the Stanford–Binet and much on Binet and Terman besides. Highlights include the increase from 12 to 16 points in the standard deviation of the L and M forms (Terman 1937) and the upward creep in IQs in the general population (due perhaps to TV). Also, see Stanley (1974).

[8]Terman acknowledges that he used Stern's idea and cites the source in a footnote. It is interesting that Stern in a lengthy autobiography (1930, pp. 335–88) never mentions the fact.

Clark University in Worcester, Massachusetts, was in its heydey under the illustrious President G. Stanley Hall, and Terman has left us a rhapsodic account of the intellectual stimulus and ideal learning conditions there (Terman 1932, pp. 312–16). Among his fellow students were Frederick Kuhlmann and Arnold Gesell. In 1905 Terman received his Ph.D.[9] with a study of seven bright and seven dull boys, and became principal of the San Bernardino (California) High School that fall (pp. 218–20). Next year he came to the Los Angeles State Normal School (now UCLA, but at that time on the old Vermont Campus), and stayed there four years.

During the summer of 1910 his friend Huey, from Clark days, who was dying of tuberculosis, visited Terman and urged him to undertake a study of Binet's new scale (pp. 322–23). Huey had already recommended Terman in his place for a job at Stanford that fall, and Terman went there, never to move again.

The next several years at Stanford were devoted to feverish work on a revision of the Binet scale in line with fresh insights Terman had and with research, writing, and refining and testing the new scale, which he modestly called the Stanford–Binet. Thus in 1916 was published the Stanford–Binet Individual Test of Intelligence, the most popular, authoritative, and (with its revisions) long-lived test of intelligence in existence, and one accorded the unprecedented honor of becoming the criterion of its own validity, for during a great portion of the present century "intelligence" has virtually been considered to be what a Stanford–Binet measures.

World War I vastly increased public interest in intelligence testing as Terman joined other experts on the psychological staff of Robert M. Yerkes, whose task force developed a group intelligence test for the Army known as Army Alpha. Given to hundreds of thousands of soldiers, it familiarized the public with the concept of an "IQ." It was not long before intelligence testing became a part of every up-to-date school system program, leading to widespread administration of individual and group intelligence tests during the 1920s.

Returning to Stanford, Terman continued to prosper. A research fellowship was granted in 1919, and Truman L. Kelley was added to the

---

[9]Other biographical notices include *Who Was Who in America* (1960, p. 846); Boring's (1959) piece with photo and bibliography; Hilgard's (1957) work with quotations from two unpublished and autobiographical papers; Seagoe's (1975) book; Murchison's full-length authorized biography (Terman 1932), which contains Terman's autobiography; and Sears' (1957) obituary notice, from which the following is quoted: "Terman was rather slight in build, with reddish hair, a soft voice, and a warm and engaging smile. He was a shy man whose outward warmth masked an inner retiringness. Social interaction seemed more fatiguing to him than to most men. . . . He was a tireless worker, despite his frail health, eager for achievement. . . . With all his gentleness, he could be a fierce fighter for his ideas. . . . What truly fascinated him was the art and science of measurement (p. 979).

staff in 1920. In 1921 the Commonwealth fund appropriated $20,000 for a study of 1,000 gifted children. This was the start of the *Genetic Studies of Genius* series, which enterprise was to occupy the rest of Terman's life and extend beyond it in perhaps the most remarkable and valuable longitudinal psychological study ever undertaken. Through the years, over a quarter of a million dollars would be raised to fund this continuing study, an interesting sidelight being that the largest part came from Terman himself in plowed-back test royalties (V, p. viii). Assistants were trained,[10] schools and pupils located (eventually there were to be 1,528 Terman children, some being present here today) (IV, p. 72), and the project was underway with the first publication of Volume I, fifty years ago in 1925.[11] It has continued long after Terman's death in 1956, as seen by the Oden (1968) follow-up of the group and chapter 3 in this volume. The study is scheduled to go on until the demise of the last Terman child during the twenty-first century.

But this history is so much better recounted by Terman himself in the first chapter of volume I that we will not further rehearse it here.[12] Instead, we shall summarize the most important or outstanding results, and then analyze his work:

1. The gifted are not homogeneous, but differ among themselves in many ways (III, p. 472). Considerable stability of IQ is one of the few commonalities (III, p. 425).

2. The stereotypes that the gifted child is either puny, asocial, or prepsychotic or that high intelligence is akin to insanity were discounted by the facts (I, chaps. 6, 8, 9, 16; IV, chaps. 3, 4, 9, 10).

---

[10]Kelley was the assistant director. The four field assistants were Florence Fuller, Florence L. Goodenough (later of *Draw a Man* Test fame), Helen Marshall, and Dorothy H. Yates. The office assistant was Giles M. Ruch. Goodenough and Ruch later took doctorates with Terman (I, p. 6).

On page 327 in his autobiography Terman (1932) names his early doctoral students Robert G. Bernreuter (author of an early test of personality), Barbara S. Burks (who coauthored one of the five volumes), Catharine M. Cox, and Arthur S. Otis.

[11]The date of the Foreword to volume I was January 15, 1925 (Terman's 48th birthday).

[12]Terman's prejudices and opinions (1932, pp. 329–30) make interesting reading, embracing as they do a belief in testing and guidance, a damnation of associationism and behaviorism, and the following controversial belief quoted verbatim: "That the major differences between children of high and low IQ, and the major differences in the intelligence test scores of certain races, as Negroes and whites, will never be fully accounted for on the environmental hypothesis." In follow-up to the Terman quote above, Hilgard (1957) in his eulogy of Terman reports that this paragraph in Terman's own copy of this book has a line through it with the following notation in Terman's handwriting: "I am less sure of this now in 1951 than I was then." Boring (1959, p. 432) reports the same. Terman was against censorship, prohibition, and "most acts of moral reformers and orthodox religion." He favored Havelock Ellis, Galton, and Binet. He "admired" Galton, but Binet was his favorite because of his "insight and open-mindedness, and his rare charm of personality" (Boring 1959, pp. 330–31).

3. The best way to identify the most intelligent child in a class was not to ask the teacher, but to consult the record book for the youngest (I, p. 33). [Cf. Stanley 1976*b*.]

4. The superiority in intelligence is maintained (V, p. 144).

5. Acceleration at all levels is beneficial (I, pp. 285, 629; IV, pp. 281; Oden 1968, p. 90).

6. Gifted students who did not attend college had the same intellectual level as Ph.D. candidates (V, p. 144).

7. Research on the difference within the gifted group between the most and the least successful men showed that socioeconomic status (SES) and college education of the father were the major factors, as well as force of character of the gifted person himself (IV, pp. 311–51, especially p. 352; Oden 1968, pp. 62, 70, 72, 77).

8. Mental age of the gifted group continues to increase through middle age (V, p. 157), especially as shown by Part I scores on the Concept Mastery Test.

9. The mean IQ of the children of the Terman group was 132.7 (IV, p. 238; V, p. 141).

10. There were several times as many very high IQ persons (over 150) in the Terman group as is predicted by the normal curve of probability (I, p. 633).

11. Males exceeded females in the general sample 116/100; in the high school sample by 212/100 (III, p. 471).

In analysis of Terman's work, the following may be said:

1. Both the Stanford–Binet Individual Test of Intelligence and the longitudinal *Genetic Studies of Genius* were epoch-making in their importance for developmental psychology. The social benefit of these two products makes them the ultimate monument to their author.

2. It is remarkable what a strong case is made for hereditary influences when one reads the five volumes consecutively. Of course, the interaction effects between the factors of environment and heredity were too little realized and investigated in Terman's time.

3. One is surprised at the neglect of the socioeconomic status factor. Of course, SES was not well understood in Terman's time, but it is obvious upon rereading the material that it is a prime interacting variable (I, p. 83; IV, pp. 183, 315). For example, the A versus C group studies (IV, pp. 311–52; Oden 1968, pp. 62–67) fairly reek with SES influence. Given Terman's interest in quantification and measurement, it is surprising that he did not go after this variable.[13]

---

[13]Compare his work with the illuminating study of Bonsall and Stefflre (1955), which showed that most of the personality variance between gifted and normal children is due to the SES interaction.

4. With the advantages of hindsight one is also surprised that Terman was not able to get a better criterion variable in the measurement of "life success." It is remarkable that interviews with grown-up gifted children did not lead to an (at least) intuitive perception of creativity or some of its correlates, such as self-actualization, or some other aspect of development as discovered later by Maslow or Erikson (V, pp. 50–51, 101, 151; Oden 1968, p. 67).

5. One is impressed with the remarkable accuracy of the Stanford-Binet and the excellent research, development, and norming that went into it. For this we are indebted to the work of three able statisticians, Truman L. Kelley, Quinn McNemar, and Giles M. Ruch.

6. The ability of Terman to administer, delegate, and inspire good morale in his staff was remarkable. This allowed the project to continue, but not, however, without a certain discursiveness in print, which is evident in the *Genetic Studies of Genius* volumes themselves. They are descriptive and factual rather than at all speculative. They plod, they report facts, they summarize. They do not theorize, explain reasons, or advocate hypotheses. Cumulatively, they are persuasive but not often eloquent.[14]

7. One is impressed with the strong Jewish component in the gifted-child population, all out of proportion to the population frequency in California at that time (I, p. 59; IV, pp. 296–310).

8. Again with the advantage of hindsight, the major mistakes or omissions which were made were as follows: (a) the consideration of intelligence as one-dimensional; (b) the lack of control of the socioeconomic status (SES) factor; (c) the neglect of creativity; (d) the lack of explicit guiding hypotheses; and (e) the failure to investigate, control, or balance the ethnic aspects. Admittedly, this is holding up a harsh standard, since most of these matters were not fully explicated at the time of the inception of the study. Perhaps it would be better to say that these are ways in which the study now seems dated.

9. The work clearly demonstrated the extreme value of longitudinal research because it brought out facts (such as the continuation of increase in vocabulary into middle life) that would have been impossible to ascertain otherwise.

10. We note for the future some issues that Terman emphasized, while the present conventional wisdom appears to discount. Time will tell if his was prejudice or prescience: (a) importance of the genetic factor; (b) method of biographical analysis employed by Cox in volume II; (c)

---

[14]Terman says in his autobiography (1932, p. 328): "I am fully aware that my researches have not contributed very greatly to the theory of mental measurement."

importance of force of character in life success (e.g., A/C research, IV, p. 352); and (d) differential in racial intelligence (Terman 1932, p. 330).

11. The evidence of these studies is that Terman was a better researcher, methodologist, and administrator than he was a theorist. He was strong on measurement but weak on rationale. With the exception of the concept of IQ (which he apparently got from Stern), he seldom shows breakthrough ideas. This is not to fault a great man unduly, but in comparison with the top figures in the field, one fails to find in his writings the kind of innovative germinal ideas found in Freud, Maslow, Erikson, or Piaget.

12. Terman's place in history is secure, but the twenty-first century may recast his role from that of the father of the gifted-child movement to a larger context as an intuitive humanistic psychologist, one of the pioneers in developmental psychology, and as a methodologist and measurement expert who laid a strong and secure foundation for the developmental measurement of the expanding abilities of man.

THE FOLLOWERS

We have given the lion his share of recognition. It is now time for summary notices of some of the lesser but nevertheless important figures in the gifted-child movement.[15]

First we should pay respects to two brilliant women, Maria Montessori and Leta S. Hollingworth, both interested in gifted children, women's rights (Shields 1975), and classroom procedures to stimulate young children properly. Hollingworth's work at the Speyer School in New York is legendary. She also wrote two influential books (1926, 1942). She was the leader of a number of dedicated women around the United States, such as Dorothy Norris (Major Work Classes, Cleveland) and Cora Danielson in Los Angeles, who did much to implement the ideas popularized by Terman in the nation's school systems in the 1930s. For an insightful biography of Leta Hollingworth by her husband, see Harry Hollingworth (1943).

Some other school personnel of note included Bristow (New York), Hobson (Brookline, Massachusetts), Bonsall and Bowman (Los Angeles), Williams (Portland, Oregon), Barbour (San Diego), and Pregler (Pittsburgh). University professors prominently interested in the gifted included Pressey, whose work on acceleration was very helpful (1949, 1954); Lehman, who did remarkable studies of age and creativity (1953); Whipple, who was involved in early National Society for the Study of

---

[15]Citations for these various persons can be found in Gowan (1965).

Education (NSSE) yearbooks on the gifted in 1920 and 1924 (1924); Witty, who was an eminent early worker with many influential doctoral students (1951); Barbe, whose book of readings was influential (1965); Cutts, Worcester, Drews, Freehill, French, and Fliegler, prominent as speakers, authors, and in associations; Goldberg, who with Passow did excellent research at the Horace Mann–Lincoln School; Laycock, the most vocal Canadian; Oswalt and Strang, popular and well-prepared writers and speakers; and Norris and Sumption, early writers in the area (Sumption, Norris, and Terman, 1950).

One wishes to note especially the many yearbooks of the National Society for the Study of Education that were devoted to the topic of the gifted; 1920, 1924, 1940, and 1950 are all examples of years when this occurred.

We must now notice some individuals outside the strictly gifted-child field who have had important impact. The first of these is Robert J. Havighurst, a University of Chicago professor whose research on the effects of SES on achievement has been very helpful. He is one of the few investigators who has dared to look at IQ in terms of SES levels. A second individual is Calvin W. Taylor, one of the earliest workers in the creativity area and the sponsor of important conferences at the University of Utah in the 1950s, as well as the editor of several books on the subject (Taylor 1964*a*, 1964*b*, 1964*c*; Taylor and Barron 1963). The third is Sidney Parnes of the University of Buffalo's Creativity Workshop. As the protégé of Alex Osborn, who got it started in 1955, the Osborn–Parnes group has had a significant and growing impact on the techniques for helping gifted children to become creative (Osborn 1954, Parnes and Harding 1962).

Among these practicalists, there is one who stands out as second only to Terman in the importance of his efforts for the gifted—Charles E. Bish of the National Education Association's Carnegie Academically Talented Project. While not advocating any new ideas, he contrived to bring the present knowledge to the education establishment in general. Approximately half a million copies of his green brochures were distributed, and his *Accent on Talent* went to virtually every schoolhouse in America for two years. He spoke the language of administrators and carried the message for the gifted all over the United States. But his most ambitious work was bringing together the leaders in the field for better communication among themselves, for concerted action, and for the rapid dissemination of new ideas. *Productive Thinking in Education* (Aschner and Bish 1968) grew out of such conferences and really popularized the Guilford Structure of Intellect (SOI) concepts. In no small part the renaissance in interest in the gifted we are now experiencing belongs to his efforts of ten years ago.

The remarkable thing about the followers of Terman during the decades from 1920 to 1960 was that so little new was discovered, and so little conceptual advance made. One reason we find little development in the field is that the gifted-child movement is not really a discipline at all but merely an applied area of the measurement of individual differences. It is hence the development section of a larger gestalt, which embraces theory and procedures for creative development of all the talents of mankind. It is consequently not complete in itself, and is best understood merely as the educational applications consequent on new ways of looking at the development of talent. For this reason the present writer has emphasized a larger whole of humanistic psychology and developmental process in the individual.

We shall therefore conclude with some sampling of important research findings in the larger area that have some semblance of theoretical advance or innovation for the education of gifted children. First we need to note the enormous changes in American life that have taken place since Terman commenced his *Genetic Studies of Genius* fifty years ago.

In comparison with those changes in American values and life styles, it is really surprising to find only modest changes in theory and research on the academically talented during this period. Perhaps this failure has been due to the fact that we have been looking in the wrong places. In the long journey of development from an art to a science, thinkers are generally saddled with a number of specious but easy-to-accept concepts that are no better than symptoms of the problem, having no real relationship to the basic underlying variables. For example, for two thousand years science slept while philosophers based their theories on the attractive but fallacious concept of the "four elements" (earth, air, fire, and water). In the nineteenth century when scientists finally came to an understanding of what elements really were (as seen in Mendeleev's periodic table), this heuristic concept fueled a blast-off of scientific advance that has now literally put mankind in orbit. It is probable that a similar escalation in behavioral science only awaits discovery of the basic parameters. Nowhere is this phenomenon better seen than in gifted-child research, which has turned up dry hole after dry hole in such investigations as (a) grouping and enrichment, (b) underachievement, and (c) personality studies of the gifted. Furthermore, we still cannot answer the following basic questions for lack of proper research and/or theory:

1. How can we intervene educationally to promote more creative adults?

2. What should differentiated curricula for the gifted be like?

3. How should programs for educating gifted children be administered, and what cost-benefit ratios should be sought?

4. What are the specific environmental details favoring or retarding the development of creativity in gifted children?

What are the significant research milestones that do stand out during this past quarter-century? I would like to select twelve such benchmarks which seem to vary from the ordinary in that they contain some definitive departure from the past.

First and foremost is Guilford's Structure of Intellect theory (Guilford 1967; and chapter 7 in the present volume). This factor-analytic advance over Spearman and Terman's unifactor concept of "*g*" has many implications for identification and curriculum intervention, most of which have not yet been explicated.

Second is the middle-life follow-up study by Terman and Oden (1959) on their gifted group, which among other things showed that (1) mental age in these persons kept increasing through age fifty, and (2) one third of the children of these "Termites" scored above the 130-IQ level. The developmental and genetic implications of these two facts need further emphasis, which can come only through more longitudinal studies, of which we have four at present. Oden's 1968 monograph is the latest published report of this work. See chapter 3 in this volume and Sears (1977) for new follow-up data.

Third is the importance of "predisposing guidance," as noted in Brandwein's (1955) forgotten classic. While we have accepted similar facts with regard to athletic coaches, Brandwein was the first to spell out the necessary parameters for the training of scientific talent.

Fourth is the remarkable study of Bonsall and Stefflre (1955) on the personality of gifted children, which showed that personality differences were not due directly to intelligence itself but instead were associated with differences in socioeconomic class. As long as we continue to ignore SES differences, we shall be in the position of the animals in Orwell's animal farm ("all the animals are equal, but the pigs are more equal than anyone else"), but if we would pay attention to this important auxiliary variable, we might find ways through early educational intervention to compensate for educationally debilitating effects of low SES.

Fifth, the Pegnato and Birch (1959) research on identification procedures deserves much more careful attention. They showed that both the efficiency and the effectiveness of various identification screens were much less than had been assumed, and thus laid the basis for sound research on identification. Unfortunately, others have generally not followed their insightful lead.

Sixth was the Getzels and Jackson study on the interrelationships between creativity and giftedness (1962). This book changed the focus of gifted-child education, making it auxiliary to the production of creative adults.

Seventh has been the multivaried investigations of Torrance (1962, 1964, chapter 8 of this volume) on developing creativity in children and his attempts to measure it by means of the Torrance tests. While we still do not know the reason for the slump in creativity at the fourth grade, his research has fueled a generation of younger scholars.

Eighth has been the Aschner (Aschner 1961) and Gallagher studies at Illinois in using the SOI in the classroom to develop curricula. It is a pity that this work was not further funded and that the professional activities of Aschner were cut short. In later times, this type of activity has been forwarded by Williams (1971), Meeker (1975), and Gray and Youngs (1975).

Ninth was the De Witt Clinton High School study of Goldberg and Passow (1959), one of the few adequate school surveys of the gifted ever recorded. It showed among other things that improvement in under-achievers required assistance with learning skills and identification with a supportive teacher.

Tenth has been the work of our host (Stanley, Keating, and Fox 1974; Keating 1976*a*) on the Study of Mathematically Precocious Youth (SMPY). Building on the work of Pressey (1949) and others, it has contributed many useful understandings about the effects of acceleration on the stimulation of particular aspects of talent that "fixes" and transforms the talent predispositions into creativity and achievement. This study has the additional advantage of being one of the few longitudinal studies recently launched. Also, it emphasizes facilitation by means of educational acceleration much more than other longitudinal studies of the intellectually gifted have done (Stanley 1976*a*, 1976*c*).

Eleventh has been the developmental theories of Erikson and Piaget on cognitive and affective developmental stages. These have been fused by the writer (Gowan 1972) into the Periodic Development Stage theory, which for the first time attempts explanation of some of the things that cause gifted children to develop as they do. (Example: The reaching of verbal readiness while still in the initiative–intuitive "fantasy" stage from age four to six gives the gifted child a much better hold on verbal creativity.)

Last but not least has been the progression of identification procedures from the Stanford–Binet type of test to biographical information as seen in the Alpha Biographical Inventory of Taylor (1964*c*), the doctoral thesis of Malone (see Malone and Moonan 1975), and some of the work of Khatena (1976) and Bruch (1968). This important advance is just beginning to make its presence felt.

As one looks at this research in an effort to classify it, one finds four items in the area of intelligence and its identification, three in the area of curriculum, and two each in the areas of development and creativity. These last four are evidently the areas that need pursuing. In an effort to make that pursuit more productive in the years ahead, we suggest that a shift should be made from *surface symptoms* to underlying *basic concepts*, as follows:

1. Surface symptom: *intelligence;* basic concept: *Structure of Intellect factors.* Research will be retarded as long as we retain the misleading stereotype of unifactor intelligence; we need to adopt fully the concept that there are many factors of intellect.

2. Surface symptom: *gifted child;* basic concept: *creative individual.* The concept that we should focus on a gifted child defined as one who has an arbitrary intelligence quotient is no longer viable. In the first place, a definition depending upon an arbitrary level of IQ is obviously superficial. In the second place, giftedness represents only potentiality; the major variable is *creativity.* We should redefine giftedness therefore as the potential to become verbally creative, and talentedness as the potential to become creative in other ways, such as in mathematics or the performing arts.

3. Surface symptom: *chronological growth;* basic concept; *developmental stages.* Development is to growth as quality is to quantity. Development is stepwise, epigenetic, and discontinuous; growth is continuous and in the form of an exponential curve (but see Keating 1976*b*).

4. Surface symptom: *acceleration, enrichment, and grouping;* basic concept: *a qualitatively differentiated curriculum capable of inducing creative performance based on the stimulation of SOI factors at appropriate developmental levels.* We use the phrase "stimulation of the factors of intellect" rather than "increase" of them, because we conceive the SOI factors to consist of discrete potentialities that, like the emulsion on a photographic film, need to be exposed to the stimulation of light (or, in this case, education by a mentor). That causes a permanent fixation in a discrete skill analogous to the exposure and development of a film. Lacking this stimulation, these potentialities, like the unexposed film emulsion, age and lose at least some of their potential. This education is the hardest task to accomplish; it requires a creative and supportive approach as well as a strong subject background and educational expertise on the part of the curriculum developer, plus knowledge both of SOI and developmental theory. It is, however, absolutely indispensible if we are properly to perform our task as teachers of the able.

Let us take a leaf from physical education, where all this is so much clearer. There a coach knows what he is looking for: athletic performance. He recruits likely candidates and stimulates whatever abilities they present; he thus both recruits and develops athletic talent. He would never think of suggesting that a man eight feet tall become a coxswain instead of a basketball player or that a man five feet tall should reverse the roles. He has a qualitatively different curriculum, which is practiced intensively, and no one regards him as an elitist for insisting that his charges have special and extra training. For him physical education is the stimulation, to their ultimate maximum, of the talents presented by his students. And when he does this, we honor him, pay him a large salary, and brag that he has produced an All-American player or an Olympic star.

When our society wakes up to the fact that the production of creative talent is equally as important as the production of professional football players, perhaps even a little more so, we will be able to face the challenges of this and the next century with a mentality somewhat advanced from that of the Roman emperors. "Bread and circuses" may have been palliative for the Roman mobs as "hamburgers and TV" are for us today, but only creative talent will solve some of the more pressing challenges of this and the next century. The youth we educate today will be just in time for that encounter. It is not a bit too early to begin our considerable task.

About eight thousand years ago prehistoric man was suddenly catapulted into history as the result of an astonishing social discovery. Previous to this, small bands of nomadic tribes had roamed a large hunting area looking for game and gathering live fruits and vegetables wild. Then someone found that if one domesticated animals and plants, one could have a ready supply of food always at hand in a confined space. Thus were agriculture and civilization born; man escalated into history, and to the possibility of a far greater population on a given land mass. We are still reaping the benefits of that change, but our continuing ecological crises show us that we are nearing the end of that period. Fortunately, we are on the brink of another momentous discovery that will have even greater impact on cultural and personal escalation.

Heretofore we have harvested creativity wild. We have used as creative only those persons who stubbornly remained creative despite all efforts of the family, religion, education, and politics to grind it out of them, in the prosecution of which men and women have been punished, flogged, silenced, imprisoned, tortured, ostracized, and killed. Jesus, Socrates, Huss, Lavosier, Lincoln, Gandhi, the Kennedys, and King are good examples. As a result of these misguided efforts, our society produces only a small percentage of its potential of creative individuals, and they are the ones with the most uncooperative dispositions. If we learn to domesticate creativity—that is, to enhance rather than deny it in our culture—we can increase the number of creative persons in our midst severalfold. That would put the number and percent of such individuals over the "critical mass" point. When this level is reached in a culture, as it was in Periclean Athens, the Renaissance, the Aufklarung, the Court of the Sun King, Elizabethean England, and our own Federalist Fathers, an escalation of creativity results and civilization makes a great leap forward. We can have a golden age of this type, such as the world has never seen; I am convinced that it will occur early in the twenty-first century. But we must make preparations now, and the society we save will be our own.

The alternatives are too dreadful for even a Huxley or an Orwell to contemplate.

In conclusion, if we may be permitted a peep at the future, we see an integrated science of human development and talent. The gestalt we are talking about there is at present at best a shore dimly seen, but it is the coming science of man of the twenty-first century. A genius is always a forerunner, and the best minds of this age foresee the dawn of that one. Then all of these branches of humanistic psychology will be welded together in a *structure d'ensemble*, greater than interest in the gifted, greater than interest in creativity, greater, in fact, than anything except the potential of man himself. We may come from dust, but our destiny is in the stars. Thoreau, the rustic seer, long ago foresaw that day; in the last sentence of *Walden* (1954) he prophesied about it saying: "That day is yet to dawn, for the sun is only a morning star." Toynbee tells us that each civilization leaves its monument and its religion. Our monument is on the moon, and the "religion" our culture will bequeath is the coming science of man and his infinite potential. This potential is truly infinite, because man may be part animal but he is also part of the noumenon. And as Schroedinger (1950), insightfully observed, "The 'I' that observes the universe is the same 'I' that created it."

The present powers of genius are merely the earnest of greater powers to be unfolded. You need not take my word for this. Listen instead to the words of the greatest genius of our age, Albert Einstein (1972):

> A human being is part of the whole, called by us "Universe;" a part limited in time and space. He experiences himself, his thoughts and feelings as something separated from the rest—a kind of optical delusion of his consciousness. This delusion is a kind of prison for us, restricting us to our personal desires and to affection for a few persons nearest us. Our task must be to free ourselves from this prison by widening our circle of compassion to embrace all living creatures and the whole of nature in its beauty. Nobody is able to achieve this completely, but the striving for such achievement is, in itself, a part of the liberation and a foundation for inner security.

REFERENCES

Allen, G. W. 1967. *William James, a biography.* New York: Viking Press.

Aschner, M. J. 1961. *The productive thinking of gifted children in the classroom.* Urbana, Ill.: University of Illinois Institute on Research on Exceptional Children. (Mimeographed.)

———, and Bish, C. E. 1968. *Productive thinking in education* (rev. ed.) Washington, D.C.: National Education Association.

Barbe, W. B. (ed.). 1965. *Psychology and education of the gifted: Selected readings.* New York: Appleton-Century-Crofts.

Bell, E. T. 1937. *Men of mathematics.* New York: Simon and Schuster.

Binet, A., and Simon, T. 1905. Méthodes nouvelles pour le diagnostic du niveau intellectuel des anormaux. *L'année psychologique* 11: 191–244.

———. 1908. Le développement de l'intelligence chez les enfants. *L'année psychologique* 14: 1–94.

Bonsall, M., and Stefflre, B. 1955. The temperament of gifted children. *California Journal of Educational Research* 6: 162–65.

Boring, E. G. 1959. Lewis Madison Terman: 1877–1956. *Biographical Memoirs of the National Academy of Sciences* 33: 414–40.

Brandwein, P. 1955. *The gifted child as a future scientist.* New York: Harcourt Brace Jovanovich.

Bruch, C. 1968. *The creative Binet.* Athens, Ga.: University of Georgia. (Mimeographed.)

Cox, C. M. 1926. The early mental traits of three thousand geniuses. *Genetic studies of genius,* vol. II. Stanford, Calif.: Stanford University Press.

Einstein, A. 1972. (As quoted in *The New York Times,* March 29, 1972, p. 24, col. 6).

Galton, F. 1869. *Hereditary genius.* London: Macmillan.

Getzels, J. W., and Jackson, P. W. 1962. *Creativity and intelligence.* New York: Wiley.

Goldberg, M., and Passow, A. H. 1959. A study of underachieving gifted. *Educational Leadership* 16: 121–25.

Gowan, J. C. 1965. *Annotated bibliography on creativity and giftedness.* Northridge, Calif.: San Fernando Valley State College Foundation.

———. 1972. *The development of the creative individual.* San Diego, Calif.: Robert R. Knapp.

Gray, C. E., and Youngs, R. 1975. Utilizing the divergent production matrix of the structure-of-intellect model in the development of teaching strategies. *Gifted Child Quarterly* 19(4): 271, 290–300.

Guilford, J. P. 1967. *The nature of human intelligence.* New York: McGraw-Hill.

Hall, G. S. 1923. *Life and confessions of a psychologist.* New York: Appleton.

Hilgard, E. R. 1957. Lewis Madison Terman. *American Journal of Psychology* 70: 472–79.

Hollingworth, H. L. 1943. *Leta Stetter Hollingworth: A biography.* Lincoln, Nebr.: University of Nebraska Press.

Hollingworth, L. S. 1926. *Gifted children: Their nature and nurture.* New York: Macmillan.

———. 1942. *Children above 180 IQ, Stanford–Binet: Origin and development.* Yonkers-on-Hudson, N.Y.: World Book.

Jastrow, J. 1930. Autobiography. In C. A. Murchison (ed.), *A history of psychology in autobiography,* vol. 1. Worcester, Mass.: Clark University Press, pp. 135–62.

Keating, D. P. (ed.). 1976a. *Intellectual talent: Research and development.* Baltimore, Md.: The Johns Hopkins University Press.

———. 1976*b*. A Piagetian approach to intellectual precocity. In D. P. Keating (ed.), *Intellectual talent: Research and development*. Baltimore, Md.: The Johns Hopkins University Press, pp. 90–99.

Khatena, J. 1976. Imagination imagery of children and the production of analogy. *Gifted Child Quarterly* 19(4): 310–15.

Lehman, H. C. 1953. *Age and achievement*. Princeton, N.J.: Princeton University Press.

Malone, C. E., and Moonan, W. J. 1975. Behavioral identification of gifted children. *Gifted Child Quarterly* 19(4): 271, 301–06.

Malone, D. 1934. Charles Sanders Peirce. *Dictionary of American Biography*, vol. VII, part 2. New York: Scribner's.

Meeker, M. 1975. *SOI in the classroom*. El Segundo, Calif.: *SOI Institute*, 214 Main Street.

Oden, M. H. 1968. The fulfillment of promise: 40-year follow-up of the Terman gifted group. *Genetic Psychology Monographs* 77: 3–93.

Osborn, A. F. 1954. *Applied imagination: Principles and procedures of creative problem solving*. New York: Scribner's.

Parnes, S. J., and Harding, H. R. (eds.). 1962. *A source book for creative thinking*. New York: Scribner's.

Pegnato, C. C., and Birch, J. W. 1959. Locating gifted children in junior high school. *Exceptional Children* 25: 300–04.

Pressey, S. L. 1949. Educational acceleration: Appraisal and basic problems. *Bureau of Educational Research Monograph No. 31*, Ohio State University, Columbus, Ohio.

———. 1954. Acceleration: Basic principles and recent research. *Proceedings of the Invitational Conference on Testing Problems*. Princeton, N.J.: Educational Testing Service, pp. 107–12.

Schroedinger, E. 1943. *What is life? The physical aspect of the living cell*. Cambridge, England: Cambridge University Press.

Seagoe, M. V. 1975. *Terman and the gifted*. Los Altos, Calif.: Wm. Kaufmann.

Sears, R. R. 1957. L. M. Terman, pioneer in mental measurement. *Science* 125: 978–79.

———. 1977. Sources of life satisfactions of Terman gifted men. *American Psychologist* 32(2): 119–28.

Shields, S. 1975. Ms. Pilgrim's progress: The contributions of Leta Stetter Hollingworth to the psychology of women. *American Psychologist* 30(8): 852–57.

Spearman, C. 1930. Autobiography. In C. A. Murchison (ed.), *A history of psychology in autobiography*, vol. 1. Worcester, Mass.: Clark University Press, pp. 299–334.

Stanley, J. C. 1974. Intellectual precocity. In J. C. Stanley, D. P. Keating, and L. H. Fox (eds.), *Mathematical talent: Discovery, description, and development*. Baltimore, Md.: The Johns Hopkins University Press.

———. 1976*a*. The student gifted in mathematics and science. *NASSP* (National Association of Secondary School Principals) *Bulletin* 60(398, Mar.):28–37.

————. 1976*b*. Test better finder of great math talent than teachers are. *American Psychologist* 31(4): 313–14.

————. 1976*c*. The case for extreme educational acceleration of intellectually brilliant youths. *Gifted Child Quarterly* 20(1): 66–75, 41.

————, Keating, D. P., and Fox, L. H. (eds.). 1974. *Mathematical talent: Discovery, description, and development.* Baltimore, Md.: The Johns Hopkins University Press.

Stern, W. 1930. Autobiography. In C. A. Murchison (ed.), *A history of psychology in autobiography,* vol. 1. Worcester, Mass.: Clark University Press, pp. 335–88.

Sumption, M. R., Norris, D., and Terman, L. M. 1950. Special education for the gifted. *Education of Exceptional Children.* Forty-ninth Yearbook, Part II, National Society for the Study of Education. Chicago: University of Chicago Press, pp. 259–78.

Taylor, C. W. (ed.). 1964*a. Creativity: Progress and potential.* New York: McGraw-Hill.

————(ed.). 1964*b. Widening horizons in creativity* (Proceedings of the 1962 University of Utah Research Conference on the Identification of Creative Scientific Talent). New York: Wiley.

————. 1964*c. Biographical information in the prediction of multiple criteria of success in science.* Salt Lake City, Utah: University of Utah. NASA Research Project, NASA-105.

————, and Barron, F. (eds.). 1963. *Scientific creativity: Its recognition and development.* New York: Wiley.

Terman, L. M. 1904. A preliminary study in the psychology and pedagogy of leadership. *Pedagological Seminary* 11: 413–51.

————. 1925. Mental and physical traits of a thousand gifted children. *Genetic studies of genius,* vol. I. Stanford, Calif.: Stanford University Press.

————. 1932. Autobiography. In C. A. Murchison (ed.), *A history of psychology in autobiography,* vol. 2. Worcester, Mass.: Clark University Press, pp. 297–332.

————. 1937. *Measuring intelligence.* Boston: Houghton Mifflin.

————, Burks, B. S., and Jensen, D. W. 1930. The promise of youth: Follow-up studies of a thousand gifted children. *Genetic studies of genius,* vol. III. Stanford, Calif.: Stanford University Press.

————, and Oden, M. H. 1947. The gifted child grows up: Twenty-five years' follow-up of a superior group. *Genetic studies of genius,* vol. IV. Stanford, Calif.: Stanford University Press.

————, and Oden, M. H. 1959. The gifted group at midlife. *Genetic studies of genius,* vol. V. Stanford, Calif.: Stanford University Press.

Thoreau, H. D. 1954. *Walden.* New York: New American Library.

Thorndike, R. L. 1975. Mr. Binet's test seventy years later. *Educational Researcher* 4(5): 3–7.

Torrance, E. P. 1962. *Guiding creative talent.* Englewood Cliffs, N.J.: Prentice-Hall.

————. 1964. *Rewarding creative behavior.* Englewood Cliffs, N.J.: Prentice-Hall.

Whipple, G. M. (ed.). 1924. *Yearbook of the National Society for the Study of Education.*

Who was who in America. 1960. Chicago: Marquis, vol. III, p. 846.

Williams, F. E. 1971. Models for encouraging creativity in the classroom. In J. C. Gowan and E. P. Torrance (eds.), *Educating the ablest.* Itasca, Ill.: Peacock, pp. 222–33.

Witty, P. A. (ed.). 1951. *The gifted child.* Boston: D. C. Heath.

3

CAREER AND LIFE SATISFACTIONS AMONG TERMAN'S GIFTED WOMEN

Pauline S. Sears
and Ann H. Barbee

ABSTRACT

Of the 671 women originally selected in 1922–28 by Terman for his gifted group (IQ 135 or above), 430 women responded to a questionnaire in 1972 (average age sixty-two). Types of satisfaction—with work pattern, with "joy in living," and with perceived success in attaining five goals in life—comprise the dependent variables.

Earlier reports (1922 to 1960) from the subjects, their parents, and their teachers were used as potential predictors of satisfaction at the current age. Hypotheses relating these experiences and feelings to current satisfactions were tested.

Two measures of satisfaction were used: of the women's work pattern and of a broader measure of life satisfaction. Comparing the income workers with the homemakers, results show the women employed outside of the home to be satisfied with their work, with the homemakers less satisfied with theirs. Especially satisfied in this respect are the head-of-household women. Homemakers report themselves more satisfied on a broader measure of satisfaction. Another large but non-gifted sample reports more satisfaction with the homemaker status. These findings are interpreted in the light of development of personality through earlier recorded experiences with parents, and with subjects' education and intelligence.

To define—and to live—a satisfying life is clearly the prime goal of most human beings, whether their IQ is 80 or 180. In the last few years we have seen an expansion of thinking with regard to women's options and choices in the pursuit of this goal. It is likely that women of differing ages, cultural backgrounds, talents, life experiences, and predispositions arrive at differing conclusions about what constitutes satisfaction in life style for them at different points in time. This study utilizes data from the fifty-year longitudinal study initiated by Lewis M. Terman,[1] and attempts to isolate those factors contributing to satisfaction in gifted women following careers, variously and in combination, as income workers, wives, mothers, and homemakers.

Description of the Sample

This research samples one cohort of women, born on the average about 1910, growing up during World War I, finishing high school just before the Great Depression, and living their early years in urban areas of California. They have most recently reported their current and retrospective life satisfactions in 1972, as they saw them at average age about sixty-two (figure 3.1).[2]

The present sample consists of 430 California women, selected in the 1920s as falling in the upper 1 percent of the population according to tested intelligence. The subjects had a minimum IQ of 135. Field contacts were made with the subjects, their parents, and their teachers in 1921, 1927, 1939, and 1950. Mail surveys were carried out in 1936, 1945, 1955, 1960, and 1972, a total of nine contacts over the fifty years.

As of 1972, the 430 women responding to the questionnaire were classified as to their marital status, work pattern, and whether or not they had children. Percentages of the total sample falling into various groups are shown in table 3.1. The large portion was currently married and living with a husband. This may not be a first husband—many divorces and second, third, and even fourth marriages have taken place in the group.

Another measure of marital status was used to separate those women who appeared to be independent or "on their own." In addition to the

---

[1] Melita Oden and Shiela Buckholtz, among others, have maintained the files over the years. Oden (1968) is the author of the publication preceding Sears (1977) and this one, and of course Lewis Terman conceived and directed the project until his death in 1956. With coauthors, he produced four volumes on the earlier development of his gifted "children" (Terman et al. 1925; Burks, Jensen, and Terman 1930; Terman and Oden 1947, 1959). As in any study of this type, much of the credit goes to the hundreds of subjects who have faithfully and conscientiously provided the information necessary to the success of this project. Robert Wolfe and Richard DeVeaux have acted as statistical consultants in the later stages of the data analysis presented here. Julian Stanley, Lee Cronbach, and Robert Sears have provided helpful criticisms of analysis and manuscript.

[2] It would be of much interest to secure additional cohorts differing in age and/or geographical location to compare with this sample. Later we shall present such comparative data as are currently available for this purpose.

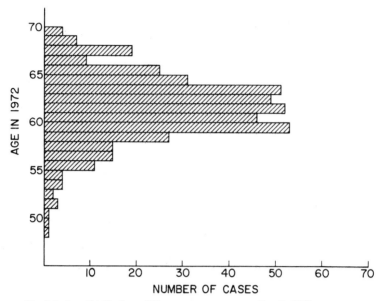

Fig. 3.1. Age distribution of Terman women responding in 1972

single women, all women who were either divorced or widowed and who had remained so since 1960 were classified as head-of-household (HH). For lack of any more appropriate term, the balance were called non-head-of-household (NHH).

The next section of table 3.1 shows that 43 percent are income workers (IW), according to a rather stringent criterion—they must have had steady work for four out of six five-year periods, 1941–72. Subjects who worked fewer than four of these periods were designated homemakers (HM). Finally, 25 percent of the entire sample were childless; 75 percent had at least one child.

The percentage differences between the Terman figures and those of the 1970 U.S. Census are insignificant except in the following instances. Among the Terman women there are somewhat more currently divorced. More Terman women are employed on a full-time basis, and of the employed, more of the Terman sample are professional. The average number of children born to married women is 1.79, a little lower than the Census reports for women in this age group. In our group the total family income shows a median of $18,000 per year (not shown in table 3.1). Sixty-eight percent reported a family income of $15,000 or better in 1971, whereas the 1970 Census figures report 27 percent at or above that figure for the U.S. population of husband–wife families.

Attrition of Sample

In longitudinal studies, attrition is always an important variable. Of the 671 women in the original 1928 sample, 573 were believed to be living in 1972. Responses to the 1972 mailing sampled 75 percent of those women, or an *N* of 430.

Since twelve years had elapsed between follow-ups, we wondered whether our current sample was self-selecting in any significant way (e.g., the most "successful" in marriage, income, career, etc.). Taking a base of response in 1960, we compared our 1972 respondents to nonrespondents on six variables: occupation, family income, marital status, health, general adjustment, and feelings of having lived up to intellectual ability. While there were some differences between those who responded and those who did not, these differences were minimal (from 1 to 5 percent as an average difference in any variable). What we did find was that generally those who had given us complete cooperation in the past continued to do so. Our fallout came largely from those subjects for whom data in 1960 were sketchy.

SATISFACTION MEASURES

Now, how do these women in different categories of martial status, occupation, and motherhood compare on the satisfactions they feel for

Table 3.1. Percentage breakdown by marital status, work pattern, and children

Category	Percent of sample
Current marital status	
Always single	9
Divorced or separated	11
Widowed	15
Married	65
Head-of-household status	
Head-of-household	19
Single (9%)	
Divorced (6%)	
Widowed (4%)	
Non-head-of-household	81
Work pattern	
Income workers	43
Homemakers	57
Children	
Childless	25
Had children	75

their life styles? (Cf. Andrews and Withey 1973.) From the 1972 returns, three measures of satisfaction with life style were devised. One involved *work pattern,* whether the work done was income-producing or not. Two other measures, broader in the sense of covering various aspects of the woman's activities, will be described later.

Work Pattern Satisfaction

This measure was derived from a question which asked the women to consider their lives as falling into one of four possible patterns: (1) I have been primarily a homemaker; (2) I have pursued a career during most of my adult life; (3) I have pursued a career except during the period when I was raising a family; or (4) I have done considerable work for needed income, but would not call it a career.

Subjects checked their pattern under a column labeled "As it was." Then they were asked to indicate the pattern that fitted their plans in early adulthood. Finally, they checked the pattern they would prefer to have been in, as they looked back.

Our measure for work pattern satisfaction came from those subjects whose answers to the first "(a) As it was" and the third "(c) As I now would choose" were identical, whichever pattern it was. (Note that homemaking is considered work, as well as income-producing jobs.) Where there was agreement, satisfaction was called high. For any sort of disagreement, the subject was considered to have a moderate or low degree of satisfaction with her work pattern in comparing her actual style with that she would now choose. Childless women who checked "career during most of adult life" as "as it was," and then "career except when raising a family" as their preference now, were coded as high satisfaction; this was only eight cases. By these criteria, 68 percent of the total sample expressed high satisfaction with their work pattern.

Our naive theory predicted that women who were married, with children, having had income-producing work, and living on a higher-than-average income would report higher satisfaction than those in the reverse groups. As with many naive theories, most of these predictions proved false. Figure 3.2 gives the data for our head-of-household/non-head-of-household categories. The percentage figures in each of the cells are *not* the number of women in that category, but rather are the percentage of women in that category who report high work pattern satisfaction. Thus, of the head-of-household subjects, 80 percent show high satisfaction. Of the non-head-of-household group, 67 percent rate

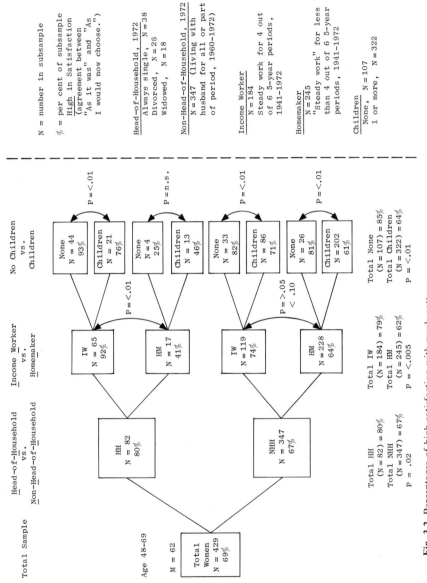

Fig. 3.2. Percentages of high satisfaction with work pattern

N = number in subsample

% = per cent of subsample
High in Satisfaction
(agreement between
"As it was" and "As
I would now choose.")

Head-of-Household, 1972
Always single, N = 38
Divorced, N = 26
Widowed, N = 18

Non-Head-of-Household, 1972
N = 347 (living with
husband for all or part
of period, 1960-1972)

Income Worker
N = 184
Steady work for 4 out
of 6 5-year periods,
1941-1972

Homemaker
N = 245
"Steady work" for less
than 4 out of 6 5-year
periods, 1941-1972

Children
None, N = 107   N = 322
1 or more, N = 322

high—with a probability of .02 for the difference between these percentages.

Income workers gave an overall figure of 79 percent high satisfaction; homemakers rated 62 percent—a very significant difference (see the bottom of figure 3.2). But note, within the cells, that those women who were head-of-household and income workers are 92 percent highly satisfied, compared to 41 percent high satisfaction in those who are also head-of-household but homemakers.

Our most surprising finding concerns the fact of having children versus childlessness. In each pair of cells (except one with very small numbers), subjects with no children show a higher percentage of satisfaction than those with children. For "always single" childless women, the percent of high satisfaction is 89 percent. Is motherhood becoming an endangered species, as one of our developmental psychology colleagues observed?

Another surprise came when we looked at family income (not shown in figure 3.2). Here the high satisfaction represents 66 percent of those below the median of $18,000 and 70 percent of those above the median, a nonsignificant difference. Since $18,000 is a pretty fair figure in itself, we separated out those in the lowest quartile of family income. Their high satisfaction figure was 67 percent—no different from those with larger incomes.

Possibly our naive theory stereotype of what life style would prove most satisfying for the women born about 1910 neglected the fact that these subjects were responding as they felt in 1972. Whereas 41 percent of the women responded "primarily a homemaker" as their work pattern in the "As it was" column, only 29 percent "would now choose" that pattern (table 3.2). Thirty percent placed themselves in the "career" category; 37 percent would now choose this option. The comparable figures for "career except when raising a family" are 12 percent and 29 percent; for the "income only" category, they are 18 percent and 5 percent. Many of these women thus would now choose a career or a career-except-when-raising-a-family, rather than the homemaker or work-for-income-only work patterns.

The proportion of women in the United States who are in the "work" (according to definition, "work" does not include homemaking) force has been steadily rising, and possibly some of the homemaker women felt that they had missed an interesting and challenging part of life. As shown in table 3.1, 43 percent of the women were coded as income workers, according to the criterion of being employed four out of six five-year periods. However, the current (1972) status shows 65 percent as either employed or recently retired from employment (48 percent working, 17 percent retired).

Table 3.2. Cross-tabulation of number of cases of "as it was" versus "as I would now choose"

As it was	As I would now choose				
	Homemaker[a]	Career[b]	Career except[c]	Income worker[d]	Row total
Homemaker[a]					
Married w/children	82	17	37	1	137
Married w/o children	7	2	1		10
Always single	1				1
Total	90	19	38	1	148
Career[b]					
Married w/children	2	38	6	1	47
Married w/o children	2	30	3		35
Always single	1	22	4		27
Total	5	90	13	1	109
Career except[c]					
Married w/children	2	6	34		42
Married w/o children		1			1
Always single			1		1
Total	2	7	35		44
Income worker[d]					
Married w/children	6	15	17	12	50
Married w/o children	2	3	2	3	10
Always single		2	1	1	4
Total	8	20	20	16	64
Column total	105	136	106	18	365[e]

[a]Full title of response category is: "I have been primarily a homemaker."

[b]Full title of response category is: "I have pursued a career through most of my adult life."

[c]Full title of response category is: "I have pursued a career except during the period when I was raising a family."

[d]Full title of response category is: "I have done considerable work for needed income, but would not call it a career."

[e]In addition to these 365 cases, 64 women responded with other answers to describe their specific work patterns.

Two Ways of Looking at Satisfaction with Life Style

Satisfaction with life style is described in two different approaches. One might be called the *demographic*, using such variables as work pattern, marital status, number of children, and income level to provide a subsample of the 430 women for a look at relative satisfaction (figure 3.2). This we have just presented. The second approach is to look back at childhood and early adulthood variables to see whether these are associated *predictively* with (1) life style, work pattern, and/or (2) satisfaction with that experienced style.

In these women now approaching ordinary retirement age, were there precursors or predictors in childhood and early adulthood of later satisfaction with their own life styles and choices? This phase of the analysis depends upon the longitudinal design of the study and the enormous files of data meticulously kept over the years. We have looked at theoretically relevant possible predictors of later satisfaction such as: education and occupation of the subjects' parents; the girls' apparent identification with their mothers and with their fathers; attitudes of their mothers, fathers, and teachers toward them; the subjects' own attitudes toward themselves in terms of ambition, self-confidence, and the like; and goals and aspects of life giving them the most satisfaction at different points in their development. These possible predictors have been related to their actual careers as income workers, mothers, and homemakers at different points in time, and to the satisfaction they felt with them.

Hypotheses to be tested involved the following groups of variables:

1. Women coming from homes in which the father and mother were well-educated and in which the father (and perhaps the mother) followed a professional or higher business career would themselves be more likely to follow suit, and show more satisfaction with their choice than those from homes in which the parents had lower levels of education and occupation.

2. Women coming from homes where parent-child relations were affectionately positive and parents' marriage a happy one would be more likely to show general satisfaction with their own lives, have happier marriages themselves, and enjoy their children more. No prediction was made with the work pattern the subject would follow in connection with this group of variables.

3. The subjects' early self-rating of self-confidence, lack of inferiority feelings, and presence of ambition should predict later feelings of satisfaction with the experiences actually encountered. More subjects with high self-ratings should fall in the income worker pattern than in the homemaker pattern.

4. As stated earlier, our naive theory predicted that for these women, marriage, number of children, and income level should be positively correlated with later satisfaction.

These hypotheses were tested for 149 variables taken from the files for 1922 to 1972. The next section and table 3.3 give significant relations between variables and work pattern satisfaction. You will recall that high satisfaction came from the subjects' indicating at average age sixty-two agreement between the experience she had actually had ("As it was"), and the response to "As I would now choose." Chi square was used because work pattern is a discrete rather than a continuous variable. Some of the

Table 3.3. Work pattern satisfaction related to other variables

Variable description	Number of categories	Date	Chi-square significance ($\leqslant.05$)
General satisfaction 5[a] (high)[b]	1.40–5.00	1972	.00
Joy in living satisfaction[a] (high)	5	1972	.00
Work pattern, income or homemaker (income)	2	1972	.00
S's occupation (professional–managerial– arts vs. clerical–sales, housewife)	3	1950	.00
S's occupation (professional–managerial– arts vs. clerical–sales, housewife)	3	1960	.00
Historical rating on general adjustment (satisfactory)	3	1960	.03
Health (very good)	5	1972	.00
Attainment: occupational success (high)[a]	5	1972	.00
Attainment: family life (high)	5	1972	.00
Attainment: cultural life (high)	5	1972	.02
Satisfying aspects of life: work	3	1950	.00
Satisfying aspects of life: income	3	1950	.03
Satisfying aspects of life: children	3	1950	.00
Satisfying aspects of life: work	3	1960	.00
Satisfying aspects of life: children	3	1960	.00
Ambition for excellence in work since age 40 (high)	5	1960	.03
Number of children (none vs. one to eight)	9	1972	.00

[a]This variable will be discussed later.
[b]Parentheses following name of variable indicate direction of relation to the criterion work pattern satisfaction. Work pattern satisfaction has two categories, high and moderate or low.

variables included are nonlinear. Note the parentheses following the name of the variable; this indicates the direction of the relationship. Thus, as we have already seen in figure 3.2, the more satisfied women tend to be childless and hold income-producing jobs. However, they also are likely to value their family and cultural lives, as well as work and income.

Apparently, we must conclude that while rewarding, income-producing work and vocational advancement are facilitated by the absence of children, still it is part of women's lives (perhaps especially those of the Terman Study generation) to wish for and enjoy their children. Later we shall discuss findings from a nationwide sample of women (not gifted) in this regard.

Turning from this issue, observe that the variables related to work pattern satisfaction generally (but not exclusively) suggest reward from work, whatever it is, a bias in favor of income-producing rather than homemaking work, a professional occupation, and ambition for excellence and advancement in the occupation.

We do not see any relations to parent- or self-ratings on feelings of inferiority, presistence, self-confidence, helpfulness of parents, and the like. Those high on work pattern satisfaction do report that one of the satisfying aspects of life is income. Possibly, more women in the income-producing work pattern brought home enough to make a decent income (to them) and were pleased to have done so.

Parents' education and occupation do not show relationships to work pattern satisfaction, but the subject's occupation does. Evidently, the women working in teaching or other professions, the arts, or who are office or property managers are more likely to show high satisfaction on this measure than those who are sales clerks, in clerical jobs, or are housewives. But the actual income (total family) does not come out as a significant correlate of work pattern satisfaction.

General Satisfaction 5

A second, and broader, measure of life satisfaction came from another question in 1972: "How important was each of these goals in life in the plans you made for yourself in early adulthood?" Columns were labeled "occupational success," "family life," "friendships," "richness of cultural life," and "total service to society." Next, the subject was asked to rate her success in each of these respects. (Note that children/marriage surveyed in earlier questionnaires were not delineated in 1972 but lumped under one category labeled "family life.") There was also a sixth area, "joy in living," which is more global than the others. It was taken as a separate criterion to be discussed later. Following a suggestion of Sanford Dornbusch (personal communication), we have weighted the individual's judgment of her success in each area by her statement as to the importance of the area to her in early adulthood. Both ratings were retrospective judgments made when she was in her early sixties.

General satisfaction 5 is the quotient obtained by multiplying the planned goal (early adulthood) by the reported success in attaining that goal, adding the five of these multiplied areas, and dividing by the sum of the planned goals for each of the areas. These scores range from 0 through 5. They are continuous, not discrete. A high score means that in those areas she considered important for herself, her success was good. It also takes into account individual differences in the choice of important goals.

Table 3.4 summarizes the results reaching the .05 level of statistical significance obtained by a one-way-classification analysis of variance for 158 variables.[3] Twenty variables, coming from reports made by subject

---

[3]A one-way classification analysis of variance of each of 158 independent variables was performed, using general satisfaction 5 scores as the dependent variable. For example, the question, "Please check to indicate your general health during 1970–1972" with five possible

and by parents in different years, appear to show positive prediction of general satisfaction in 1972. These fall into certain groups, as earlier hypothesized.

1. There are quite a number indicating positive relations with *parents* in earlier years. These come both from favorable ratings of the subject *by* parents, and ratings of her father's and mother's qualities *by* the subject. Examples are the 1928 parents' rating of the child subject as high in self-confidence and low in feelings of inferiority. Subjects high in general satisfaction 5 in 1972 rated their parents favorably in 1950 on understanding and helpfulness. They showed admiration for their mothers.

2. As expected, favorable ratings of self qualities by the subject appear as early as 1940 and again later. These self-concept reports are rather highly correlated over the years.[4] It seems unlikely that the subjects could remember in 1972 how they responded in 1940 or 1950; thus a considerable stability in self-regard is indicated. These ratings were self-confidence, which was high, and feelings of inferiority, which were low.

3. Aspects of life reported as satisfying in earlier years (1950, 1960)—marriage, children, social contacts, community service—are associated with general satisfaction in 1972.

4. Good health and professional work appear as positive predictors of satisfaction, as do level of education and occupation of husband, and subject's opinion of vocational success of her father. Time devoted to volunteer work also comes out associated with general satisfaction 5, as does a staff rating on general adjustment.

It is unfortunate that those variables *not* predictive of satisfaction cannot be reported completely here.[5] Some, of course, came close to, but

---

answers—very good, good, fair, poor, very poor—constitutes a five-level independent variable for the ANOVA. Variation among the means of responses "very good" vs. "good" vs. "fair" vs. "poor" vs. "very poor" is analyzed, as shown in table 3.4. There, F with 4 and 412 degrees of freedom is statistically significant at the .05 level.

[4]Self-rating correlations over different years of report give some indication of the consistency or rough reliability of these measures. For example:

Variable number	Description	N	Correlation with		
			2	3	4
1	Self-confidence (1940)	384	.56	-.49	-.46
2	Self-confidence (1950)	377		-.38	-.54
3	Feelings of inferiority (1940)	383			.55
4	Feelings of inferiority (1950)	375			

[5]Complete code books are available to qualified persons. Appendix 3.1 lists 149 of the variables entered into the analyses reported in tables 3.3 through 3.9.

Table 3.4. General satisfaction 5 (five areas) related to other variables

Variable description	Number of categories	Date	ANOVA probability, $F \leqslant .05$
Work pattern satisfaction (high)[a]	2	1972	.00
Joy in living satisfaction[b] (high)	5	1972	.01
Health (very good)	5	1972	.05
S's occupation (professional–managerial–arts vs. clerical–sales, housewife)	3	1940	.05
Historical rating, general adjustment (satisfactory)	3	1960	.00
Percent time volunteer work, 1966–72 (high)	0–40	1972	.00
Feelings about present vocation (good)	5	1950	.01
Parent rating: self-confidence (high)	1–13	1928	.00
Parent rating: feelings of inferiority (low)	1–11	1940	.00
Parent/teacher rating: perseverance, desire to excel (high)	34	1928	.00
S rates: understanding with mother (high)	4	1950	.01
S rates: helpfulness of father (high)	4	1950	.01
S rates: vocational success of father (high)	4	1950	.00
S rates: admiration for mother (high)	4	1950	.04
Self-rating: feelings of inferiority (low)	1–11	1940	.00
Self-rating: persistence (high)	1–11	1950	.05
Education of spouse (AB or better)	3	1940	.00
Occupation of spouse (professional)	3	1940	.03
Satisfying aspects of life: marriage	3	1950	.00
Satisfying aspects of life: children	3	1950	.03
Satisfying aspects of life: community service	3	1950	.00
Satisfying aspects of life: marriage	3	1960	.00
Satisfying aspects of life: social contacts	3	1960	.02
Satisfying aspects of life: community service	3	1960	.03

[a]Parentheses following name of variable indicate direction of relation to the criterion general satisfaction 5. General satisfaction 5 is a continuous variable with scores from 1.40 to 5.00.

[b]This variable will be discussed later.

did not quite meet, the significance criteria. Among those which showed no relationship to satisfaction were number of children; 107 of the 430 women were childless but had nearly as high general satisfaction scores as those who had from one to eight children. Income and ambition for financial gain also do not show up in relation to general satisfaction. We have here in general satisfaction 5 several dimensions of life experiences which are not tapped by work pattern satisfaction.

Joy in Living Satisfaction

The simplest of our measures of satisfaction, Joy in Living Satisfaction, was derived from the subjects' answers in 1972 to the question of how successful they had been in pursuit of that goal. A five-point scale was used, ranging from "had excellent fortune in this respect" down to "found little satisfaction in this area." Predictors of this measure of satisfaction were found by use of chi squares instead of analysis of variance.

Joy in living scores correlate .51 with general satisfaction 5 scores, and many of the same predictors appear in relation to both criteria (table 3.5). Positive relations with parents and positive self-ratings are signifi-

Table 3.5. Joy in living satisfaction related to other variables

Variable description	Number of categories	Date	Chi-square significance, ≤.05
General satisfaction 5 (high)[a]	1.40–5.00	1972	.00
Work pattern satisfaction (high)	2	1972	.00
Work pattern, income or homemaker (income)	2	1972	.00
Health (very good)	5	1972	.00
Energy and vitality level (vigorous)	5	1972	.00
Historical rating, general adjustment (satisfactory)	3	1960	.00
Feelings about present vocation (good)	5	1950	.05
Teacher's rating of arithmetic (very superior)	6	1922	.00
Conflict w/father before S's marriage (none)	5	1940	.01
S rates understanding with mother (high)	5	1940	.01
S rates father's self-confidence (high)	5	1950	.00
S rates admiration for mother (high)	5	1950	.01
S rates rebellious feelings toward father (none)	5	1950	.05
S rates father's encouragement of independence (high)	5	1950	.04
Self-rating: feelings of inferiority (low)	1–10	1940	.00
Self-rating: feelings of inferiority (low)	1–11	1950	.03
Education of spouse (AB or better)	3	1940	.02
Satisfying aspects of life: community service	3	1950	.00
Satisfying aspects of life: marriage	3	1960	.00
Satisfying aspects of life: religion	3	1960	.02
Ambition for excellence in work, age 30–40 (high)	5	1960	.00
Ambition for excellence in work, since age 40 (high)	5	1960	.00

[a]Parentheses following name of variable indicate direction of relation to the criterion joy in living satisfaction. Joy in living satisfaction has five categories.

cantly related to both satisfaction measures. However, income workers, as contrasted with homemakers, score higher in joy, which was not the case on the broader measure of general satisfaction 5. Further, ambition for excellence in work, both in early and later adulthood (as recollected in 1960) is associated with joy. Of interest to those working with mathematically precocious children is the fact that teachers reported special ability in math as early as 1922 for those subjects high in joy.

Reliability of Satisfaction Measures

These 1972 measures are a one-shot type of response. Additionally, they are based on combinations of separate responses. Conventional reliability is impossible to determine. We offer instead some indication of the consistency of certain measures of satisfaction, repeated over a ten-year period, as evidence that at least some satisfaction variables are not subject-quixotic but represent some moderately stable indication of the subjects' feelings at different points in their lives.

Self-ratings on self-confidence and feelings of inferiority, coming from 1940 and 1950, correlate .56 and .55, respectively. In 1950 and 1960, subjects were asked to rate certain aspects of life which were satisfying to them. Correlations between the two sets of responses showed the following: for work, .41; for marriage, .56; for children, .69; and for social contacts, .39.[6]

FACTOR ANALYSIS

For reduction in the huge number of variables contained in the reports over the fifty years 1922–72, certain variables were submitted to factor analyses. First, since the interest was in life-style satisfactions of these women, variables were selected which theoretically should relate to the three types of satisfaction measured in later life: (1) Work pattern satisfaction (including both income workers and homemakers); (2) general satisfaction 5, covering five areas of possible satisfactions; and (3) joy in living, another general type of satisfaction. The variables selected were thought to be possibly predictive of these satisfactions in later life: they included earlier attitudes toward homemaking and income-producing work, ambition, children, self-confidence, marriage, volunteer work, attachment to parents, and the like.[7]

[6]The complete correlation matrix is given in appendix 3.2.

[7]In all, four factor analyses were done: (1) with 78 variables, using an orthogonal design with varimax rotation; (2) also with 78 variables, using oblique rotation, $\Delta = .3$, the Rao factor; (3) 50 variables (leaving out those which appeared to duplicate one another), using PA2 factor with oblique rotation, $\Delta = .3$; and (4) also 50 variables using oblique rotation, $\Delta =$

The first analysis resulted in ten meaningful factors; these will be reported here. The other three resulted in the following numbers of factors, respectively: 26, 19, and 19. Many of these incorporated only single variables, and told little more than analysis of variance and the chi-squares with single variables and satisfaction scores.

Table 3.6 gives the chief variables in the ten factors, the percent of variance in the analysis accounted for by each factor, and the correlation of each factor with the three measures of satisfaction in 1972. These ten factors account for about 74 percent of the common variance expected from the correlation matrix of seventy-eight variables. Fifty-three of the seventy-eight variables correlated .35 or better with a factor. These are reported here.

It can be seen that one factor emphasizes income-producing work, and two factors (5 and 9) group variables involving marriage and children. These are not completely antithetical, as seen earlier in table 3.3, work pattern satisfaction. Although number of children is lower in the income-worker group than in the homemaker, children appear to be one of the satisfying aspects of life (1950, 1960) as related to work pattern satisfaction.

Factor 2 illustrates the clustering of positive self-ratings, and is somewhat related to both general measures of satisfaction. These two measures of satisfaction are also self-rating, but are reported at a time up to thirty years later than some of the self-confidence measures. If this clustering is due to response set, it is remarkably enduring over time. More likely, there is a true prediction: If a woman feels self-confident early in life, she is more likely to order her life in a way that promotes later satisfaction. Note that such women also consider themselves ambitious for vocational advancement.[8]

Factors 3 and 6 represent attachment to parents. Here the prediction to later satisfaction is not clear for attachment to mother, although there is some relation in the extent of positive regard for the father. Likewise, mother's occupation (factor 4) does not correlate highly with satisfaction.

Factor 8 presents the highest correlation with a satisfaction measure. This is more suspect with regard to response set, since two of the predictors came from the same year (1972) as the satisfaction measures.

Finally, factor 9, while contributing much less variance to the total than factor 1, shows that rewards from marriage constitute a fair prediction of general satisfaction later in life.

.3, and the Rao factor. All were done using SPSS programs. See *SPSS: Statistical Package for the Social Sciences* (Nie et al. 1975), pp. 468–86.

[8]In our search for approximations to consistency of response measures, several of these factors are illuminating, since they represent responses from many different years which cluster together in the factors.

Table 3.6. Factor analysis of seventy-eight variables[a]

Factor number (% variance)	Description	*r* with factor >.10		
		General satisfaction (five areas)	Work pattern satisfaction	Joy in living satisfaction
1 (21.5%)	Income worker (1941–72),[b] occupation high level (1940), low time volunteer work—1960–65 (1972), work is rewarding (1950, 1960), ambitious for vocational advance—age 30–40 (1960)		+.26	
2 (17.1%)	Self-rating: self-confidence (1940, 1950), persistence (1950), ambitious for vocational advance—age 30–40 and since 40 (1960)	+.16		+.21
3 (11.8%)	Attachment to mother (1940, 1950)			
4 (10.1%)	Mother's occupation, high (1922, 1927, 1936, 1940)			
5 (9.2%)	Had children (1972), wanted them (1940), found them rewarding (1950, 1960), would do it again (1950)		−.19	
6 (7.0%)	Attachment to father (1940, 1950), parents' marriage happy (1940)	+.19		+.12
7 (6.7%)	S's education good (1940), husband's education and occupation high (1950)	+.17		
8 (5.9%)	Feels good about work (1972), good health (1972), not ambitious for excellence in work—age 30–40 (1960)	+.31	+.17	+.45
9 (5.7%)	Married (1972), likes it (1950, 1960)	+.33	+.17	+.32
10 (4.9%)	S gets satisfaction from recognition of work (1950) and social contacts (1950, 1960)	+.13		

[a]This analysis used an orthogonal design with varimax rotation. Variables are not reported if correlation was less than .35 with the factor.

[b]Date is that of subject's response.

ANALYSIS OF SUBSAMPLES

A final analysis divides our sample into categories according to current marital status, work pattern, and presence of children. Table 3.7 gives percentages of the sample thus divided who reported *high* (favorable) ratings on a number of variables early and late in time. Since the categories for subsamples are those of 1972, many of the earlier responses were made *before* the woman was divorced or widowed. We shall look at the proportions of women in each category for suggestions as to dynamics or circumstances underlying their position in one or another category. Numbers in parentheses refer to variables listed in table 3.7.

Single Women

Not many in this group rated their parents' marriage as more happy than average (1), but more than in other groups reported that both father and mother encouraged independence in the child subject (2, 3). Few considered their mothers very self-confident (4). Their mothers were rarely in professional or managerial occupations (8). When we add in the fact that these single women were distinctly better educated than the other groups (9), a picture emerges of a woman without a strong maternal role model but encouraged to be independent by her parents, and finding her own satisfactions in work for which she has been well prepared by education. These single women liked arithmetic very much as children (17) and were rated by their teachers as superior at it (18).

Married Women

This group showed a much higher percentage who felt their parents' marriage was very happy (1). The subjects' level of education is much lower than that of the single women (9), perhaps partly because marriage and/or children interrupted educational plans and goals, or perhaps because the women were willing to have them interrupted. A large proportion of these women take great satisfaction in marriage, family life, and children (10, 11, 12, 13). Interestingly, the percentage taking "great" satisfaction in children increased substantially from 1950 to 1960 (10, 11). Absence of older children from the home may make the heart grow fonder, and grandmothers are notorious for their love of children. In this group the husbands are well educated (15) and often hold professional or managerial jobs (14). The family income is high (16).

Divorced Women

To these women, their parents' marriage was seen as less happy (1), and the subjects believed that their fathers and mothers did not encourage independence in them to any great extent (2, 3). A relatively large number considered their mothers as very self-confident (4), and many of their

Table 3.7. Percentages of subsamples scoring high on selected variables, 1922-72[a] (top figure is number reporting; bottom is percent of that subsample high)

Variable (year) % of total	Current marital status				Work pattern		Children	
Sample reporting high:	Single	Mar.	Div.	Wid.	IW	HM	No	Yes
Work pattern satisfaction (1972) 69%	38 89%	280 68%	46 72%	65 63%	184 79%	245 62%	107 85%	322 64%
General satisfaction, five areas (1972) 53%	35 43%	274 57%	44 39%	64 50%	180 51%	237 55%	102 52%	315 53%
(1) Rates parents' marriage as happier than average (1940) 56%	36 39%	246 60%	38 47%	56 54%	161 52%	215 59%	90 47%	286 58%
(2) Father encouraged independence (1950) 47%	33 58%	229 47%	35 29%	52 52%	149 50%	200 44%	86 50%	263 46%
(3) Mother encouraged independence (1950) 51%	33 64%	246 50%	37 41%	57 53%	158 53%	215 50%	87 55%	286 50%
(4) Considers mother very self-confident (1950) 13%	33 6%	243 13%	39 21%	58 16%	158 13%	215 14%	88 7%	285 15%
(5) Deep feeling of under-standing w/father (1950) 14%	33 9%	234 15%	36 11%	54 19%	153 14%	204 15%	86 14%	271 14%
(6) Felt very close to father (1940) 19%	33 24%	230 19%	35 11%	51 25%	147 16%	202 21%	81 16%	268 21%
(7) Felt very close to mother (1940) 28%	35 26%	241 30%	35 20%	55 29%	158 22%	208 34%	84 29%	282 28%
(8) Mother employed as pro-fessional or manager (1940) 15%	32 3%	223 14%	39 31%	47 13%	140 14%	201 15%	83 14%	258 15%
(9) Education—AB or better (1940) 67%	34 92%	278 64%	46 72%	65 62%	181 68%	245 66%	106 78%	320 63%
(10) Great satisfaction from children (1950) 51%	— —	218 51%	29 48%	45 53%	97 44%	195 54%	— —	292 51%

[a]In order not to overburden this table, the P values for differences between percentages have not been given. The text reports differences which are generally greater than 10 percent. Some examples of comparisons involving small and large numbers in the subsamples are given in appendix 3.3 to help the reader estimate the probabilities of true differences.

mothers had been employed in professional or managerial positions (8). Apparently, the subjects did not feel very close to either father or mother (6, 7). Obviously, very few felt great satisfaction with their marriages (12) and family life (13). Income is low for most (16). For these women, for whatever reason, the proportion who liked arithmetic very much as a child is small (17).

Table 3.7. *(Continued.)*

Variable (year) % of total Sample reporting high:	Current marital status				Work pattern		Children	
	Single	Mar.	Div.	Wid.	IW	HM	No	Yes
(11) Great satisfaction from children (1960) 66%	— —	226 68%	27 63%	45 58%	100 60%	198 69%	— —	298 66%
(12) Great satisfaction from marriage (1960) 51%	— —	262 61%	41 12%	58 47%	172 37%	226 56%	63 51%	298 53%
(13) Highly satisfied with family life (1972) 45%	31 6%	273 56%	42 14%	65 38%	176 30%	235 56%	98 31%	313 50%
(14) Spouse employed as professional or manager (1960) 77%	— —	240 78%	14 71%	32 75%	92 64%	195 83%	42 81%	245 76%
(15) Spouse's education— AB or better (1950) 58%	— —	206 61%	34 50%	54 48%	107 44%	190 64%	40 48%	254 59%
(16) Family income greater than $18,000/year (1971) 52%	25 36%	233 66%	33 21%	53 15%	143 46%	201 56%	78 47%	266 54%
(17) Liked arithmetic very much (1922) 44%	28 54%	203 48%	35 29%	58 36%	141 48%	183 41%	83 47%	241 43%
(18) Superior rating by teacher in arithmetic (1922) 60%	18 67%	152 60%	27 56%	39 62%	94 66%	142 56%	55 65%	181 59%
(19) High energy level (1972) 37%	38 42%	280 35%	46 43%	66 38%	184 42%	246 33%	107 36%	323 37%
(20) General health excellent (1972) 44%	38 34%	279 43%	46 41%	65 57%	183 45%	245 43%	105 40%	323 46%
(21) Volunteer time 10%+ from 1960 to 1965 (1972) 23%	32 19%	256 26%	39 21%	61 16%	159 11%	229 32%	90 18%	298 26%
(22) Volunteer time 10%+ from 1966 to 1972 (1972) 24%	32 28%	250 26%	38 18%	60 18%	158 12%	222 34%	90 26%	290 24%

Widows

In this group, the parents' marriage was believed to be relatively happy (1); the proportion rating father and mother as encouraging independence is high (2, 3). In 1940, these women considered themselves to be close to both father and mother (6, 7). Their level of education was the least of all the groups (9), and their income in 1972 the least, on the average (16). It is provocative to observe a discrepancy for these women between their reports of health—the highest proportion of "excellent" responses of all the groups (20)—and a less favorable self-report of energy and vitality (19). These two variables correlate .70, so considerable correspondence is expected. Possibly the widowed women felt less energy, although health was good, because of the loss of their spouse and consequent sadness and depression. These women are not older than those of the other groups.

Income Workers Compared to Homemakers

Income workers are the group that has had rather steady employment during much of their lives. By marital status, we find the following percentages of income workers: 89 percent of the single women, 65 percent of the divorced, 45 percent of the widows, and only 32 percent of the married. Subtracting from 100 percent, we find the reverse percentages for the chiefly steady state of homemaker in each of the marital-status categories.

There are not early differences between the reports from these groups. The homemakers rate their parents' marriage as a little happier (1), and more of them felt close to their mother than did the income workers (7). Homemakers report more satisfaction from children, marriage, and family life (10, 11, 12, 13) than do income workers, as expected from the marital-status figures above. Their family income is generally higher (16). An interesting difference between the two groups is in energy level, on which the income workers rate themselves higher (19). On health, the two groups report no difference (20). The homemakers spent more of their time on volunteer work than did the income workers; but it is interesting to note that single women, and those without children, increased in proportion of time spent on this in the twelve years preceding the 1972 questionnaire (21, 22). They got older, and some retired. Finally, on the child and teachers' view of arithmetic superiority, the income workers are a little higher (17, 18).

Childless Women Compared to Those with Children

Here again, the marital status intervenes in the figures. The childless group is composed of 100 percent of the single women, 30 percent of the divorced, 23 percent of the widows, and 14 percent of the married. The reverse figures from 100 percent indicate those who have one or more children. Of the childless, 72 percent are income workers and 28 percent are homemakers.

In this comparison, the women with children rate their parents' marriage as happier than those without children (1). Their mothers' self-confidence is rated higher (4). Husbands' occupation and education (14, 15) and family income are higher (16). Satisfaction with family is higher (13). Somewhat more volunteer time was spent in the early 1960s by those with children than by those without, but the two groups are essentially equal by the latter part of the decade (21, 22).

COMPARISON OF THE TERMAN SAMPLE
WITH TWO NATIONWIDE PROBABILITY SAMPLES

Earlier, we presented some data comparing the Terman group with U.S. Census statistics. Unfortunately, the Census does not ask much about *satisfaction* in the life as it is lived, and that is our major concern here.

Campbell Study

At the Institute for Social Research at Michigan, Angus Campbell and coworkers *have* done just this. Their data, published by the Russell Sage Foundation in 1975, mesh in certain ways with the data of our Terman women.

Campbell used one of Michigan's Survey Research Center's representative samples of 2,164 adults over seventeen. There are breakdowns for men, women, age groups, marital status, children, employed, and the like. Since the Survey Research Center's methods of selecting a sample representative of the U.S. population are precise, we feel confident that we can compare our gifted women with their women at roughly comparable ages. Their publication, entitled *The Quality of American Life*, aims at "capturing the feelings of satisfaction or dissatisfaction that Americans draw from different parts of their lives and with how these specific experiences combine to produce satisfaction with life in general" (Campbell, Converse, and Rogers 1975).

They obtained their data from a lengthy personal interview in 1971 with people of the selected representative sample. One thousand two hundred forty-nine women were interviewed. Of these results, the older women ($N=669$) most comparable to our sample are used for comparison. The average age of these older women in Campbell's sample is less than that for the Terman women (the latter average age sixty-two in

1972), but most of this subgroup of Campbell's sample were over forty-five. The time of response is close, however: Campbell in 1971 and Terman in 1972. In both cases the number is large (Campbell 669; Terman 430), but the selection criteria are quite different.

Our question then becomes: How do the gifted women of the Terman sample resemble or differ from a representative sample of U.S. women of all IQ levels—somewhat younger, to be sure, but otherwise classified in ways that we can match with our sample? We shall first compare the dimensions of marital status, employment, and education. Second, we shall look at similarities and differences in the two samples as to the degree of satisfaction they feel with their lives.

Demographic Variables.   Table 3.8 gives the comparison on the demographic dimensions. With regard to marital/children status, fewer of the Terman sample were currently widowed or divorced; more of the Terman group were currently married and had children. This may have resulted from more remarriages in our group, which on the average is somewhat older than Campbell's.

More of the Terman group were employed, whatever their marital status. A great many more had obtained a college degree: 67 percent of our sample as compared to 8 percent of Campbell's. However, the percentage of the two samples who were college graduates and also employed, is very similar on the level of job held. In all probability, many of Campbell's 8 percent were as "gifted" in IQ as our sample.

Those subjects with some college short of obtaining a degree present an interesting comparison. In the Terman group, many more are at a higher level of employment (professional, managerial, arts, as compared to clerical, sales) than those in Campbell's group. Campbell's data suggest that his group having some college fare little better in level of employment than those with only a high school diploma.

The Terman data show the following percentages of professional, managerial jobs by groups having differing education: college graduate, 87 percent; some college, 67 per cent; and high school graduate, 58 percent. Campbell's sample shows these figures: college graduate, 82 percent; some college, 16 percent; and high school graduate, 8 percent. The Terman data suffer from low numbers at the lower levels of education; the Campbell figures are based on low numbers at the higher education levels.

We are inclined to draw the speculative conclusion that the women of high IQ are able to prove themselves capable on the job, perhaps have higher vocational goals and aspirations because of their family background, and hence succeed in higher-level jobs and in more employment overall in the labor force than do the women in Campbell's representative sample. Also to be kept in mind is the fact that the Terman women are

Table 3.8. Percentages of samples, Terman and Campbell groups

	Terman ($N = 430$), age ±62	Campbell ($N = 669$), age 30+
Current marital status		
Married, children, age ±62	56% (240/430)	
Married, youngest child over 17, age 45+		33% (218/669)
Married, childless, age ±62	9% (40/430)	
Married, childless, age 45+		7% (50/669)
Always single, age ±62	9% (38/430)	
Always single, age 30+		8% (53/669)
Widowed, age ±62	15% (66/430)	
Widowed, age 55+		33% (220/669)
Divorced, separated, age ±62	11% (46/430)	
Divorced, separated, one-half under age 45		19% (128/669)
Current employment		
Housewives, homemakers	34% (147/430)	46% (450/974)
Total employed	66% (283/430)	54% (524/974)
Of employed: married	37% (158/430)	30% (293/974)
Of employed: single, widowed, divorced	29% (125/430)	24% (231/974)
Education		
College graduate	67% (284/424)	8% (58/737)
Of college graduates: homemakers	35% (98/284)	43% (25/58)
Of college graduates: employed	65% (186/284)	57% (33/58)
Of college graduates, employed:		
Professional, managerial	87% (162/186)	82% (27/33)
Clerical, sales	13% (24/186)	12% (4/33)
Some college	24% (101/424)	14% (101/737)
Of some college: homemakers	37% (37/101)	51% (52/101)
Of some college: employed	63% (64/101)	49% (49/101)
Of some college, employed:		
Professional, managerial	67% (43/64)	16% (8/49)
Clerical, sales	33% (21/64)	67% (33/49)
High school graduate	8% (35/424)	44% (329/737)
Of high school graduates: homemakers	26% (9/35)	59% (193/329)
Of high school graduates: employed	74% (26/35)	41% (136/329)
Of high school graduates employed:		
Professional, managerial	58% (15/26)	8% (11/136)
Clerical, sales	42% (11/26)	59% (80/136)

older than those of Campbell; the proportion of the Terman women employed has been increasing over the last twelve years, and no doubt the same will be true of his sample.

Satisfaction Variables. The Campbell satisfaction measure reported here was as follows: "We have talked about various aspects of your life, now I want to ask you about your life as a whole these days. Which number on the card comes closest to how satisfied or dissatisfied you are with your life as a whole?" A seven-point scale from "completely satisfied" to "completely dissatisfied" was used. High satisfaction was defined as points 1 and 2 at the completely satisfied end of the scale.

The three satisfaction measures for the Terman group have been described earlier. Work pattern satisfaction and general satisfaction 5 correlate only .21 and, as we have seen, tap quite different aspects and correlates of satisfaction with life style. General satisfaction 5 takes into account a broader spectrum of life satisfactions than does work pattern satisfaction. As such, the general measure seems more comparable to Campbell's question on life as a whole. However, the percentages of high satisfaction are not meaningful in comparing the two Terman and one Campbell measures (table 3.9).[9] Therefore, the most appropriate way to make the comparisons is on the rank order of the various groups of women *within* one measure and without attempting comparisons across columns of "high" satisfaction for different measures.

Marital status and satisfaction. Here we get fairly close correspondence between the two samples on Terman general satisfaction 5 and Campbell's results. Most satisfied with their lives are the married women, with or without children, followed by the widowed, then single, with divorced in the lowest position on satisfaction.

For our work pattern satisfaction, the ordering of the Terman women is quite different. Single, and then childless married women are most satisfied, followed by divorced, married with children, and widowed. All results so far show that absence of children contributes to satisfaction with work, at least in this group of sixty-year-old women. The strain of thinking and acting on children's development (even when the children are adults themselves?) apparently contributes to less whole-hearted devotion to work and satisfaction in it. More single women have achieved better education and higher professional level of employment, which has been shown to promote more satisfaction in work. Women with children may have come later, and with less preparation, to the jobs which might be rewarding to them personally.

Employment and satisfaction. Here again, there is agreement between the Terman general satisfaction 5 and the normative Campbell sample. Married housewives (homemakers) are the most satisfied, while married employed and single/divorced/widowed women follow. The time released from job requirements no doubt permits the housewives to gain more satisfactions from other aspects of life: friendships, cultural activities, volunteer service to the community, and perhaps children and

---

[9]Campbell had other measures, which are not reported here.

Table 3.9. Satisfaction in life style, Terman and Campbell samples compared

	Terman		Campbell
	Work pattern satisfaction high[a]	General satisfaction high[b]	How satisfied w/ life these days?[c]
Current marital status			
Married, children, age ±62	64% (159/240)	54% (129/237)	
Married, youngest child over 17, age 45+			69% (148/215)
Married, childless, age ±62	85% (34/40)	65% (26/40)	
Married, childless, age 45+			69% (34/49)
Always single, age ±62	89% (34/38)	41% (15/37)	
Always single, age 30+			53% (28/53)
Widowed, age ±62	62% (40/65)	50% (32/64)	
Widowed, age 55+			56% (121/215)
Divorced, separated, age ±62	72% (33/46)	38% (17/45)	
Divorced, separated, one-half under age 45			33% (42/128)
Current employment			
Married, housewives	64% (78/121)	57% (69/121)	69% (311/450)
Married, employed	70% (110/158)	55% (86/156)	66% (195/293)
Single, widowed, divorced: employed	74% (92/125)	44% (54/123)	47% (107/231)
Total employed	71% (202/283)	50% (140/279)	58% (302/524)
Education			
College graduate	69% (197/284)	52% (147/284)	
Of c.g.: married, housewives	60% (48/81)	53% (43/81)	56% (14/25)
Of c.g.: married, employed	71% (68/96)	57% (55/96)	79% (26/33)
Total c.g. employed	76% (141/186)	53% (98/186)	77% (24/31)
Professional, managerial	77% (124/162)	52% (84/162)	81% (22/27)
Clerical, sales	71% (17/24)	58% (14/24)	50% (2/4)
Some college	68% (69/101)	54% (54/101)	
Of s.c.: married, housewives	81% (26/32)	72% (23/32)	69% (36/52)
Of s.c.: married, employed	66% (27/41)	56% (23/41)	69% (34/49)
Total s.c. employed	61% (39/64)	47% (30/64)	68% (28/41)
Professional, managerial	74% (32/43)	49% (21/43)	62% (5/8)
Clerical, sales	33% (7/21)	43% (9/21)	70% (23/33)
High school graduate	71% (25/35)	49% (17/35)	
Of h.s. grad.: married, housewives	43% (3/7)	43% (3/7)	72% (139/193)
Of h.s. grad.: married, employed	81% (13/16)	50% (8/16)	69% (94/136)
Total h.s. grad. employed	77% (20/26)	46% (12/26)	71% (65/91)
Professional, managerial	73% (11/15)	33% (5/15)	55% (6/11)
Clerical, sales	82% (9/11)	64% (7/11)	74% (59/80)

[a] $N = 429$.

[b] $N = 423$.

[c] $N = 669$ age 30+. High satisfaction was determined by those subjects who answered with the two highest points on a seven-point scale to the question, "How satisfied are you with your life as a whole these days?"

husbands. In regard to work pattern satisfaction, the most satisfied are the employed women (whatever their marital status), with housewives lower.

Education and satisfaction. Here are the most conspicious differences between our gifted and the normative groups. Fortunately for the Terman group, 67 percent of its women were able to achieve college graduation, even in the days of the Great Depression. Eight percent of the Campbell sample did so, even though they were younger. On all three satisfaction measures, college-graduate housewives were lower on satisfaction than are employed married college graduates.

For those who had some college without graduation, the Campbell data show no difference in satisfaction between housewives and married employed women. Within the Terman group, housewives are more satisfied than the employed on both measures of satisfaction. Those employed in professional jobs report more satisfaction than those in clerical or sales work.

The high school graduates constitute only a small percentage of the Terman group, though nearly half of the Campbell sample. For the latter, the satisfaction for housewives and married employed women is very close. In the Terman sample, small numbers report the employed as more satisfied than the housewives on both measures of satisfaction.

Spreitzer Study

Another nationwide probability sample survey was carried out in 1973 by Spreitzer, Snyder, and Larson (1975). Questionnaire items tapping life satisfaction included the following: (1) "Taken all together, how would you say things are these days—would you say that you are very happy, pretty happy, or not too happy?"; (2) "In general, do you find life exciting, pretty routine, or dull?"; and (3) "Taking things all together, how would you describe your marriage? Would you say that your marriage is very happy, pretty happy, or not too happy?"

Eight hundred two women respondents covered the age range 18 to 71+, but most of the analyses of interest for comparison to the Terman group did not control for age. We have, however, figures on satisfaction by marital status and by employment, with education controlled for the whole age range.

Marital Status. High perceived happiness (question 1) was reported most frequently by married women, followed by widowed and then single women, with divorced women distinctly lower. The Terman figures on general satisfaction 5 show the same ordering by status (table 3.7), but the groups are much closer together, with divorced women not nearly so low. On our work pattern satisfaction measure, the order is quite different: single women much the highest, divorced next, then married, and widowed as the lowest.

Employment Status. This was trichotomized into full-time work, part-time work, and full time homemaking. No significant associations were found with the three indices of satisfaction. Nor did the introduction of marital status as a control variable produce significance.

However, level of education as a control variable resulted in interesting findings. Women with no college education engaged in full-time homemaking reported the most perceived happiness. Those with at least a year of college showed the highest percentage of perceived happiness associated with part-time work, and the college women were higher on perceived excitement in life, particularly in association with part-time work.

Summary of Comparison

These two surveys obviously leave much to be desired as comparative data to the Terman material. The Terman women are older, have much better education and more professional jobs when they are employed, have a higher rate of employment, and have higher family incomes (as compared to Census data); those married have husbands with more education and more professional occupations. This is in addition to IQ as a selection device. Finally, the measures of satisfaction are different.

In both normative studies, the effect of education as interacting with level of employment has been suggested as relating to life satisfaction. Education and IQ can be said to be correlated without saying that one or the other is causative. It is interesting to find this education variable cropping up in all three studies.

GENERAL DISCUSSION AND SUMMARY

The objectives of this study were (1) to delineate the current status of the 430 "gifted" women reporting in 1972 (these were selected for the study when they were children in 1922 and 1928 because of their having an IQ of 135 or higher), and (2) to investigate earlier variables in their life experiences and feelings that might predict satisfaction with their life style and situation when in 1972 they averaged about sixty-two years of age.

Method

Material dating from 1922 to 1972—obtained from mail surveys at five periods and field contacts at four periods—was culled for variables theoretically relevant to life satisfaction as reported in 1972. Such satisfaction was measured in three ways, two rather global, tapping different areas of life experiences (general satisfaction 5—covering the five areas of occupational success, family life, friendships, richness of cultural life, and total service to society—and joy in living satisfaction), and one involving satisfaction in the pattern of work actually adopted or experienced earlier as homemaking, career, career except when raising a family, or working for needed income without career implications (work pattern satisfaction). These three variables were used as criteria against which earlier experiences and feelings could be assessed for their predictive value.

The Sample

The demographic variables of current and historical status—marital, occupational, and production of children—showed no great differences from Census data or from two national surveys conducted on probability samples which did not use IQ as a selection device. At average age sixty-two, however, the Terman women showed a higher percentage employed as compared to full-time homemakers than did the normative samples, more of the married women in the Terman group were childless, more had relatively high incomes, and far more had better education and more professional levels of employment than did the other samples.

Comparative Results

Lopata (1973) suggested that the roles of wife and mother are seen as "basic and the only really important ones for adult women." This is not the case, he believed, for comparable male roles as viewed by men, for whom occupation is the major role. In contrast, Yockey (1975) proposed a model predicting a future reduction in family size as a result of contemporary role change, with increased female employment outside the home and increased sense of personal efficacy in employed women.

The Terman women were past child-rearing age in 1972, but they were not in 1941 when the records of employment used in an historically oriented classification of income worker versus homemaker begin. The normative samples cited here do not give clear breakdowns by age for employment, children, and satisfactions, which would permit direct comparison with the Terman group in late middle age or later maturity. And one must remember that if the Terman women had borne children, by 1972 nearly all of those children were grown and away from home.

Some things can be clearly compared: the situation of the women at average age sixty-two whom we have characterized as head-of-household (single, divorced, or widowed, and in that status for twelve years or more) is clearly more satisfying to them on work pattern than it is to the non-head-of-household group (those who have been married for all or some portion of the twelve-year period).

This is in distinct contrast to the normative samples, in which the divorced, widowed, and employed women come out lower on general happiness than do the married housewives. We suggest that for high-IQ women, the independence from an unhappy marriage, the challenge of making one's own life alone as a widow or single person, activates over time feelings of competence rather than depression. The absence of children, with their needs for parental involvement, no doubt contributes to the ease with which this satisfaction is achieved. Good health and energy are also significant when care of children and concommitant outside employment are both involved.

In a number of recent studies of high school and college-age women, the distinction has been made between those "traditionally" oriented and those "nontraditionally" oriented. In one, O'Leary and Hammack (1975), traditional subjects generated more traditionally feminine characteristics on a self-rating scale than did the nontraditional in terms of femininity–masculinity, role activities they find acceptable for themselves as women, and career activities they consider more appropriate for men than for women.

Within the Terman group (which attended high school and college in the 1920s and 1930s), we may be seeing some of the same distinctions between traditional and nontraditional sex-role orientation.

Some of the ten factors produced by factor analysis on this group represent traditional or nontraditional views (and/or actions) on sex-role orientation. Consider factor 1 (table 3.6). The following variables contribute to the factor: income worker (1941–1972), occupation high level (1940), low time volunteer work (1960–65), work is rewarding (1950, 1960), and ambitious for vocational advancement at age thirty to forty and since age forty (1960).

Women scoring high on this factor also generally showed high scores on work pattern satisfaction; it should be remembered that in this context homemaking is considered "work" in the same sense as is work outside the home.

Another factor (number 5) also correlated fairly well in a negative direction with work pattern satisfaction. Here are the variables for that factor: had children (1972), wanted them (1940), found them rewarding (1950, 1960), and would do it again (1950).

Factor 8 includes: feels good about work (1972), good health (1972), and not ambitious for excellence in work at age thirty to forty (1960). This factor has the highest relation of any of the ten factors to the criterion joy in living satisfaction. Factor 9 has the highest correlation with general satisfaction 5: married (1972), and likes it (1950, 1960).

It is clear that these gifted women achieved life-style satisfactions by different routes. Note that not all the variables reaching significance are contemporary as of 1972, nor retrospective from that date. Some are actual reports in 1940, when the women were on the average thirty years old. This is a longitudinal study of the same women over half a century.

Terman Results

Studying prediction of life-style satisfaction at average age sixty-two by reports made in early and middle adulthood was hypothesized to reveal certain characteristics and experiences contributing to the variance, and others irrelevant to it. The following hypotheses were posed. The actual results follow.

1. Women coming from homes in which both father and mother were well educated and in which father (and perhaps mother) followed a professional or higher business career would themselves be more likely to follow suit and show more satisfaction with their choice than those from homes in which the parents had lower levels of education and occupation.

This expectation was not confirmed, with the exception of a rating by the subjects, made in 1950, of their opinions of the vocational success of their father (high), which was a significant predictor.

On the contrary, rather than emphasizing parents' occupational achievements, the predictors reaching significance on the association with the three measures of satisfaction emphasize the subject's own level of education, occupation, health, and ambition. Education and occupation of the married women's husbands also reached statistical significance, but not those of her parents.

The foregoing results are correct for the total sample of 430 women, although when taking subsamples by marital status, some exceptions occur. Single and married childless Terman women rated their parents' marriage as less happy than did married women with children.

Divorced women's mothers, significantly more than those of other groups, had been in professional and managerial positions, and more of the divorced subjects considered their mothers to be very self-confident. One may speculate that this example of the mother's occupational achievement stimulated these subjects to get out on their own rather than to remain in an unhappy marriage. We have seen earlier that divorced women from this sample appear to be more satisfied with life than those divorced women from the general population.

2. Women coming from homes where parent–child relations were affectionately positive, and where the parents' marriage was happy, were predicted to be more likely to show general satisfaction with their own lives, have happier marriages themselves, and enjoy their children more. No prediction was made as to the work pattern the subject would follow in connection with this group of variables.

No parent–child relations variable reached significance in the prediction of work pattern satisfaction, but a great many did for general satisfaction 5 and for joy in living satisfaction. These included the subjects' ratings (most of them in 1950) of the understanding and helpfulness of parents, encouragement of subjects' independence by parents, and subjects' admiration for their parents. In addition, parents' ratings of their child subjects' feelings of self-confidence and lack of inferiority feelings were high (1922, 1928) in connection with general satisfaction, suggesting a child-rearing climate of mutual affection and admiration between parents and child.

Also in connection with high general satisfaction, there occurs a larger proportion of married than not-married women, with marriage and children named as important aspects of life satisfaction. As has been stated earlier, subjects higher on general satisfaction 5 considered their parents' marriage to be happier.

3. The third prediction was as follows: the subject's early feelings of self-confidence, lack of inferiority feelings, and presence of ambition should predict 1972 feelings of satisfaction with the experiences actually encountered over the years. More subjects with high early self-ratings should fall in the income work pattern than in the homemaker.

The results: earlier ambition for excellence in work and vocational advancement from age forty on appear as predictors of all three measures of later satisfaction. For general satisfaction 5 and joy in living, high self-ratings on self-confidence, persistence, and low feelings of inferiority appear also as early as 1940. Not confirmed was the prediction that early-self-confident women would appear more frequently later as income workers than as homemakers.

4. Our first, naive theory predicted that marriage, children, and income level should be positively related to later satisfaction. For general satisfaction 5, but not for the other two measures, married women came out higher than did the other groups. But on work pattern satisfaction they were surpassed by both the single and the divorced women.

Total family income was high in the Terman sample (median $18,000 in 1971) as compared to the general population. The actual level of income did not relate significantly to any of the three satisfaction measures. However, it was mentioned as one of the satisfying aspects of life in connection with work pattern satisfaction. So also were children, in spite of the preceding finding of greater satisfaction among the childless.

Summary

Finally, disregarding the specific hypotheses, what can we say about the factors that have contributed to the joy and well-being of these gifted women over the last half-century? Clearly, there is no single path to glory. There are many women with high satisfactions, both in the general sense and with respect to their work, who belong to each of the subgroups we have distinguished.

What does stand out is that happiness under various circumstances depends on one's earlier experiences. Married women with children are more likely to be happy if their own parents' marriage was a good one, and if there was an affectionate and warm relationship between them and their parents. But such a relationship does not guarantee happiness at average age sixty-two, if the life style followed by the gifted woman was one that led her into a single life or a childless married life. Or, to put the matter in the other direction, the conditions that led to a life style producing single status simply did not include any reference to the family state of affairs in their own childhood. Indeed, with reference to life satisfaction, one comes inescapably to the conclusion that the degree of satisfaction, either in general or specifically with reference to work alone, is part and parcel of a total developing personality. The life style which brings happiness to one woman with one kind of life experience does not necessarily bring it to another woman with a different experiential background.

The foregoing might be said about any woman growing up in the era under consideration. In the comparisons with a less gifted population of women, however, there are various suggestions that our gifted sample in many instances identified circumstances which would allow for the possibility of a happy life on their own without a husband, took advantage of these, and were able to cope comfortably with their lives thereafter. It may well be that the coping mechanisms that enable the gifted women to adapt flexibly to a variety of conditions, and in whatever condition to find good satisfactions, are related to the intelligence they bring to their life situations.

REFERENCES

Andrews, F., and Withey, S. B. 1973. *Developing measures of perceived life quality: Results from several national surveys.* Paper presented at the annual meeting of the American Sociological Association, New York.

Burks, B. S., Jensen, D. W., and Terman, L. M. 1930. The promise of youth: Follow-up studies of a thousand gifted children. *Genetic studies of genius,* vol. 3. Stanford, Calif.: Stanford Universtiy Press.

Campbell, A., Converse, P. E., and Rodgers, W. L. 1975. *The qualtiy of American life.* New York: Russell Sage Foundation.

Lopata, H. Z. 1973. Self-identity in marriage and widowhood. *Sociological Quarterly* 14: 407–18.

Nie, N. H., Hull, C. H., Jenkins, J. G., Steinbrenner, K., and Bent, D. H. 1975. *SPSS: Statistical Package for the Social Sciences* (2nd ed.). New York: McGraw-Hill.

Oden, M. H. 1968. The fulfillment of promise: 40-year follow-up of the Terman gifted group. *Genetic Psychology Monographs* 77: 3–93.

O'Leary, V. E., and Hammack, B. 1975. Sex-role orientation and achievement context as determinants of the motive to avoid success. *Sex Roles* 1(3): 225–34.

Sears, R. R. 1977. Sources of life satisfactions of the Terman gifted men. *American Psychologist* 32(2): 119–28.

Spreitzer, E., Snyder, E. E., and Larson, D. 1975. Age, marital status, and labor force participation as related to life satisfaction. *Sex Roles* 1(3): 235–47.

Terman, L. M., assisted by B. T. Baldwin, E. Bronson, J. C. DeVoss, F. Fuller, F. L. Goodenough, T. L. Kelley, M. Lima, H. Marshall, A. H. Moore, A. S. Raubenheimer, G. M. Ruch, R. L. Willoughby, J. B. Wyman, and D. H. Yates. 1925. Mental and physical traits of a thousand gifted children. *Genetic studies of genius,* vol. 1. Stanford, Calif.: Stanford University Press.

———, and Oden, M. H. 1947. The gifted child grows up. *Genetic studies of genius,* vol. 4. Stanford, Calif.: Stanford University Press.

———. 1959. The gifted group at mid-life. *Genetic studies of genius,* vol. 5. Stanford, Calif.: Stanford University Press.

Yockey, J. M. 1975. A model of contemporary role change and family size. *Sex Roles* 1(1): 69–81.

Appendix 3.1

Variables Used in Data Analyses

Variable number	Description
003	Age at 1972 birthday
004*	Marital status at present (1972)
007*	Number of children born to subject, adopted, or stepchildren
010*	Classification of subject as income worker or homemaker (1972)

Appendix 3.1 (continued)

Variables Used in Data Analyses

Variable number	Description
011*	Level of satisfaction with work pattern (1972)
019*	1972 occupational classification, simplified
029*	Feelings about work at present (1972)
041*	Total family income, 1971
043	Importance of goals planned: occupational success (1972)
044	Importance of goals planned: family life (1972)
045	Importance of goals planned: friendships (1972)
046	Importance of goals planned: richness of cultural life (1972)
047	Importance of goals planned: total service to society (1972)
048	Importance of goals planned: joy in living (1972)
049	Satisfaction with attainment: occupational success (1972)
050	Satisfaction with attainment: family life (1972)
051	Satisfaction with attainment: friendships (1972)
052	Satisfaction with attainment: richness of cultural life (1972)
053	Satisfaction with attainment: total service to society (1972)
054*	Satisfaction with attainment: joy in living (1972)
055*	Percent time spent in volunteer work: 1960–65 (1972)
056*	Percent time spent in volunteer work: 1966–72 (1972)
057*	Rating on general health, 1970–72
059*	Energy and vitality level (1972)
060	Subject's self-rating of interest in algebra (1922)
061	Subject's self-rating of interest in arithmetic (1922)
069*	Teacher's comparison with average in arithmetic (1922)
073*	Teacher rates math as best or worst subject (1924)
074	Becoming more like father or mother (1950)
075	Father's choice of vocation for subject (1950)
076	Mother's choice of vocation for subject (1950)
081*	Conflict with father regarding career choice (1950)
082	Conflict with mother regarding career choice (1950)
084*	Mother's occupation (1922)
085*	Mother's occupation (1927)
086*	Father's occupation (1936)
087*	Mother's occupation (1936)
088*	Parents' marital status (1936)
089*	Mother's occupation (1940)
090	Parents' opinion of best occupation (1936)
091	Favorite parent (1940)
092	Amount of conflict with father (1940)
093*	Amount of attachment to father (1940)
094*	Amount of conflict with mother (1940)
095*	Amount of attachment to mother (1940)
096*	Subject rates happiness of parents' marriage (1940)
098*	Subject's opinion on how often punished (1940)
101	Ever wished to be a member of the opposite sex? (1940)
109*	Did you want children? (1940)
114	Parents' report on amount of punishment used (1922)
118*	Subject's level of education (1940)
119*	Subject's occupation (1940)
120*	Combined quotient on Stanford Achievement Test (1922)

Appendix 3.1 (continued)

Variables Used in Data Analyses

Variable number	Description
121*	Stanford Achievement Test: arithmetic quotient (1922)
122*	1922 Intellectual traits
123	1922 Volitional traits
124	1928 Intellectual traits
125	1928 Volitional traits
126*	Parent report on special ability in math (1922)
130	Father's occupation (1922)
131	Amount of schooling of father (1922)
132	Amount of schooling of mother (1922)
133	Parents' marital status (1922)
134	Father's occupation (1928)
135	Parents' marital status (1928)
136	Attitude toward present job (1940)
137	Was present work chosen or drifted into? (1940)
139*	Education level of spouse (1940)
140*	Occupation of spouse (1940)
142	Parents' rating of subject's traits: feelings of inferiority (1940)
143*	Parents' rating of subject's traits: persistence (1940)
144	Parents' rating of subject's traits: integration (1940)
145	Parents' marital status (1940)
146*	Self-rating on traits: self-confidence (1940)
147	Self-rating on traits: persistence (1940)
148	Self-rating on traits: integration (1940)
149*	Self-rating on traits: feelings of inferiority (1940)
163*	Extent of understanding with father (1950)
164*	Extent of understanding with mother (1950)
165	Subject's rating of father's self-confidence (1950)
166*	Subject's rating of mother's self-confidence (1950)
167	Subject's rating of father's helpfulness (1950)
168	Subject's rating of mother's helpfulness (1950)
169	Subject's rating of father's friendliness (1950)
170	Subject's rating of mother's friendliness (1950)
172	Opinion on vocational success of father (1950)
173*	Satisfying aspects of life: work (1950)
174*	Satisfying aspects of life: recognition (1950)
175*	Satisfying aspects of life: income (1950)
176*	Satisfying aspects of life: activities/hobbies (1950)
177*	Satisfying aspects of life: marriage (1950)
178*	Satisfying aspects of life: children (1950)
179*	Satisfying aspects of life: religion (1950)
180*	Satisfying aspects of life: social contacts (1950)
181*	Satisfying aspects of life: community service (1950)
182*	Satisfying aspects of life: other (1950)
183*	Self-rating on self-confidence (1950)
184*	Self-rating on persistence (1950)
185	Self-rating on integration (1950)
186*	Self-rating on feelings of inferiority (1950)
187*	Subject rates admiration for father (1950)
188*	Subject rates admiration for mother (1950)

Appendix 3.1 (continued)

Variables Used in Data Analyses

Variable number	Description
189	Subject rates rebellious feelings toward father (1950)
190	Subject rates rebellious feelings toward mother (1950)
191*	Subject rates father's encouragement of independence (1950)
192*	Subject rates mother's encouragement of independence (1950)
193	Subject rates father's resistance of independence (1950)
194	Subject rates mother's resistance of independence (1950)
195	Subject rates father's rejection (1950)
196	Subject rates mother's rejection (1950)
197	Subject rates how solicitous was father (1950)
198	Subject rates how solicitous was mother (1950)
199*	Subject rates how domineering was father (1950)
200*	Subject rates how domineering was mother (1950)
201	Subject rates father's intelligence (1950)
202	Subject rates mother's intelligence (1950)
203*	Feelings about present vocation (1950)
204*	Subject's occupation (1950)
205*	Spouse's occupation (1950)
208*	Number of children same as planned? (1950)
210*	If life lived over, how many children? (1950)
223*	Prefer duties of housewife to other occupation (1922)
224*	Subject's occupation (1960)
225*	Spouse's occupation (1960)
226*	Historical rating on general adjustment (1960)
229*	Subject's ambition: excellence in work, age 30–40 (1960)
230*	Subject's ambition: excellence in work, since 40 (1960)
231	Subject's ambition: recognition, age 30–40 (1960)
232	Subject's ambition: recognition, since age 40 (1960)
233*	Subject's ambition: vocational advancement, age 30–40 (1960)
234*	Subject's ambition: vocational advancement, since 40 (1960)
235	Subject's ambition: financial gain, age 30–40 (1960)
236	Subject's ambition: financial gain, since 40 (1960)
237	Change in ambition for excellence in work (1960)
238	Change in ambition for recognition (1960)
239	Change in ambition for vocational advancement (1960)
240	Change in ambition for financial gain (1960)
241	Increase in responsibilities or work pressure (1960)
242*	Satisfying aspects of life: work (1960)
243	Satisfying aspects of life: recognition (1960)
244	Satisfying aspects of life: income (1960)
245	Satisfying aspects of life: activities/hobbies (1960)
246*	Satisfying aspects of life: marriage (1960)
247*	Satisfying aspects of life: children (1960)
248	Satisfying aspects of life: religion (1960)
249*	Satisfying aspects of life: social contacts (1960)
250	Satisfying aspects of life: community service (1960)
251	Satisfying aspects of life: other (1960)
252*	Satisfaction 5: measure of general satisfaction using variables 43–47 and 49–53 (1972)

Asterisk indicates variable used in factor analysis (table 3.6).

Appendix 3.2

Correlations Between Satisfying Aspects of Life—1950 and 1960

	1950 ($N = 381$)				1960 ($N = 398$)			
	Work	Mar- riage	Chil- dren	Social contacts	Work	Mar- riage	Chil- dren	Social contacts
1950								
Work		−.07	−.20	.12	.41	−.15	−.31	.13
Marriage			.47	.09	−.14	.56	.32	.01
Children				.11	−.17	.29	.69	.04
Social contacts					.06	−.03	−.03	.39
1960								
Work	.41	−.14	−.17	.06		−.12	−.15	.09
Marriage	−.15	.56	.29	−.03			.40	.00
Children	−.31	.32	.69	−.03				.00
Social contacts	.13	.01	.04	.39				

Appendix 3.3

Probabilities of Differences Between Subsamples in Table 3.7

Variable number	Description	Subsamples	Probability
1	Parents' marriage happy	Single vs. married	.02
1	Parents' marriage happy	No children vs. children	<.10 to >.05
2	Father encouraged independence	Single vs. divorced	.02
2	Father encouraged independence	Single vs. married	>.10
3	Mother encouraged independence	Single vs. divorced	.02
3	Mother encouraged independence	Single vs. married	>.10
4	Mother very self-confident	Single vs. divorced	<.10 to >.05
4	Mother very self-confident	Single vs. married	>.10
8	Mother professional	Single vs. divorced	<.01
8	Mother professional	Single vs. married	>.10
16	Family income over $18,000	IW vs. HM	<.10 to >.05
19	Energy level high	IW vs. HM	.05

4

A MUSICALLY
AND ARTISTICALLY TALENTED
FAMILY NEARLY HALF
A CENTURY LATER[1]

Phyllis Brown Ohanian

ABSTRACT

Since the Terman testing of forty-seven years ago, P.J.B. has evinced several traits noted in early childhood, especially in music. She has performed musically all her life, and has published two song books plus other material. All her children are musical; one is a professional musician. P.J.B. finished college while her children were young, taught school, and later became a school librarian, which position she still holds.

M., her sister, showed early promise in art and writing. Her interests have been maintained, though not professionally. Her daughter is a talented artist.

C., a brother, excelled in music and academic subjects. He is now chairman of the economics department at the Massachusetts Institute of Technology. One of his daughters is on the staff of a city museum for children.

Cn., youngest sister, is creative in art. She has won awards for original designs. Her daughter is an artist and jewelry maker.

L., younger brother, showed artistic promise very early. He is a costume designer in New York City in the field of television, stage, ballet, and opera. L. is also highly interested and knowledgeable in the field of music.

The parents of this family were involved with their children. They supported but did not push, maintaining a climate for achievement and creativity.

---

[1]This is the follow-up of the case studies of two sisters who were tested and observed at Stanford University in 1928, when the elder (the author of this sequel, then named Phyllis Jane Brown) was fifteen years old. See Burks, Jensen, and Terman (1930, pp. 340–57, 479).

Terman tested P.J.B. at age fifteen, in 1928. Forty-seven years later she is married, the mother of three and grandmother of two, and actively working full-time as a high school librarian, with music as her primary avocation.

During her high school years following the testing she was involved in many areas of school activity. She was a member of the girls' tennis team, editor of the high school newspaper, and active in the local Camp Fire Girls organization, spending two summers as a junior counselor at the San Joaquin County Camp Fire Girls camp in the high Sierras. She played baritone horn in the high school band, and was concertmistress of the school orchestra. During these years she was pianist for the Congregational Church in her town, playing for services and accompanying soloists. She gave several joint recitals as a pianist, and gave her own recital during her junior year in high school.

The year after the testing she was graduated from high school as valedictorian of the class. During that year she played first violin in a nearby community symphony orchestra, while continuing the study of piano at a college conservatory as a special student. At the end of her senior year she won the speed-typing championship of the state, as well as the California State Spelling Contest at the state fair. The typing award carried with it a chance to compete in Virginia at the International Typing Contest, which she did, winning second place in the United States in the main event, novice class. She was international winner in the subsequent one-minute competition (110 words without error).

As the country was by then feeling the effects of the Great Depression, the family moved to a university city so that the children might live at home and attend college. Her father left the field of school administration and joined the faculty of a junior college in southern California, which after a year of business training (with a view to working her way through college) P.J.B. attended, with her sister M. as a classmate and their brother C. one year behind them. P.J.B. worked part-time as an author's secretary to pay her college bills and to help her sister through.

During these two years she began the study of organ and played first violin in the local community orchestra. She and her sister were active in campus politics, M. being elected vice-president of the student body and P.J.B. serving a term as president of the associated women students. The sisters graduated as members of the honor society, and then attended the University of California at Los Angeles (UCLA). M. graduated with a major in English. P.J.B. married after her junior year and went to live in New England. Here she taught piano, continued her studies in organ and

---

Two younger siblings were also tested then. Greatest interest centered on a detailed record of the first twenty-five months of P.J.B.'s life that her father had kept and used as the thesis for his master's degree.

composition, and served as a church organist. After her first son was born, she composed children's songs for several school song-book series and wrote an operetta that was presented at the local high school as well as at the junior college she had attended in California.

P.J.B. and her husband were divorced during the war years. She returned to secretarial work, first at the Radiation Laboratory of the Massachusetts Institute of Technology, and later in Washington, D.C., at the Office of Scientific Research and Development. Later she remarried and again moved to New England, at which time music became her vocation. She held a position as church organist for eight years, accompanied her husband's high school and community choruses, taught piano privately, and became the mother of two more sons.

She coauthored a book of children's songs, published simultaneously in hardcover and paperback, followed by a book of nursery songs and several children's anthems, which brought her a listing as a composer in the early editions of *Who's Who of American Women*.

At this point she realized her wish to finish college, which she managed to do in a year plus a summer session. She earned a B.S. in Education degree and was hired to teach in a local elementary school. Feeling after some time that this was not her exact niche, she began studying toward a master's degree in library science while working as a school librarian on the elementary level. For the past few years her position has been on the high school level. Her composing has not been given up, as she has written music for children's story records during the past few years. P.J.B. and her violinist husband[2] learned to play recorder, and for the past several years have played with a baroque group that has weekly meetings and performs upon occasion.

Of her three sons, the eldest (D.C.F.) is a full professor of linguistics at Temple University. Author of several published works, he is married and has two children. He has his Ph.D. degree in English and is listed in the *Directory of American Scholars,* 6th edition. The second son plays French horn in the Boston Symphony and is listed in the 1974–75 *Who's Who in America*. He is married. The third son is a specialist in high-fidelity and stereo components and considers music to be his avocation. All three sons could sing at a very early age, and music is an important part of their lives.

In the forty-year follow-up of the Terman group as adults, the statement is made that they have continued to cultivate a wide range of interests and activities not directly related to their vocations. Certainly this is true of P.J.B., as her activities include not only reading and music, but golf, creative needlework, gourmet cooking, travel (many trips to

---

[2]He is listed in the *International Who's Who in Music.*

Europe; two years spent in Hawaii), and active membership (chapter president 1974–76) in an international women's honorary educational society.

P.J.B.'S SISTER M.

M. was graduated from high school the year after P.J.B., having excelled in art, creative writing, and scholarship. Her designs won blue ribbons at the state fair. She won several regional awards for typing accuracy and played bassoon in the high school band. At the Shakespearean declamation contests she won the regional title once; in the state contest she placed second one year and first the next year. She was also active in the Camp Fire Girls organization.

Joining her sister as a freshman at junior college, she continued to write, her poetry appearing in *First the Blade,* an anthology of verse by Southern California students. She was also active in dramatics, appearing in several plays. M. entered UCLA, majoring in English, and was graduated with honors at the age of twenty. She won second place in the Harper's National College Essay Contest her junior year and placed second the following year in the Atlantic Monthly Essay Contest.

M. married shortly after graduation and took graduate courses at the University of California at Berkeley while her husband finished law school. They then moved to Washington, D.C., in the prewar years. There she completed her work for a junior high school teaching credential and worked as a school attendance officer. During these years she continued to write poetry.

Shortly before World War II began her husband left government service for a corporation position, and their home has been in California ever since. (He is listed in *Who's Who in America.*) They have three children: one son is an attorney practicing in Florida, the second is a junior high school science teacher in Oregon, and their daughter is an artist. M. is now grandmother of three.

For eight years M. was a docent at the Los Angeles County Museum of Art, which job involved writing student preparatory material sent out to Los Angeles children. She also wrote courses of study for a new program for inner-city children. M. was for several years a member of the Los Angeles Area Board of Camp Fire Girls.

M.'s creativity has shown itself in all facets of her life: her home, her handwork, her outside interests. Not primarily a musician, she was, however, part of a recorder group that practiced together for several years. She has always been intensely interested in the theater. M. is a "collector" of poetry—she has memorized hundreds of lines in English and French, which she recites to herself at odd moments, and which she treasures. Her latest activity has been the intensive study of French, preparatory to spending the first year of retirement with her husband in France. She says that she has always been in love with the sound of words, and enjoys putting just the right ones together to express a thought.

P.J.B.'S BROTHER C.

The third of the siblings mentioned in the Terman report is C., who is a year younger than M. The results of the Terman Group Test at age ten years two months gave him an IQ of 157. C. graduated from a much larger high school than did his two older sisters. His academic record was excellent, and he was a member of the tennis team. Before that, he had played solo clarinet in the high school band and orchestra. He, too, attended junior college, and there his interest in economics led to his transferring to the University of California at Berkeley, where he graduated as an economics major and a member of Phi Beta Kappa.

After a year of graduate school, during which time he married, he transferred to Harvard University to begin work for his Ph.D. degree. The war intervened, and he spent several years with the Treasury Department in Washington. Returning to Harvard afterward, he finished his advanced degree and joined the faculty of the Massachusetts Institute of Technology, where he has remained. C., now chairman of the economics department, is listed in *Who's Who in America.*

C.'s early interest in art and music have persisted through the years, and he is still an avid tennis player. He has two daughters. One of these, a former elementary school teacher, is now on the staff of a city children's museum and the wife of a Ph.D. candidate. The other, formerly a teacher in inner-city Philadelphia, is now the wife of a physician in that city. C. has two grandchildren.

P.J.B.'S YOUNGEST SISTER, CN.

Cn., another sister, three years younger than C., attended junior college and UCLA. She sang in various church and school groups and played the piano and clarinet in her earlier school days. Cn. is married to the Dean of Student Services at a large California city college. Cn. has always been extremely artistic and innovative—a quilt of her own design and handiwork won an award in 1973. Her main hobby is handwork, but others are as varied as sailing, community service, and music.

She has two children. One is a son with a Ph.D. degree in zoology, doing laboratory research in a large midwestern university science department. He has been musical since babyhood, and enjoys playing piano and guitar. Her daughter is an artist and jewelry maker in Colorado. Cn. has two grandchildren by her son.

P.J.B.'S YOUNGER BROTHER, L.

L., the youngest of the family, and unmarried, was one month old when P.J.B. and M. were tested at Stanford in 1928. He showed artistic and musical promise at a very early age, as well as high intelligence; his Stanford–Binet IQ was computed to be 167 when he was four years old. Entering school at the age of six, he was promoted to second grade at the end of the first week and third grade the following week. His great interest as a child was the designing and making of puppets and putting on puppet shows. He attended UCLA as a fine arts major, then did his graduate work in theater arts. This was followed by a sojourn in the army, after which he moved to New York City and began his work there in which he continues to the present time. A costume designer for television, ballet, the Broadway stage, and the films, he has costumed several NBC operas, as well as many special productions. He takes short leaves from New York to do plays about the country (e.g., at the Guthrie Theatre in Minneapolis, the Stratford Shakespeare Theatres in Connecticut and Ontario, and in the Los Angeles area). His latest contract will take him to Europe to design an opera.

In January 1966, L. was written up in the *American Artist* magazine as an "Artist in the Theatre." His vocation is his avocation; being constantly on the prowl for inspiration, he is an avid theater and museum buff. Music is a constant delight to him, and living in New York he has ample opportunity to sample all the offerings of a great cultural center.

CONCLUDING REMARKS

These, then, are the five B. children, the two oldest of whom were tested by Terman's staff in 1928. The creativity and achievement found in the siblings and their children is now beginning to show itself in their grandchildren, as P.J.B.'s granddaughter has had drawings done by her at the age of three published in a magazine devoted to school arts. The other eight grandchildren are younger, and so far no studies have been made on them.

P.J.B. recalls her parents as "caring": a mother who after a full day of teaching sat nightly with her children around the study table, correcting her own papers and giving what help was needed in the early school years. She believed in reading aloud to her children, and singing to and with them; music was a daily experience. Her father was never too busy to answer questions or to drive twenty miles to take children to music or tennis lessons or to concerts. He himself played tennis with those of his children who were interested in the game. P.J.B.'s mother bought piano duet books, and the mother–daughter duet playing continued for years. Both parents believed that the best books, musical instruments, art supplies, and sports equipment they could afford were a good investment —plus, of course, the teachers to go with them. Their discipline was fairly strict. They liked their children to be "doers" and creators, and their interest was always active. P.J.B. does not view her parents as "pushers" —rather as "expecters." They maintained a climate for achievement and expected the best efforts their children could put forth.

REFERENCE

Burks, B. S., Jensen, D. W., and Terman, L. M. 1930. The promise of youth: Follow-up studies of a thousand gifted children. *Genetic studies of genius*, vol. III. Stanford, Calif.: Stanford University Press.

II
TWO LONGITUDINAL STUDIES AT THE JOHNS HOPKINS UNIVERSITY: THE STUDY OF MATHEMATICALLY PRECOCIOUS YOUTH AND THE INTELLECTUALLY GIFTED CHILD STUDY GROUP

5

RATIONALE OF THE STUDY OF MATHEMATICALLY PRECOCIOUS YOUTH (SMPY) DURING ITS FIRST FIVE YEARS OF PROMOTING EDUCATIONAL ACCELERATION

Julian C. Stanley

ABSTRACT

The Study of Mathematically Precocious Youth (SMPY) began officially at The Johns Hopkins University in September 1971 under a five-year grant from the Spencer Foundation. Its staff, headed by Professor (of psychology) Julian C. Stanley, seeks highly effective ways to facilitate the education of youths who reason extremely well mathematically. To do so, it is of course necessary first to identify such youths and understand them well. During SMPY's initial five years, much service was rendered to the mathematically talented in the State of Maryland, especially seventh and eighth graders in the Greater Baltimore area. This enabled the SMPY staff to develop and refine principles, techniques, and practices with which to improve the education of intellectually talented students there and elsewhere. SMPY's underlying rationale is not fully obvious from the two books that report its substantive achievements. Thus it seems desirable to state that rationale clearly so that its assumptions can be examined by all persons who consider using SMPY's practices. This chapter is the initial attempt to set forth explicitly the point of view guiding SMPY's activities.

Results of the first year of the Study of Mathematically Precocious Youth at The Johns Hopkins University were reported in a book entitled *Mathematical Talent: Discovery, Description, and Development* (Stanley, Keating, and Fox 1974). Findings during the following three years are contained in a larger book entitled *Intellectual Talent: Research and Development* (Keating 1976). In this paper I shall not attempt to summarize the twenty-seven chapters of those two books, but instead shall present the rationale of the study as it has been worked out by me in close collaboration with a number of associates, especially Lynn H. Fox, Daniel P. Keating, Susanne A. Denham, Linda K. Greenstein, William C. George, Cecilia H. Solano, and Sanford J. Cohn. The reader will see how our extreme emphasis on educational acceleration has greatly helped many youths who were *eager* to move ahead academically.

WHY MATHEMATICAL REASONING IS THE INITIAL BASIS FOR IDENTIFICATION

The Study of Mathematically Precocious Youth (abbreviated SMPY) began informally at The Johns Hopkins University during the summer of 1968 when Doris K. Lidtke, an instructor in computer science, called my attention to a twelve-year-old boy just out of the seventh grade who was doing remarkable things in the computer laboratory. It started slowly and without a name.

Emphasis on the mathematical and physical sciences began early, however. Persons often ask us why we chose mathematical reasoning ability rather than something else, or even why we decided to concentrate on one type of talent rather than studying all sorts. We wanted to steer a careful course between excessive specialism and overly broad coverage.

Sharply limited resources made this decision inevitable. Even for the first two years after the study was funded by the Spencer Foundation in 1971 it did not have a single full-time worker, and after that there was just one. During the 1976–77 academic year our entire regular staff consisted of William C. George, the full-timer; Cecilia H. Solano, a fourth-year doctoral student in psychology who worked ten hours per week on the study; Sanford J. Cohn, a second-year doctoral student in psychology who worked twenty hours weekly; me, who devoted to it as much time as being a professor of psychology with unreduced teaching responsibilities permitted; the administrative secretary, Lois Sandhofer; and a part-time secretary, Laura Thommen. Small wonder that we did not also select initially for other talents such as verbal reasoning ability, athletic prowess, musical talent, and leadership potential! No matter how hard we might work (and we do indeed put in long hours), relatively little could be done by us for that varied a group.

In response, however, to persistent inquiries about verbal reasoning ability after SMPY was funded, we encouraged JHU psychology professors Catherine J. Garvey, Robert T. Hogan, and Roger A. Webb to obtain from a philanthropic foundation a five-year grant (1972–77) with which to pioneer in that area. For reports of their work see Hogan et al. (1977), Viernstein et al. (1977), McGinn (1976), Viernstein and Hogan (1975), and Webb (1974).

Given that we must specialize, it seemed sensible to choose an ability closely related to major subjects in the academic curricula of public and private schools in the United States. Because we planned to help intellectually talented youths improve their education, it appeared wise to start at as early a grade and age level as the developing of the chosen ability permitted. In order to capitalize on the precocious development of this ability by greatly accelerating school progress in the subject-matter area concerned, it was necessary to choose school subjects much more highly dependent for their mastery on manifest intellectual talent than on chronological age and the associated life experiences. These considerations led to our choosing mathematical reasoning as the ability and the best of the standard courses in mathematics, the mathematical sciences, and the physical sciences as the subjects on which to focus directly. We did not want to develop curricula in mathematics, but instead to help mathematically talented boys and girls use their abilities more effectively in the various academic areas.

We were aided in this choice by more than just armchair considerations. Great precocity in mathematics and the physical sciences is documented by such writers as Harvey C. Lehman (1953), Catharine M. Cox (1926) in the second volume of Terman's *Genetic Studies of Genius* series,[1] Eric Temple Bell (1937), and Edna Kramer (1974). The only clear competitor was musical composition, where the almost unbelievably early accomplishments of Saint-Saëns, Mozart, and Mendelssohn are well known (see Schonberg 1970). This does not articulate well with school curricula, however, nor do we have the knowledge or facilities to nurture young composers. We eliminated chess because it is not an academic discipline.

Two who helped begin the study (Lynn H. Fox and I) had been teachers of high school mathematics, and I of chemistry and general science also. My undergraduate major had been physical science, and much of my graduate and postdoctoral work has been in statistics at three

---

[1]It is well for the reader to keep in mind the nature of these five volumes, the years in which they appeared, and the fact that their publisher (the Stanford University Press) has kept the whole series in print for more than half a century. References are as follows: Terman (1925), Cox (1926), Burks, Jensen, and Terman (1930), and Terman and Oden (1947, 1959). They have been extended by Oden (1968) and by chapter 3 in this volume. Further analyses of the 1972 follow-up survey are being conducted by Robert R. Sears (1977) and Lee J. Cronbach.

universities. As a Fellow of the American Statistical Association and of the American Association for the Advancement of Science, I felt competent to help students make decisions in the areas of mathematics and science, aided of course by consultation and collaboration with high school and college teachers, supervisors, and administrators.

Also, I had a master's degree in educational and vocational counseling and guidance and much background in evaluation and testing. These proved invaluable.

My interest in intellectually gifted youths began at the University of Georgia during the summer of 1938, after my first year of teaching in high school (see Stanley 1976a, pp. 6–9). It smouldered from then on, coming to the level of publication occasionally (e.g., Stanley 1954a, b; 1958; 1959a, b). Not until 1969, however, did I begin helping intellectually talented youngsters systematically (Stanley 1974, pp. 12–14; 1976a, p. 9).

It is interesting to note here as an aside that the SMPY staff has had little difficulty in planning closely with top-flight mathematicians and scientists, but has met with distrust from some mathematics supervisors and teachers who do not understand how university psychologists could know anything about their subjects. There is an element of defensiveness in this, of course, because we have prodded school personnel to do much more for mathematically highly talented students than is usually done.

Thus we settled upon mathematical reasoning ability developed to a high level at an early age as the basis for initial selection of students to be studied considerably more and helped to develop fast and well in mathematics and related subjects. We did this for logical, empirical, and personal reasons. Somewhat more of our rationale can be gleaned from Stanley (1954a, b; 1958; 1959a, b; 1974; 1976a–f).

We would not have begun this kind of project had we not agreed fully with Thomas Gray ("Elegy Written in a Country Churchyard," 1751, line 53) that

> Full many a gem of purest ray serene
> The dark unfathomed caves of ocean bear;
> Full many a flower is born to blush unseen,
> And waste its sweetness on the desert air.

WHY SAT-M SCORE IS THE INITIAL CRITERION

We wanted to find youths who at an early age (mostly twelve or thirteen) were already able to reason extremely well with simple mathematical facts, students who even before taking or completing the first year of algebra would reason mathematically much better than the average male twelfth grader does. We gave applicants for the talent-search contest plenty of practice materials for the forthcoming test so that they would be on essentially the same footing with respect to opportunity to score well. Because reasoning mathematically involves reasoning with some mathematics, however elementary, this was essential in order to smooth out at least partially their differences in mathematical training and outside-of-school experiences. We did not want scores to depend much on rote knowledge of mathematical concepts or on computational ability, as the usual test of mathematical "aptitude" does, because we surmised that these could be taught readily and quickly to students whose mathematical reasoning ability is splendid. It seemed to us likely that the reasoning test would predict success in later mathematics, at least through advanced calculus and linear algebra, far better than items measuring rote memory and computational speed and accuracy would.

Thus we needed a mathematical reasoning test difficult enough that the average participant in our contest would score on it halfway between a chance score and a perfect score. For example, if there were sixty items and scores were "corrected for chance," we wanted the mean score of our examinees, a highly able group, to be about 30. Also, the test should have enough "ceiling"—be difficult enough for even the ablest entrants into the contest—so that virtually no scores of 60 would occur.

In addition to the considerations of reasoning content and appropriate difficulty, we wanted a professionally prepared, carefully standardized, reliable test for which several well-guarded ("secure") forms existed and for which well-known, meaningful interpretations of scores were available. High scores on the test should command immediate attention and respect at both the high school and college levels, because they could be compared with scores on the same test earned by superior high school seniors.

These considerations led to pilot studies of the mathematical part of the College Entrance Examination Board's Scholastic Aptitude Test (SAT-M).[2] Our first examinee, an obviously brilliant thirteen-year-old eighth grader, scored 669, which was then the 96th percentile of a random sample of male twelfth graders. On the verbal part of SAT, abbreviated SAT-V, he scored 590, the 93rd percentile of the same norm group. The next thirteen-year-old eighth grader on whom we tried the test scored 716 on M and 608 on V. Others scored similarly, some even higher. None scored near the perfect score of 60 right on M or 90 right on V. It seemed likely, then, that SAT-M would be excellent for identifying the level of mathematical reasoning ability we sought among seventh and eighth graders. SAT-V could be used with the high scorers on SAT-M to assess verbal reasoning ability, which seemed likely to be more closely related to

[2]For its history and rationale, see Downey (1961).

speed of thinking and of taking tests than is SAT-M. As has been shown in several publications, especially Stanley, Keating, and Fox (1974) and Keating (1976), for the students we tested SAT-M and SAT-V did indeed prove suitable in both content and difficulty. The mean on each was appropriately between the chance- and perfect-score levels. The highest scores were never perfect. Only an occasional examinee scored as high as 55 out of 60 on SAT-M. A twelve-year-old did score 58, and a thirteen-year-old scored 59, but these were the extreme exceptions among some 3,000 youths tested.

More importantly, SAT-M and SAT-V proved to have great value for predicting which students would be able to accelerate their mathematical education radically. Of course, motivational factors—especially, willingness to do difficult homework well—proved crucial within the high-scoring group, but without considerable ability of the SAT-M and SAT-V types students could not race ahead successfully in mathematics and related areas.

We have learned that the SAT-M score scale is valid right up to the top-reported score, 800, *if* the criteria themselves have enough "ceiling" for the group. For instance, in the usual eighth- or ninth-grade algebra I class, variation in this ability would probably make little difference in apparent success of students at SAT-M levels 500, 600, 700, or 800, because all of these exceed the mathematical-reasoning demands of the course. Paying attention and bothering to do homework and tests carefully are probably better determiners of grades among these high-scorers than are differences of the order of even 100 to 300 points. Put a 500-scorer into a fast-paced, homogeneously grouped 700-level algebra III class, however, and he is unlikely to be able to keep up at all. In general, most reports that a test of appropriate difficulty loses its validity at some point short of the top of its score scale are actually commentaries on the lack of ceiling of the criterion, rather than intrinsic dropping off of validity of the predictor. This seems especially true when both the predictor and the criterion variables are ability-test scores.

We realize that a factor analysis of SAT-M scores would show several factors, perhaps somewhat different for our youths than for the usual older examinees (see Pruzek and Coffman 1966). Because the criteria we use are also factorially heterogeneous, however, this is probably at least as much an asset as a liability.

The setting and rules of the mathematics talent searches tended to attract interested, mathematically able students who liked keen competition. The entrants were probably about the upper 1½ percent of their age group in mathematical reasoning ability (i.e., the top 1 in about 67). It would be foolish to administer the SAT-M to twelve- to thirteen-year-old students much less able than that, and even more unwise to test them with SAT-V, because SAT is designed for above-average eleventh and twelfth graders.

SAT-V proved rather difficult for some of the seventh graders who scored extremely high on SAT-M. Verbal reasoning ability seems more closely related to age than mathematical reasoning ability is and also more closely related to the verbal ability of the child's parents and their socioeconomic level. Nevertheless, splendid mathematical reasoners who were seventh or eighth graders seldom scored lower on SAT-V than the average twelfth grader does. For example, in the first mathematics and science talent search the 35 top boys out of the 265 male entrants averaged the 95th percentile of a random sample of high school seniors on M and the 87th on V. Of course, that type of regression (here, .4 of a standard deviation) is to be expected in any group chosen on one variable and then examined on another variable not perfectly correlated with it.

It would be rare, indeed, for a person to have excellent mathematical *reasoning* ability and yet be inferior to average thinkers in verbal *reasoning* ability. SMPY does not seek mere calculating freaks (Barlow 1952). Though its participants are not chosen explicitly for high IQ, virtually none of them have average or below-average IQs.

Most persons who upon entering their teens already reason extremely well mathematically, as indicated by a high score on SAT-M, will not become "pure" mathematicians. Far less than half of them will even major in mathematics as college undergraduates. Instead, most of the boys and some of the girls will specialize in the physical sciences (especially physics), engineering, computer science, mathematical statistics, operations research, economics, and other areas in which a good grasp of mathematics is essential. Some will go into medicine because of the prestige and financial compensation it usually offers, even though few persons holding M.D. degrees can make much use of great talent for mathematics. Medicine and law seem more likely choices for girls than for boys, because even yet the former tend to shy away from mathematics, engineering, and the physical sciences. A large percentage of the boys will probably work toward Ph.D. degrees.

Whenever one uses a test and has a fixed point above which the examinee is considered "successful" and below which he is considered "unsuccessful," the issue of false positives and false negatives arises. Some students will have a good day and equal or exceed the criterion, whereas others will have a bad day and drop below it. On another occasion the former would have failed and the latter have succeeded. SMPY guards against false positives by retesting at a later date with an extremely heavy battery of difficult tests all those persons who attained the criterion—e.g., SAT-M score of 640 or more during the second or third talent searches. The initially lucky scorer will be detected easily. Thus, for the retested group positive errors of measurement (see Stanley 1971) are not much of a problem, nor is the inevitably somewhat-less-than-perfect validity of SAT-M itself.

There will, however, be some youths inappropriately consigned to the below-640 group. A score of 630 represents only a point or two less, out of the possible 60 points, than a score of 640 does. The 10-point difference between 630 and 640 is only about one third of a standard error of measurement. Obviously, small fluctuations in score at this level will make the difference between being identified as an excellent enough mathematical reasoner to warrant being studied considerably more and helped a great deal and being consigned to the less mathematically brilliant group. This problem is unavoidable, no matter what score criterion is used. The 640 was chosen because it screened in just about as many students (about 7 percent of those who entered the contest) as it was feasible to test further and work with closely. Also, it was only about 20 points below the average SAT-M score as eleventh and twelfth graders of Johns Hopkins's freshmen, an impressive figure indeed for seventh and eighth graders.

There are several justifications for not worrying inordinately about the false negatives:

1. If seventh graders, they were eligible to enter the contest again the next year as eighth graders and were encouraged to do so. This worked, however, only for seventh graders tested in the March 1972 and January 1973 (i.e., the first and second) contests, because the January 1974 contest was the last of the initial series. (The contest resumed, with seventh graders only, in the fall of 1976.)

2. SMPY offered a great deal of help to all contestants who scored 420 or more, and most of them did.

3. It was unlikely that a student who scored as low as 630 would with better luck have exceeded 700, so probably few of the false-negative eighth graders would have been among the very highest scorers.

4. Relatively few students scored in the 610–630 range.

5. Nearly all of the students entering the contests would later, as eleventh graders or earlier, take both the Preliminary SAT and the SAT and recalibrate their levels of mathematical aptitude.

6. The SAT-M scores from the SMPY contest did not "count" anything for school or other purposes. Most such scores made the student look good and gave his parents and teachers evidence with which to argue that special provisions in mathematics for him/her were desirable. For example, 420 on SAT-M exceeds the score earned by approximately 57

percent of male eleventh and twelfth graders. To be that apt three to five years early is impressive.

SMPY FOCUSES ITS EFFORTS

SMPY is developmental and longitudinal but not retrospective. Its staff identifies at the seventh- or eighth-grade level students who are already superior reasoners mathematically and observes their development (while trying to influence it) over the ensuing years. Its staff does not have the time or interest to delve deeply into the "whys" of their precocity. While not wholly without interest to us, questions such as "Is mathematical talent mainly inherited?" are largely outside SMPY's scope. We are concerned mostly with capitalizing on the high-level reasoning ability and the motivation to use it that can be found among youths twelve or thirteen years old. It is already-evident ability we seek, rather than some presumed underlying potential that has not yet become manifest. We leave it to others to study the origins of such ability, the effects of nature and nurture on it during the early years, the failure of mathematical ability to arise in what are otherwise bright children, and the treatment of "underachievers." These are important topics, but strenuous efforts to help the vastly neglected hordes of well-motivated mathematically apt youths who are caught in the interest-killing traps of routine mathematics classrooms leave us little time for them.

We are, however, greatly interested in the nature of mathematical talent as it develops and unfolds, especially from age twelve or so onward. We do care, too, how intellectual prodigies of the past have turned out (e.g., Wiener 1953 and Montour 1976*a, b*). Some books that we have found helpful are Bell (1937), Krutetskii (1976), and Skemp (1971). Also, see Fox (1976*c*).

WHY IDENTIFICATION USUALLY
BEGINS AT THE JUNIOR HIGH SCHOOL LEVEL

Elementary mathematics is, from the standpoint of the learner, heavily an algorithmic and deductive system, though for those who create it there are usually strong intuitive and aesthetic elements. Unlike understanding philosophy or great novels such as Tolstoy's *War and Peace*, personal experience outside the classroom and maturation closely tied to chronological age are not essential for learning mathematics well. Certain types of reasoning ability necessary for mastering subjects such as high school algebra develop at vastly different ages. A precocious ten-year-old may be superior in this respect to most adults. To him or her, mathematics and related subjects such as computer science may be seen as interesting games, little related to the real world of experience.

A startling example will illustrate this. At age ten one of SMPY's participants made the highest grade in a state college introduction-to-computer-science course, competing with seven of our exceptionally able older students and twelve adults. Before his eleventh birthday he completed at Johns Hopkins most of a second-level computer course on which he earned a final grade of A. At age eleven he earned, by examination, credit for two semesters of the calculus at Johns Hopkins. This is no ordinary boy, of course. His Stanford–Binet IQ at age eight was 190, and he had been in our special fast-mathematics classes for two years. Even he is not the most precocious youth we have discovered.[3] Furthermore, at age twelve to thirteen, when the typical child is in the seventh or eighth grade, there are quite a few students able to forge through all of precalculus mathematics *far* quicker than schools ordinarily permit them to do.

The first year of algebra usually causes serious problems for youths who are among the ablest few percent of their classmates in mathematical reasoning ability. Regardless of how advanced their ability is, seldom are they permitted to take this subject before the eighth or ninth grade. Then, no matter how much algebra I the student can already do or how quickly he or she could learn the material and go on to second-year algebra, the student is usually lockstepped into approximately 180 forty-five- or fifty-minute daily periods throughout the school year. Mathematically highly precocious youths need vastly less exposure to what is for them an extremely easy subject. This is especially true when the student has already had one or more years of "modern" mathematics that may have included much algebra covertly. Several examples from our experience will illustrate the mathematically talented youth's dilemma.

A twelve-year-old seventh grader who scored extremely high in one of SMPY's annual contests asked permission to join his junior high school's eighth-grade algebra I class in February but was refused on the grounds that he already had missed more than half the course. He insisted on being given a standardized test covering the first year of the subject. On this he made a perfect score, 40 right in forty minutes, which is two

---

[3]Even more psychometrically precocious was the boy of Chinese background who at age ten years one month scored 600 on SAT-V and 680 on SAT-M, and a year later scored 710V and 750M. SMPY's youngest college graduate thus far is Eric Robert Jablow, born 24 March 1962, who received his B.S. degree in mathematics *summa cum laude* from Brooklyn College in June of 1977. In the fall of 1977 he became a doctoral student in mathematics at Princeton University.

points above the 99.5th percentile of national norms for ninth-grade students who have been in this type of class all year. Upon seeing this achievement, the teacher agreed with the boy that he was indeed ready to join the class! Instead, he took a college mathematics course that summer and easily earned a final grade of A.

At the end of the sixth grade a student took second-year algebra in summer school without having had first-year algebra; his final grade was A. By the end of the eighth grade he had earned credit by examination for two semesters of college calculus. A year later he had completed third-semester calculus by correspondence from a major university, earning A as his final grade.

A student learned two and one-half years of algebra well by being tutored while in the fifth and sixth grades. He continued, by means of tutoring, with a high-level course in geometry. His tutor in geometry was a sixteen-year-old freshman at Johns Hopkins who enrolled for honors advanced calculus (final grade, A) and other subjects that most nineteen-year-olds would find extremely difficult. He, too, condensed his mathematics radically.

Several girls have accelerated their progress in mathematics considerably, though not as much as the boys discussed above. One of them graduated from high school a year early while being one of the best students in SMPY's second high-level college calculus class.

Many other such examples could be given (e.g., see Stanley 1974, 1976 *a-f*) to show that the usual high school pace in algebra I to III, geometry, trigonometry, analytic geometry, and the calculus is far from optimum for boys and girls who reason extremely well mathematically. Algebra I is a particularly virulent culprit, because being incarcerated in it for a whole year gives the apt student no really appropriate way to behave. He or she can daydream, be excessively meticulous in order to get perfect grades, harass the teacher, show off knowledge arrogantly in the class, or be truant. There is, however, no *suitable* way to while away the class hours when one already knows much of the material and can learn the rest almost instantaneously as it is first presented. Boredom, frustration, and habits of gross inattention are almost sure to result.

We are amazed that even more youths do not sustain obvious academic injury, and we suspect that the damage is greater than it seems. At least, it appears uncomfortably likely that motivation for mathematics may suffer appreciably in all but those few students devoted to the subject. After such snail-pacing in high school precalculus and calculus—often, five and one-half years or more—the number of top minds still excited by mathematics may be few.

The remedy for this unfortunate situation is conceptually simple but seldom employed. It consists of the regular and appropriate use of tests.

First, those students with great mathematical reasoning ability are found. Then various tests of achievement in mathematics are administered to them. This enables mathematics teachers to determine what a particular talented student does not yet know and arrange for him or her to learn those points, and those only, fast but well.

Seldom, though, does the teacher of beginning algebra use an achievement test during the first week of class to locate the students who might, with a little individual help, move into second-year algebra right away. Also, not nearly enough use is made of the mathematics scores from the achievement batteries that most schools administer. Those tests are not difficult enough to differentiate adequately among the top several percent of the group, but at least they do single out potentially exceptionally able youths.

In special classes where students are grouped homogeneously according to high mathematical reasoning ability, SMPY has found that first-year algebra can be mastered in from nine to twenty two-hour weekly periods—and, as noted above, some exceptionally able students do not need even that much. Details about this are contained in Fox (1974*a*, 1976*b*) and Stanley (1976*b*). Other precalculus courses and the calculus can also be learned quickly by mathematically apt youths, as George and Denham (1976), George (1976), and Stanley (1976*b*) document rather fully.

To go beyond first-year algebra, youths need certain better-developed mental qualities, especially excellent reasoning ability and Piagetian formal-operations status. SMPY's testing and experience with special instructional programs and the studies by Keating (1975) and Keating and Schaefer (1975) indicate that the intellectually top 1 or 2 percent of students as low as the fifth grade probably already have these abilities well enough developed to learn algebra II and other precalculus courses well. Speed of learning them is dependent on level of ability, quality of instruction and pacing, stimulation by classmates or tutor, and the mysterious ingredient called motivation that makes the student willing (or, ideally, eager) to do a great deal of homework excellently between classes.

For these reasons SMPY conducted its three annual mathematics talent searches among seventh and eighth graders, but also did special work among sixth graders and a few students even younger than that. Students whose mathematical reasoning abilities proved to be superb were encouraged to move fast through the high school mathematics sequence, beginning with algebra I or skipping it and ending *soon* with calculus so well learned that college credit for it could be obtained. Somewhat less able entrants were given less drastic suggestions, but nevertheless encouraged to speed up their progress in mathematics and science. Experience of several years has shown that youths able and eager to move ahead can do so readily if they and their parents are resolute and persistent in their search for suitable ways.

Tentative physiological evidence concerning the suitability of the age period twelve to thirteen for accelerating educational progress was suggested rather recently by Epstein (1974a, b). He found spurts in both brain development and mental age, one of them at chronological ages ten to twelve. Mental age seemed to grow especially slowly during the years twelve to fourteen and then to spurt again for the final time at fourteen to sixteen. Thus junior high school students (grades seven to nine) may be on a mental plateau. We do not know, however, whether his findings characterize precocious youths, who might spurt at different times than average students do. It seems congruent with our experience to postulate that by age twelve some youths already have great learning potential that seems to accelerate to the point that by age fourteen to sixteen they are fully ready to succeed in a selective college. We have not noticed any tendency for SMPY participants to have merely reached a rather high level of ability early and to remain there. Obviously, though, the developmental curve for a given ability might differ greatly from one person to another, depending on genetically programmed potential, environmental stimulation, and the interaction of these two.

WHY NOT CONDUCT A CONTROLLED EXPERIMENT?

Because experimentation is a strong force in psychology and in my own background (e.g., Campbell and Stanley 1966; Stanley 1973), we were tempted to set SMPY up as a rigorously controlled experiment. Upon reflection, however, we came to believe that there were cogent reasons for not doing so. Some of those considerations were the following:

1. We were rather sure that the smorgasbord of accelerative educational opportunities we planned to offer the "experimental" subjects in the study were much more likely to help than to harm them. Therefore, it would be inadvisable to withhold such opportunities from a portion of the subjects (probably half of them) who in a controlled experiment would be assigned randomly to a "control" group.

2. There were not likely to be enough extremely high scorers to make the numbers in both the experimental and the control group sufficiently large to yield statistically powerful or precise comparisons between groups and subgroups. It seemed more sensible to take the N ablest subjects and mass the experimental efforts on them.

3. The procedures, principles, and techniques that SMPY planned to develop would be disseminated widely by the press and in speeches, letters, articles, books, and newsletters, so withholding knowledge of opportunities from a control group of subjects would be impossible. The control group would be substantially exposed to influences designed only for the experimental group, and that type of contamination would greatly weaken or even nullify the experiment.

4. By not having a control group from which certain presumably beneficial opportunities and information were withheld, it is possible to keep the study completely on an above-board basis, with no need to deceive anyone about anything. This openness is important in gaining the confidence of the students, their parents and teachers, and the general public.

5. Certain comparisons could be made by matching and other quasi-experimental procedures. Fox (1976*b*) did this in her study of sex differences in mathematical aptitude and achievement, as have other SMPY researchers in trying to determine how well a certain special procedure worked.

SMPY plans to use a completely controlled experimental design in its attempt to increase interest in chemistry among mathematically talented youths, but not to deceive either group about the nature of the study. Members of the control group will get equivalent educational stimulation, though not in chemistry. The staff of SMPY is not at all sure in advance that the chemistry "treatment" will be effective, so it seems reasonable to withhold it from some of the ablest youths (with their knowledge and consent) while giving them the same amount of attention in certain other areas. Of course, despite SMPY's best efforts, this experiment will be contaminated somewhat by knowledge of its nature and by whatever spillover of chemistry influence from the experimental to the control group that may occur, but if the experimental variables are not potent enough to triumph over these, they are probably not of great practical value. Careful attention to the sources of invalidity spelled out by Campbell and Stanley (1966) will help keep the experiment as unbiased as possible. Experimentation with humans in important, relevant "field" situations is seldom as easy or neat as experimentation under laboratory conditions can be. Often, however, it yields more important, albeit perhaps somewhat equivocal, information.

6. A great deal of SMPY's analysis of the results of its programs depends heavily on case-study clinical methods, using all known information about each individual with as much insight as can be mustered on the basis of considerable experience with many mathematically precocious youths (see Hudson 1975). Burt (1975, p. 138) states this point especially clearly:

With human beings, when the problem is primarily psychological, statistical studies of populations should always be supplemented by case studies of individuals: early histories will often shed further light on the origin and development of this or that peculiarity. Tests should be supplemented by what Binet called the *méthode clinique*, and interpreted by introspective observations, designed to verify the tacit assumption that they really do test what they are intended to assess. After all, each child is a complex and conscious organism, nor a mere unit in a statistical sample.

Fortunately, many of SMPY's procedures yield results so different from the usual ones that the effects are obvious. For instance, it is almost preposterous to suggest that if SMPY had not found a certain youth when he was an over-age sixth grader and helped him in many ways to move ahead educationally fast and well he would, nevertheless, have been graduated from a major university at barely seventeen years of age. The youngest recipient of a bachelor's degree in 1971 at Johns Hopkins was nineteen years ten months old (Eisenberg 1977). Two years later, under SMPY's influence, the youngest was seventeen years seven months old, and three months later he had completed a master's degree also. Now seventeen-year-old graduates are frequent. Similar strong observations could be made about most of SMPY's programs, such as the effects of the fast-math classes (Fox 1974*b*; George and Denham 1976; Stanley 1976*b*).

THREE SEQUENTIAL ASPECTS OF SMPY: D³

The first book-length report about SMPY's initial work (Stanley, Keating, and Fox 1974) was entitled *Mathematical Talent: Discovery, Description, and Development*. To emphasize the three D's, we sometimes abbreviate that title, pseudo-mathematically, as MT:D³. Discovery is the identification phase during which the talent is found. Description is the study phase during which the most talented students are tested further and otherwise studied a great deal. This leads to the prime reason for SMPY, the development phase. During it the youths who were found and studied are continually helped, facilitated, and encouraged. Each is offered a smorgasbord of educational possibilities (see Fox 1974*a*, 1976*a*; Stanley 1976*a*) from which to choose whatever combination, including nothing, that best suits the individual. Some splendid mathematical reasoners try almost everything at breakneck speed, whereas others do little special. SMPY offers as much educational and vocational counseling and guidance as its resources permit, both via memoranda and its newsletter—ITYB, the *Intellectually Talented Youth Bulletin*—and individually as requested.

Most studies of intellectually gifted children are heavy on description but light on educational facilitation. From the start the SMPY staff has been determined to intervene strongly on behalf of the able youths it found. Thus discovery and description were seen as necessary steps leading to strong emphasis on accelerating educational development, particularly in mathematics and related subjects.

WHY ACCELERATION RATHER THAN
ENRICHMENT IS STRESSED

There were both logical and empirical reasons why we chose to emphasize educational acceleration rather than enrichment. Some of them are implied above, such as that mathematically highly apt students can move through the standard mathematics curriculum much faster and better than they usually do. Fears expressed by teachers or parents about their missing important concepts or techniques because of the speed are usually groundless and, indeed, often merely a rationalization for inaction. Such students are likely to doze through the 5 percent they do not know when it is camouflaged by the 95 percent they already know, because under these circumstances there is no incentive for them to be alert. SMPY has evidence (see Fox 1974*b*, George and Denham 1976; Stanley 1976*b*) that students who reason extremely well mathematically learn first-year algebra considerably better in a few two-hour periods with their intellectual peers than they do in regular all-year classes.

There seem to be four main kinds of educational enrichment: busy work, irrelevant academic, cultural, and relevant academic. In our opinion, for reasons to be stated below, only the third (cultural) is well suited to mathematically highly precocious youths; it does not, however, meet their needs in mathematics itself or in the other usual academic subjects.

Busy work is a well-known way for some teachers to keep their brightest students occupied while the class goes on with its regular work. In a common form it consists of having them do a great deal more of the subject in which they are already superb, but at the same level as the class they have surpassed. One of our eighth graders, whose Stanford–Binet IQ as a kindergartner was 187, was asked by his algebra teacher to work every problem in the book, rather than just the alternate problems that the rest of the class was assigned. He already knew algebra I rather well and therefore needed to work few problems, so he resented this burdensome chore. The busy work proved to be a powerful motivator, however, because after that year he took all of his mathematics at the college level. First, though, during the second semester of the eighth grade and while he was still twelve years old this precocious youth took the regular introductory course in computer science at Johns Hopkins and earned a final grade of A. During the summer, still twelve until July, he took a course in college algebra and trigonometry at Johns Hopkins, earning a B. From then on for two academic years and two more summers he took college mathematics through the calculus and linear algebra and two years of college chemistry, with all A's. At age 15 1/6 years he entered Johns Hopkins as a full-time student with 30 percent of the sophomore year completed. During his first year at Hopkins he earned eight A's and one B on difficult courses, majoring in electrical engineering. Thus in a rather perverse sense his teacher had done him a great favor, but without his having been discovered by SMPY, he would probably have been forced to sit a whole year in each of numerous high-school mathematics courses far below his capabilities.

In May 1976 this remarkable young man completed his junior year at Johns Hopkins with an impressive record in both his studies and research. On his sixteenth birthday, July 10, 1975, he had begun work for the summer with General Electric. During the summer of 1976, while still sixteen, he was a full-time researcher at the Bell Telephone Laboratories. He is scheduled to receive a baccalaureate from Johns Hopkins a couple of months before his eighteenth birthday—that is, four years ahead of the usual age-in-grade progression—and continue on to earn a Ph.D. degree in electrical engineering by age twenty or twenty-one. Radical educational acceleration is certainly paying off well for him—academically, professionally, and personally. In March 1977 he was awarded a three-year National Science Foundation graduate fellowship to study electrical engineering at the Massachusetts Institute of Technology.

One of his classmates (who skipped grades seven, nine, ten, twelve, and thirteen) completed his baccalaureate work at Johns Hopkins in December 1976, a few days after his seventeenth birthday, with a major in quantitative studies and considerable work in political science, economics, and astronomy. He plans to start work toward the M.B.A. and Ph.D. in economics at the University of Chicago while still seventeen.

Another of their quite bright classmates received his bachelor's degree in electrical engineering while still 17 2/3 years old, and a physics major reached only 18 1/2. Both of these were elected to Phi Beta Kappa, and both won three-year National Science Foundation fellowships.

Irrelevant academic enrichment consists of not determining precisely what types of advanced stimulation the brilliant student needs, such as faster-paced mathematics for the mathematically precocious, but instead offering all high-IQ youths a special academic course such as high-level social studies or essentially nonacademic work such as games (e.g., chess) or creative training largely divorced from subject matter. Of course, while this may be splendid that year for those whose major interest is touched on, it does not assuage the mental hunger of the mathematically oriented. (See Stanley 1954*a*, 1958, 1959*a*.) Also, if the enrichment is academic, special efforts need to be made to alter later courses, or else the enriched students may be more bored than ever in subsequent years.

Cultural enrichment consists of providing certain "cultural" experiences that go beyond the usual school curriculum and therefore do not promote later boredom. Examples are music appreciation, performing arts, and foreign languages such as Latin and Greek (see Mill 1924 and Packe 1954). Early experiences with speaking modern foreign languages and learning about foreign cultures can also fit this pattern and may be a type of stimulation that parents and teachers of high-IQ youths should provide from the early years. These do not, however, meet the specialized academic needs of the intellectually talented.

This may be the place to decry what we at SMPY perceive to be vast overemphasis on the Stanford–Binet or Wechsler-type overall IQ in planning academic experiences for brilliant children. If one takes a group of students who all have exactly the same Stanford–Binet IQ (say, 140), one does not have a group homogeneous with respect to such special abilities as mathematical reasoning. The IQ is a global composite, perhaps the best *single* index of general learning rate. One can, however, earn a certain IQ in a variety of ways, e.g., by being high on memory but much lower on reasoning, or vice versa. *It is illogical and inefficient to group students for instruction in mathematics mainly on the basis of overall mental age or IQ.* Often this is done and then the students who lag behind in the class are accused of not being well motivated, when in fact they simply do not have as high aptitude for learning mathematics as some in the class who have the same IQ. These considerations also apply to other academic subjects, such as history or English literature.

It is difficult to form a group of students really homogeneous for instruction in a given subject even when one uses all the psychometric and other knowledge about them that can be gathered. To rely primarily on the IQ for this purpose, as quite a few city and state programs for the intellectually do, seems to us curious indeed. An obvious corollary is that students should be grouped for instruction separately for each subject and that these groupings should be subject to change from year to year. Probably administrative or political convenience is the cause of undue reliance on a single grouping measure such as IQ. Now that computer scheduling is available, however, this justification for an ineffective process is weakened.

The fourth and last type of enrichment is what we term *relevant academic*. It is likely to be both the best short-term method and one of the worst long-term ones. Suppose, for instance, that an excellent, forward-looking school system provides a splendid modern mathematics curriculum for the upper 10 percent of its students from kindergarten through the seventh grade, and then in the eighth grade these students begin a regular algebra I course. How bored and frustrated they are almost sure to be! It is not educationally or psychologically sound to dump these highly enriched students into the mainstream, and yet that kind of situation often occurs. Only if the kindergarten through twelfth-grade curriculum is considered can this failure of articulation be prevented. Even then, a superb thirteen-year mathematics program without strong provisions for college credit would merely defer the boredom and frustration until the college years.

For the preceding logical reasons we feel strongly that any kind of enrichment except perhaps the cultural sort will, without acceleration, tend to harm the brilliant student. Also, there is excellent support for acceleration in the professional literature. Wiener (1953, 1956), Fefferman (Montour 1976b), Bardeen (Young 1972), Wolf (Keating 1976, see index; Montour 1976a), Watson (1968), and others have benefited greatly from it professionally. Norbert Wiener had his baccalaureate at fourteen and his Ph.D. degree at eighteen. Charles Louis Fefferman had his baccalaureate at seventeen and his doctorate at barely twenty; by age twenty-two he was a full professor of mathematics at the University of Chicago. Five years later he was the first winner of the National Academy of Sciences $150,000 Waterman Award.

John Bardeen, twice a Nobel Laureate in physics, completed high school at age fifteen. Merrill Kenneth Wolf, now a prominent neuroanatomist and talented musician, was graduated from Yale University shortly after becoming fourteen years old. James Watson had his Ph.D. degree at age twenty-three and had earned a Nobel prize before he became twenty-five. These examples could go on and on. Counterexamples, such as the ill-fated William James Sidis (Montour 1975, 1977), who was graduated from Harvard College at age sixteen but failed badly thereafter, are rare.

Lehman (1953), a psychologist, teamed up with a specialist in each of various fields to study the ages at which their greatest creative contributions were made by eminent scientists, scholars, and prodigies of other kinds. The typical age at which eminent mathematicians and physical scientists made their most highly rated achievements was lower than the average age at which the Ph.D. degree in those fields is awarded in the United States. Many brilliant young men and women are still students when according to logic and history they should be more independent researchers.

Terman and Oden (1947, pp. 264–66) found that the typical member of Terman's gifted group was graduated from high school about a year early. They advocated a moderate amount of acceleration for gifted youths. Hollingworth (1942), who worked with even abler children than the average of Terman's group, recommended considerable acceleration for them.

The University of Chicago's extensive experience with early entrance and fast progress in college during the 1930s showed that this was indeed a feasible approach for certain students. After this program was largely abandoned because of financial and other reasons, the Fund for the Advancement of Education (1953, 1957) set up studies at a number of colleges and universities to admit well-qualified students at the end of the tenth or eleventh grade. These were judged to be markedly successful.

Hobson (1963) and Worcester (1956) showed that, when properly arranged, early entrance to public school was beneficial. It seems to me especially unfortunate that their work is not well known to most educational administrators, because its scope, practicality, and clarity make the findings hard to ignore.

The most comprehensive study of educational acceleration was the splendid monograph by Pressey (1949). Anyone who can read it carefully and still oppose such acceleration certainly has the courage of his or her preconvictions. Pressey, Hobson, Worcester, and others reveal that opposition to acceleration is founded on emotionalized prejudices rather than facts. (Also, see Friedenberg 1966.) We do not know of a single careful study of actual accelerants that has shown acceleration not to be beneficial, though armchair articles against it abound (see Daurio 1977).

In SMPY's experience, the eagerness of the brilliant student himself or herself to move ahead rapidly seems crucial. If the youth is reluctant to take a particular accelerative path, such as going into algebra II early without bothering with algebra I, taking a college course, or skipping a grade, probably he or she should not be urged to do so. Unfortunately, many boys and girls are not allowed by their teachers, guidance counselors, principals, or even sometimes their parents to make a calm, rational decision about such matters. They may get so much bad advice that they give up in confusion. Many are simply forbidden to use a particular method of acceleration. It takes an unusually strong-willed youth to buck this adult obfuscation and tyranny.

From its inception SMPY has tried to communicate directly with the youths themselves, rather than through their parents. Reports of the results of the testing competition have gone to them, even including discussion of percentile ranks on national norms and the like. We have also written letters to them in response to their queries or their parents'. In the few instances where we have deviated from this policy—chiefly, with quite young boys and girls who came to our attention by way of their parents rather than through the formal talent search—the youngster's motivation has seemed to suffer. We believe that contacts of the facilitating agency such as SMPY should be mainly through the youth, even though he or she may be only nine or ten years old. After all, a child that age whose Stanford–Binet IQ is 170 or more (and SMPY seldom deals with any that young unless they are that bright) has a mental age of at least fifteen years. He or she will be as able to understand our communications as many parents are. We want the youths to take charge of their own academic planning early and to use their parents and us as means for implementing their own decisions. Some parents object to this approach, of course, because they want to keep their children dependent, but if communication from the beginning is with the student, such friction between SMPY and the parents will not usually be great.

In summary, the SMPY staff believes that offering each splendid mathematical reasoner a varied assortment of accelerative possibilities and letting him or her choose an optimum combination of these to suit the individual's situation is far superior to so-called special academic enrichment. Of course, we would be pleased to see individual courses and curricula improved and special accelerative classes set up by school systems for their intellectually talented students.

SELF-PACING AS INAPPROPRIATE NEOENRICHMENT, VERSUS GROUP PACING

When we propose accelerative opportunities for mathematically highly talented youths, the school is likely to counter by offering to let them proceed "at their own pace." In practice this usually means still sitting in the too-slow class, such as first-year algebra, while working ahead in the book and perhaps into algebra II. Common sense and observation tell us that this is not likely to work well for most students, no matter how able. Any student that autonomous and well motivated would probably have little use for school. Our model is definitely not self-pacing, whether in the crude way described above or by means of programmed instructional materials, except for an occasional highly unusual student.

We have found that stimulation by one's intellectual peers within a homogeneously grouped class which is fast-paced by the teacher produces astoundingly good results for about half of the students enrolled. Skeptics should read about some of SMPY's fast-mathematics classes: Wolfson I (Fox 1974*b*; Stanley 1976*b*); Wolfson II (George and Denham 1976); and McCoart calculus (Stanley 1976*b*).

Our model is somewhere between the high-ability athletic team that stimulates its members to great achievement against an opposing team, and individual competition such as tennis singles or running the hundred-yard dash. The difference between SMPY's special fast-mathematics classes and athletic events is that the mathematically precocious youths have an opponent against which all of them can win and be stars—namely, national norms on standardized achievement tests. Though they pace each other fast, and students who proceed too slowly may have to leave the group, the SMPY students are not competing directly with one another or with any other team except the anonymous national one.

Programmed instructional materials are almost sure to contain too many steps, and too small ones, for mathematically extremely apt students, who will therefore tend to be bored and frustrated by them. Also, such materials do not usually lend themselves to group-paced stimulation. Most of our precocious youths do not perform well against an abstract standard such as number of chapters or frames completed, just as a track man does not usually run well alone or a tennis player perform his or her best against a weak opponent. Most of our students who have tried self-pacing or correspondence-study courses move far less swiftly and well than they do in special fast-mathematics classes. Therefore, we consider the group-pacing feature essential for most persons (cf. Macken et al. 1976).

EMPHASIS ON COUNSELING AND TUTORING THE INDIVIDUAL

All of SMPY's efforts are directed toward helping each youth use his/her mathematical and other abilities best for the ultimate benefit of the person—and, we assume, thereby for society itself. The smorgasbord of accelerative educational possibilities that SMPY develops, tries out, and refines is meant to be adapted flexibly to each student. No one program, in mathematics or other educational areas, could possibly serve many of this highly able group well.

This approach makes the "description" (i.e., the study) phase of SMPY follow crucially from the "discovery" (i.e., identification) phase and lead naturally to the "development" (i.e., facilitation) efforts. Without intensive study of the aptitudes, achievement, interests, values, and attitudes of the youths who scored quite high on SAT-M, appropriate counseling would not be possible. Such study continues, of course, during the entire period that the youths are being helped and followed, but a massive initial assessment program helps begin the counseling process. (See Stanley, Keating, and Fox 1974; Keating 1976.)

Part of this studying is done via diagnostic testing and the ensuing specific teaching of just those points not yet known by the student. For example, many seventh- or eighth-grade youths who reason extremely well mathematically can score high on a standardized test of knowledge of first-year high school algebra even though they have not yet studied a school subject entitled "Algebra I." If, for example, such a student can answer correctly thirty out of forty items on Form A of Educational Testing Service's Cooperative Mathematics Algebra I Test in the forty-minute time limit, he has scored better than 89 percent of a random national sample of ninth graders did after studying algebra I for a whole school year. Then the youth is handed back the test booklet, told which ten items he missed, and asked to try them again. If he still misses, say, six items, they are examined carefully and he is helped by a tutor to learn quickly those points that he does not know. After suitable instruction on *just those points* and on any other points in the test about which he was unsure (e.g., items guessed right), he takes Form B of the test under standard conditions and his success is studied. In this way an able youth can often go on to algebra II within a few hours, rather than wasting nearly all of a long, tedious 180-period school year on algebra I. He already knows most of the material of the first course or can learn almost any not-yet-known point almost instantaneously. This type of diagnostic testing and teaching of superior mathematical reasoners makes so much sense that we cannot understand why it is tried so seldom. SMPY has formalized the procedure into a day-long "algebra tutorial clinic."

As a valuable part of its smorgasbord, SMPY has begun to develop into expert tutors mathematically talented youths who are not much older than the persons they tutor. This one-to-one relationship, modeled on the tutorial system of Oxford and Cambridge universities rather than the remedial tutoring arrangement more common in the United States, is proving to be the fastest and best way to move the typical quite young, mathematically highly apt youth ahead fast and well in mathematics.

For example, a seventh grader who scored 720 on SAT-M was tutored by a brilliant eleventh grader less than two years older than he through algebra I to III and geometry easily on Saturday mornings during eight months of the school year. The tutored youth then entered the ongoing Wolfson II fast-math class that summer and was its best student in trigonometry. He skipped the eighth grade and at barely fourteen years of age received by examination credit for two semesters of college calculus. As a tenth grader he made A's on both calculus III and differential equations. At fifteen he took complex-variable theory in the Johns Hopkins summer session and made a final grade of A. Besides all that, he had completed college courses in oceanography and computer science! After the eleventh grade, two years accelerated, he will enter college with sophomore standing or more at the ancient age of 16½ years. Think how much boredom this extremely able, well-motivated young man would undoubtedly have suffered had his mother not "discovered" SMPY when he was beginning the seventh grade.

ARTICULATION WITH THE SCHOOLS

SMPY is not a curriculum-development project. We decided early not to attempt altering the best of the standard school courses and textbooks. That in itself would be a multimillion-dollar project. Fortunately, in the wake of Russia's Sputnik I from 1957 until recently many programs such as SMSG mathematics, BSCS biology, and PSSC physics were carried out on a comprehensive scale by specialists. Elements of these have been incorporated into most high school courses and textbooks. It would be unnecessary and presumptuous of SMPY to engage in curriculum construction.

Thus we work within the better school mathematics curricula, usually in the conventional order of algebra I to II, geometry, college algebra and trigonometry, analytic geometry, and calculus. The special mathematics classes move through these extremely rapidly at a high level of rigor, abstraction, and proof, using standard textbooks. (For calculus a college textbook is used.) Creativity in these courses is promoted by the subject matter itself, the creative skills of the teacher, and the influence of able classmates, rather than by training for so-called creativity itself. We do not deny that such training can probably be useful for some students in certain courses or grades, but for our purposes the direct approach to creative performance in mathematics itself seemed preferable. Actually, until even the brightest students get into mathematics of at least number-theory or advanced-calculus level, much of their learning is algorithmic—how to perform processes and why these processes work. Originating proofs and derivations can be encouraged early, but for quite a while most students will be kept rather busy trying to understand the algorithms and proofs that the instructor and the textbook introduce, rather than devising their own.

A caution is in order here: Before a young student abandons pre-algebra mathematics, including arithmetic, for algebra (which, if he or she is able enough, may be easy), diagnostic testing should be done to discover specifically what this particular student does not yet know about arithmetic concepts and computation so that this material can be taught fast and well on an individual basis. This point has been mentioned earlier in another context; it is especially relevant when, for example, a nine-year-old enters a fast-mathematics class such as the one described by Fox (1974*b*).

Our early rejection of curriculum revision as a goal of SMPY has enabled us to save schools considerable time and money and still not upset their sequences of courses. If, for instance, a student learned all of precalculus mathematics well in one of our special classes while still a seventh or eighth grader, the next stage would simply be finding a high school (or college) calculus course for him or her. Most senior high schools are cooperative about this. The greatest problem occurs in the three-year junior high schools (grades 7 to 9), some of which offer algebra I and II, whereas others offer algebra I and plane geometry. Few provide courses in both algebra I and II and geometry, so the student who completes both years of algebra or algebra I and geometry while a seventh or eighth grader may be left without any mathematics to take for a year or two unless a senior high school is nearby. Some friction between certain junior high schools and SMPY has resulted because of this, but sincere efforts by both parties reduced it.

Our initial purpose was to try out procedures that would augment the usual work of the schools. SMPY was meant to be prototypal, producing exportable principles, techniques, and programs that public and private schools could adopt and adapt for their own uses. We were not going into business as an educational agency except to develop, try out, and improve whatever special procedures mathematically highly gifted youths seemed to need. We did not want to criticize the schools' performance of their usual functions, but merely to offer them ways to meet the highly special needs of a relatively small but extremely important group of their students. Thus articulation of our methods with theirs was important from the start.

Being aware of the vast and often cumbersome bureaucracy of educational systems, however, we did not want to get enmeshed in prolonged deliberations with supervisory personnel of city and country school systems. We planned to work with the youths themselves, and, through them, with their parents. As noted above, our communications are addressed directly to the students. As we said somewhat facetiously, the students are free to share our memoranda and letters with their parents, who in turn might share them with teachers, counselors, and principals if they wish to do so. Usually, we send an extra copy of each memorandum, to make that easy. We believe that this is the desirable way for us to proceed, because more change can be effected quickly for particular individuals at the child–parent–teacher–counselor–principal level than by trying to institutionalize innovations in a school system. Also, such innovations, even if finally adopted, tend to differ from the original model in what we would consider unfortunate ways. We want to develop our own innovations with minimum demands on the schools and then offer *them* for adoption throughout the country, not just in the Baltimore area.

We departed from this plan with one school system that contacted us early and expressed interest in cooperating. This resulted in many long high-level meetings that took much of our limited time and did not seem productive enough. Supervisory personnel may be quite cautious about proposed innovations, preferring to express their concerns and reservations about them rather than to take positive action. Such talk often serves mainly to delay or fend off the innovation.

This is not to say that school systems cannot be led or forced to change curricular policies. Often they can, especially if a sizable group of determined, well-informed parents whose mathematically highly talented children attend the schools concentrate on attaining specific objectives. Outsiders such as SMPY have far less political leverage, but by working directly with students and their parents they can help initiate pressure for needed policies and programs.

Excellent private schools can often provide well for students who are somewhat above average, e.g., those with IQs of 120 to 140. For youths with IQs much above 140 or so, however, the small size of most private schools and their social nature (usually more intimate than that of public schools) may make them less flexible in dealing with extremely gifted youths than public schools can be. Especially, faculty members of many private schools are even more opposed to educational acceleration than most public school teachers are.

In any event, private schools are no automatic panacea for the intellectually extremely talented. Parents who expect *any* school to provide optimally for their 160- to 225-IQ child without much help from them simply do not understand the extreme nature of such brightness. In an important sense, an IQ of 160 is the mirror image of an IQ of 40, because both deviate 60 points from the average IQ of people in general. A child with an IQ of 160 is about as bright as a child with an IQ of 40 is dull. Both need much special attention if they are to utilize their respective abilities effectively. A great deal of the thinking and planning for a brilliant child must come from its parents or other interested persons bent on supplementing the efforts of the school.

SMPY is not primarily a service project. It is meant to be prototypal —that is, to develop principles, techniques, and practices that can be used widely to improve the mathematical and other education of youths who reason extremely well mathematically.

BENEFITS TO STUDENTS

The benefits to SMPY's participants are numerous. Among them are the following:

1. Increased zest for learning and life, reduced boredom in school, and therefore a better attitude toward education and other activities.

2. Enhanced feelings of self-worth and accomplishment.

3. Reduction of egotism and arrogance. At first this may seem counterintuitive, but repeatedly we have observed that SMPY students who compete with their intellectual peers in rigorous settings such as special fast-mathematics classes tend to develop more realistic under-standing of their ability. These youths learn that, compared with national norms on standardized tests, they are superb, but less spectacular relative to each other. In regular mathematics classes the typical SMPY partici-pant earns such good grades with little effort that the temptation to feel superior is strong. For example, the 190-IQ boy who by age eleven had done so well in two college computer-science courses and on the Ad-vanced Placement Program examination in college calculus seems far less egotistical than he was before entering one of our special precalculus classes at age ten. In the SMPY courses he had to work hard to maintain an average rank, whereas as an accelerated sixth grader he was vastly overqualified for all his regular subjects.

4. Becoming far better prepared educationally than they otherwise would be, especially in mathematics, which is basic to many disciplines.

5. Better preparation for the most selective colleges and improved chance of being admitted to them. For example, in the fall of 1975 four of the students whom SMPY had helped entered Harvard or Radcliffe Colleges, two of them two years early each and one of those as a highly prestigious National Scholar.

6. Getting into college, graduate school, and a profession earlier, thus having more time and energy for creative pursuits.

7. Increased opportunities to explore more specialties and hobbies.

8. More time to explore various careers before marriage.

9. Less cost. Most accelerative procedures save the student and/or the parents money. Even skipping the last year of junior high school and going into senior high school a year early eliminates a year that the student must be supported at home. Eight credits earned by means of a $32 Advanced Placement Program examination in calculus were worth $1000 of tuition at Johns Hopkins in the fall of 1977, and such costs tend to rise almost every year. Graduating from college in three years rather than four saves about one-fourth of all costs and can lead to paid full-time employment a year earlier than otherwise.

10. Being an unusually well-prepared, advanced entrant to college often brings the student to the attention of professors who help him or her get started on important research early. This, in turn, usually leads to better graduate-school opportunities, including improved financial sup-port there. For example, five of SMPY's six radically accelerated youths who were graduated from college in 1977 at ages fifteen to eighteen won National Science Foundation three-year graduate fellowships.

11. Ultimately, we hope, considerably greater success in life, both professionally and personally.

BENEFITS TO SOCIETY

Presumably, whatever helps a sizable group of talented individuals use their abilities better should also benefit the larger society. It is easy to see that a number of the points made above about benefits to SMPY participants themselves fall into this category. Below we shall list a few other, somewhat related gains that society itself can expect from the three D's of SMPY and similar programs.

1. Students superbly prepared to major in the mathematical sciences, physical sciences, quantitative social sciences, and other areas where mathematical talent and keen analytical ability are essential or helpful.

2. More years of professional contribution and effective adulthood.

3. Happier, more effective citizens who will understand better how to educate their own children.

4. Reduced cost of education. The types of policies and activities that SMPY espouses save school systems and colleges money, rather than increasing educational expenditures. When a student who already knows first-year algebra is moved into algebra II, room for another pupil is created in the algebra I class, or the teacher can probably work more effectively with the lesser number because a potential distracter and irritant has been removed. When a student skips an entire school grade, the cost of educating him or her that year is saved. If four and one-half years of precalculus mathematics can be learned in a year, a great saving is likely to ensue. Passing introductory college calculus by examination increases room in the class and enriches the next mathematics course by moving an able, well-motivated student directly into it. Students who go through selective colleges in three years rather than the usual four enable those schools to handle more students.

Of course, it would be naive to assume that special policies and provisions for mathematically highly talented youths do not require any extra efforts. Of course they do, but the more effectively the facilitators of these students work, the greater the savings that can accrue to the school system, above and beyond their salaries and other expenses. Much of the identification, study, and implementation can be done by regular personnel in the mathematics supervisor's office. Even if in a strict cost-accounting sense the mathematically precocious were to cost a little extra, it would be an almost negligible amount relative to the expenditures for other types of special education within most school systems.

An often overlooked factor reducing the cost of working with intellectually gifted youths is the tremendous output that one gets for inputs which take little time. A few instructional minutes spent with a brilliant youth can produce amazing results. This contrasts sharply with the much greater amount of time that one must devote to a slow learner in order to get even moderate gains. Similarly, counseling SMPY participants and their parents by memorandum, telephone, letter, or case conference does not usually require a great deal of time but often produces striking changes in their education.

An added advantage is that most intellectually precocious youths have bright parents who can and will read counseling information before asking questions, thereby saving the advisers considerable time.

The two sentences with which I ended the first chapter of the first volume of SMPY's *Studies of Intellectual Precocity* (this is the third) seem appropriate here: "Expensive curricular adjustments are made, quite justifiably, for slow learners. It is past time that fast learners get the much less costly 'special education' they deserve" (Stanley, 1974, p. 19).

SCARCE RESOURCES AND ELITISM

But even after the above points some readers may still feel that any special attention to mathematically highly precocious youths is an unwarranted and unnecessary diversion of scarce special resources. Won't the talented boy or girl get along rather well with the regular resources of the school? Don't elective courses such as algebra I, offered specially in the eighth grade of some school systems, and the considerable array of honors-type subjects in senior high school (calculus being a strong example) take care of the needs of the gifted satisfactorily? Why provide more for those who already have so much? Isn't that elitism and therefore contrary to the American way of life? One could argue endlessly about the philosophical content of these questions. Empirically, however, the answer is clear: many of the youths in the top few percent of their age mates with respect to mathematical reasoning ability can learn mathematics and related subjects faster and better than the curricula of most schools permit. If held to the age–grade lockstep, a large percentage of them will develop poor work habits and lose interest in the area. Even those who do not would usually benefit from better opportunities.

An example, not highly unusual for SMPY, may serve to illustrate the point that quite a few students lag undesirably far behind their capabilities in the usual school setting. We discovered a certain young man at the end of the summer after he had completed the seventh grade of a public junior high school. Standardized testing showed that without actually having had an algebra course he already had almost perfect knowledge of the first year of that subject. In September he entered our first fast-mathematics class, which had begun in June and had covered algebra I quickly during the summer (see Fox 1974*b*, Student No. 1; Stanley 1976*b*, app. 7.2). By the next August—that is, in about fifty two-hour Saturday-morning classes—he had completed algebra II and III, geometry, trigonometry, and analytic geometry well. That fall, as a ninth grader, he entered a selective independent school in the Baltimore area. It took considerable effort by us to convince the calculus teacher that he should be allowed in that twelfth-grade subject. As the year wore on he became one of the very best students in the class. At age 14 he took the higher-level (BC) national calculus examination of the Advanced Placement Program and made a grade of 4 (meaning that he was "well qualified" for two semesters of college credit). Only a few of the twelfth graders at that excellent school did as well. While a tenth grader at a public senior high school he took a two-semester course in *advanced* calculus at a state college and made A's. Besides that, he has taken several other college courses and made excellent grades. In the fall of 1976 he entered Johns Hopkins as a sophomore after completing the eleventh grade.

If we had not intervened, it is extremely likely that this boy would have been required to take algebra I (which he did not need) as an eighth grader, algebra II as a ninth grader, and plane geometry as a tenth grader. He could have done splendidly on these with virtually no effort, but probably without any zest, either. From his case and many others one sees that a laissez-faire policy for education of the mathematically talented is misguided and harmful to them. Perhaps "genius will out," but much of the superior talent with which SMPY deals is unlikely to do so if unaided. Valuable time and energy will be squandered in the usual too slowly paced courses.

RELATIONSHIP TO TERMAN'S LONGITUDINAL STUDY

SMPY owes a heavy debt to Terman's five *Genetic Studies of Genius* volumes and Oden's (1968) monograph. They provided many of the ideas and cautions that undergirded SMPY's initial efforts. It is natural, then, that there should be a number of similarities. Because of the half-century that intervened between the start of Terman's study in 1921 and SMPY's official beginning in 1971, however, it is natural, too, that there should be substantial differences. Some of the similarities, most of which have already been implied in this paper, are the following:

1. Both studies sought approximately the ablest 1 in 200 youths. For some purposes SMPY dipped down to the top 15 in 1,000, and for others went up to the ablest 1 in 1,000 or more. Terman also had special subgroups, though not below IQ 135.

2. Participants in both studies were chosen via standardized tests.

3. Both studies were conducted state-wide, California for Terman and Maryland for SMPY, over a several-year period.

4. Both are longitudinal. Terman's group, born on the average in 1910, is still being followed up. SMPY's first three groups, born as early as 1955 (but chiefly from 1958 to 1961), are meant to be followed until at least the end of this century.

5. Both sexes are involved.

6. No quota was set for representation of any sex or other group.

7. Identification was only the first step. After being found, students were studied extensively.

8. Results of both studies are reported in books, articles, and speeches. Terman's (1925) first book appeared four years after he began. SMPY's first one came out in three (Stanley, Keating, and Fox 1974).

9. Both studies were based in departments of psychology. This may seem somewhat ironic; many of the prime considerations in both belong to the area called educational psychology, which in recent years has involved the gifted all too little. Also, mathematics educators in most universities seem far more interested in curriculum development and textbooks for the average and somewhat-above-average student than for facilitation of the mathematically highly talented. We have detected more interest among some heads of mathematics departments in senior high schools and some college teachers of mathematics.

Certain differences between the studies are indicated above. Others are as follows:

1. SMPY tries to help its participants greatly educationally, rather than just observing their natural progress over the years. We intervene on their behalf vigorously, often, and in varied ways.

2. SMPY's initial screening is by a difficult mathematical reasoning test, rather than an intelligence test. Tests that yield IQs are not used for its later testing, either, though sometimes intelligence-test information is furnished us through the parents. But few of our prime group of about 200 students would have Stanford-Binet IQs much less than 140, and two of them reached 212.

3. We are working rather intensively with about 250 youths, whereas Terman started with more than 1,500. About 1,800 more of SMPY's students are getting considerable counseling and suggestions from us, though. This secondary group represents approximately the upper 1.5 percent of the age group with respect to mathematical aptitude.

4. Nearly all of SMPY's participants entered the difficult test competitions of a mathematical talent search sponsored by SMPY at Johns Hopkins. Thus there is probably a strong volunteering bias that makes our youths somewhat more academically aggressive and self-confident than were quite a few of Terman's. Also, a majority of them are definitely oriented toward academic subjects that involve considerable mathematics.

5. Most of our participants were eleven to thirteen years old and in the seventh or eighth grade when first tested. Terman's ranged across all the school grades.

6. Because of SMPY's initial selection procedure, emphasizing mathematical reasoning ability, most of the high scorers in the contest also score well on other reasoning tests, both nonverbal and verbal.

7. In various ways, including a printed newsletter appearing 10 times per year,[4] we encourage SMPY participants to accelerate their educational progress, particularly in the mathematical and physical sciences. SMPY has devised and tried out many special programs for its students. Terman's study was not meant to be interventional.

TALENT VERSUS GENIUS

Many persons seem hostile toward intellectually talented youths, perhaps a little less so toward those splendid in mathematics than toward the verbally precocious. This contrasts sharply with their generally favorable attitudes toward prodigies in music and athletics. Friedenberg (1966) and Stanley (1974), among others, have discussed how deep-seated this prejudice is. Expressions such as the following abound in literature back to Shakespeare's time: "Early ripe, early rot"; "So wise so young, then say, do never live long"; "For precocity some great price is always demanded sooner or later in life"; and "Their productions . . . bear the marks of precocity and premature decay" (Stanley 1974, pp. 1–2).

We noted earlier that one disguise for dislike of the intellectually talented is to argue that they need no special help; it is assumed that they will succeed well educationally without it. Another tactic we have noticed is the comparison of a highly able youth with Gauss, Euler, Fermat, Galois, Pascal, Newton, or (especially) Einstein, a sort of *reductio ad absurdum* denigration of talent by asserting that it is not the rarest genius. Terman encountered a great deal of this. Some reviewers criticized him because in his frontier-state sample, identified in a short while, he did not discover someone who later became a worthy successor to the greatest

[4]It is called *ITYB*, the *Intellectually Talented Youth Bulletin*.

musicians, artists, and writers. [Some insight into problems of defining and predicting genius may be obtained from Albert (1975) and Bell (1937).]

Obviously, in the State of Maryland during a three-year period we do not expect to have located or helped to produce a Nobel Laureate, much less a successor to Gauss. To have in the sample someone even of the caliber of Norbert Wiener (1953, 1956) is perhaps more than we can reasonably expect. On his sixteenth birthday, however, one young man already through the sophomore year of college began important research in electrical engineering. Another, at age nineteen, did original research in mathematics. At age seventeen another solved an important problem in computer science. Because SMPY's participants were identified young recently, only nine had been graduated from college by June 1977. Achievements of participants will be studied for at least the next twenty years.

On the other hand, we do believe that SMPY is helping a number of exceptionally able young men and women to go far beyond what they would probably have done without our intervention. That is sufficient for us: strong enhancement of talent, rather than the creation of genius. We might have been able to help a lonely, awkward person such as Wiener use his great talents better at an earlier age, and probably Einstein would have scored quite high in a contest like ours had he deigned to enter it, but those two men are examples of persons who somehow achieved magnificently anyway. If one has already thrown a coin and it has landed with the "head" side up, what is the probability of *that* occurrence? This is a foolish question, of course, but no sillier than reasoning from the success of Einstein and Wiener that great intellectual talent will lead inevitably to success. Those country churchyards chronicled by Thomas Gray hold their share of "mute, inglorious" Wieners and Einsteins as well as of Miltons. We suspect that many classrooms also serve as premature tombs for mathematical talent.

A STRONG BOND

SMPY's top 200 participants differ considerably in most personal characteristics except age. Some are tall and others are short. Some are introverted and others are extroverted. Some are much better verbal reasoners than others. Some are males and others are females. In fact, they probably differ at least as much from each other as do youths their age who are only average mathematically. These students have one important thing in common, however: they entered a challenging mathematical-aptitude competition and scored extremely well on a difficult mathematical reasoning test designed to be used with above-average students three to five years older than they. This is a powerful commonality that reminds me of the famous lines from Rudyard Kipling's "The Ballad of East and West":

> Oh, East is East, and West is West, and never the
> twain shall meet,
> Till Earth and Sky stand presently at God's great
> Judgment Seat;
> But there is neither East nor West, Border, nor
> Breed, nor Birth,
> When two strong men stand face to face, though
> they come from the ends of the earth!

Read Kipling's male-chauvinistic "two strong men" as "mathematically highly precocious youths" and you have a summing up of the rationale for SMPY. We believe that mathematical talent does transcend sex, circumstance, and nationality and mandates special educational treatment of mathematical prodigies with respect to their area(s) of great talent. We consider accelerative procedures crucial because—to paraphrase Robert Browning—"a mathematically precocious youth's reach should exceed his/her grasp, or what's an educational system for?" We at SMPY will continue helping to extend both the reach and the grasp of youths who reason extremely well mathematically.

REFERENCES

Albert, R. S. 1975. Toward a behavioral definition of genius. *American Psychologist* 30(2): 140–51.

Barlow, F. 1952. *Mental prodigies: An enquiry into the faculties of arithmetical, chess and musical prodigies, famous memorizers, precocious children and the like, with numerous examples of "lightning" calculations and mental magic.* New York: Philosophical Library.

Bell, E. T. 1937. *Men of mathematics.* New York: Simon and Schuster.

Burks, B. S., Jensen, D. W., and Terman, L. M. 1930. The promise of youth: Follow-up studies of a thousand gifted children. *Genetic studies of genius,* vol. III. Stanford, Calif.: Stanford University Press.

Burt, C. L. 1975. *The gifted child.* New York: Wiley.

Campbell, D. T., and Stanley, J. C. 1966. *Experimental and quasi-experimental designs for research.* Chicago: Rand McNally.

Cox, C. M. 1926. The early mental traits of three hundred geniuses. *Genetic studies of genius,* vol. II. Stanford, Calif.: Stanford University Press.

Daurio, S. P. 1977. Educational enrichment versus acceleration: A review of the literature. Baltimore, Md.: Study of Mathematically Precocious Youth, Department of Psychology, The Johns Hopkins University.

Downey, M. T. 1961. *Carl Campbell Brigham: Scientist and educator.* Princeton, N J.: Educational Testing Service.

Eisenberg. A. R. 1977. Academic acceleration and the relationships between age and gradepoint average. Baltimore, Md.: Study of Mathematically Precocious Youth, Department of Psychology, The Johns Hopkins University.

Epstein, H. T. 1974*a*. Phrenoblysis: Special brain and mind growth periods. I. Human brain and skull development. *Developmental Psychobiology* 7(3): 207–16.

———. 1974*b*. Phrenoblysis: Special brain and mind growth periods. II. Human mental development. *Developmental Psychobiology* 7(3): 217–24.

Fox, L. H. 1974*a*. Facilitating educational development of mathematically precocious youth. In J. C. Stanley, D. P. Keating, and L. H. Fox (eds.), *Mathematical talent: Discovery, description, and development.* Baltimore, Md.: The Johns Hopkins University Press, pp. 47–69.

———. 1974*b*. A mathematics program for fostering precocious achievement. In J. C. Stanley, D. P. Keating, and L. H. Fox (eds.), *Mathematical talent: Discovery, description, and development.* Baltimore, Md.: The Johns Hopkins University Press, pp. 101–25.

———. 1976*a*. Identification and program planning: Models and methods. In D. P. Keating (ed.), *Intellectual talent: Research and development.* Baltimore, Md.: The Johns Hopkins University Press, pp. 32–54.

———. 1976*b*. Sex differences in mathematical precocity: Bridging the gap. In D. P. Keating (ed.), *Intellectual talent: Research and development.* Baltimore, Md.: The Johns Hopkins University Press, pp. 183–214.

———. 1976*c*. Women and the career relevance of mathematics and science. *School Science and Mathematics* 76: 347–53.

Friedenberg, E. Z. 1966. The gifted student and his enemies. In E. Z. Friedenberg, *The dignity of youth and other atavisms.* Boston: Beacon Press, pp. 119–35.

Fund for the Advancement of Education of the Ford Foundation. 1953. *Bridging the gap between school and college.* New York: Research Division of the Fund.

———. 1957. *They went to college early.* New York: Research Division of the Fund.

George, W. C. 1976. Accelerating mathematics instruction for the mathematically talented. *Gifted Child Quarterly* 20(3): 246–61.

———, and Denham, S. A. 1976. Curriculum experimentation for the mathematically talented. In D. P. Keating (ed.), *Intellectual talent: Research and development.* Baltimore, Md.: The Johns Hopkins University Press, pp. 103–31.

Hobson, J. R. 1963. High school performance of underage pupils initially admitted to kindergarten on the basis of physical and psychological examinations. *Educational and Psychological Measurement* 33(1, Spring): 159–70.

Hogan, R., Viernstein, M. C., McGinn, P. V., Daurio, S., and Bohannon, W. 1977. Verbal giftedness and socio-political intelligence: Terman revisited. *Journal of Youth and Adolescence,* 6(2): 107–16.

Hollingworth, L. S. 1942. *Children above 180 IQ, Stanford-Binet: Origin and development.* Yonkers-on-Hudson, N.Y.: World Book.

Hudson, L. 1975. *Human beings: The psychology of human experience.* Garden City, N.Y.: Anchor Press/Doubleday.

Keating, D. P. 1975. Precocious cognitive development at the level of formal operations. *Child Development* 46: 276–80.

——— (ed.). 1976. *Intellectual talent: Research and development.* Baltimore, Md.: The Johns Hopkins University Press.

———, and Schaefer, R. A. 1975. Ability and sex differences in the acquisition of formal operations. *Developmental Psychology* 11(4): 531–32.

Kramer, E. A. 1974. *Nature and growth of modern mathematics.* New York, N.Y.: Fawcett World Library (2 vols.).

Krutetskii, V. A. 1976. *The psychology of mathematical abilities in schoolchildren.* Chicago: University of Chicago Press.

Lehman, H. C. 1953. *Age and achievement.* Princeton, N.J.: Princeton University Press.

Macken, E., van den Heuvel, R., Suppes, P., and Suppes, T. 1976. *Home-based education: Needs and technological opportunities.* Washington, D.C.: National Institute of Education, U.S. Department of Health, Education, and Welfare, pp. 49–71, "Home-based computer-assisted instruction for gifted students."

McGinn, P. V. 1976. Verbally gifted youth: Selection and description. In D. P. Keating (ed.), *Intellectual talent: Research and development.* Baltimore, Md.: The Johns Hopkins University Press, pp. 160–82.

Mill, J. S. 1924. *Autobiography of John Stuart Mill.* New York: Columbia University Press.

Montour, K. M. 1975. Success vs. tragedy. *ITYB* (Intellectually Talented Youth Bulletin, published by SMPY) 1(9, May 15): 3.

———. 1976a. Merrill Kenneth Wolf: A bachelor's degree at 14. *ITYB* 2(7, Mar. 15): 1–2.

———. 1976b. Charles Louis Fefferman: Youngest American full professor? *ITYB* 2(8, Apr. 15): 2.

———. 1977. William James Sidis, the broken twig. *American Psychologist* 32(4): 265–79.

Oden, M. H. 1968. The fulfillment of promise: 40-year follow-up of the Terman gifted group. *Genetic Psychology Monographs* 77 (1st half, Feb.): 3–93.

Packe, M. S. J. 1954. *The life of John Stuart Mill.* New York: Macmillan.

Pressey, S. L. 1949. Educational acceleration: Appraisals and basic problems. *Bureau of Educational Research Monographs No. 31,* The Ohio State University, Columbus, Ohio.

Pruzek, R. M., and Coffman, W. E. 1966. A factor analysis of the mathematical sections of the Scholastic Aptitude Test. *Research Bulletin 66–12,* Educational Testing Service, Princeton, N.J., April.

Schonberg, H. C. 1970. *The lives of the great composers.* New York: W. W. Norton.

Sears, R. R. 1977. Sources of life satisfactions of the Terman gifted men. *American Psychologist* 32(2): 119–28.

Skemp, R. R. 1971. *The psychology of learning mathematics.* Baltimore, Md.: Penguin Books.

Stanley, J. C. 1954a. Is the fast learner getting a fair deal in your school? *Wisconsin Journal of Education* 86(10): 5–6.

———. 1954b. Identification of superior learners in grades ten through fourteen. *Supplementary Educational Monograph No. 81,* University of Chicago, December, pp. 31–34.

———. 1958. Providing for the gifted by means of enrichment of the curriculum. *Bulletin of the Wisconsin Association of Secondary School Principals,* Spring, pp. 5–7.

———. 1959a. Enriching high-school subjects for intellectually gifted students. *School and Society* 87 (2151): 170–71.

———. 1959b. Test biases of prospective teachers for identifying gifted children. *School and Society* 87 (2151): 175–77.

———. Reliability. 1971. In R. L. Thorndike (ed.), *Educational measurement* (2nd ed.). Washington, D.C.: American Council on Education, pp. 356–442.

———. 1973. Designing psychological experiments. In B. B. Wolman (ed.), *Handbook of general psychology.* Englewood Cliffs, N.J.: Prentice-Hall, pp. 90–106.

———. 1974. Intellectual precocity. In J. C. Stanley, D. P. Keating, and L. H. Fox (eds.), *Mathematical talent: Discovery, description, and development.* Baltimore, Md.: The Johns Hopkins University Press, pp. 1–22.

———. 1976a. Use of tests to discover talent: In D. P. Keating (ed.), *Intellectual talent: Research and development.* Baltimore, Md.: The Johns Hopkins University Press, pp. 3–22.

———. 1976b. Special fast-math classes taught by college professors to fourth-through twelfth-graders. In D. P. Keating (ed.), *Intellectual talent: Research and development.* Baltimore, Md.: The Johns Hopkins University Press, pp. 132–59.

———. 1976c. The student gifted in mathematics and science. *NAASP* (National Association of Secondary School Principals) *Bulletin* 60 (398, Mar.): 28–37.

———. 1976d. Test better finder of great math talent than teachers are. *American Psychologist* 31(4, Apr.): 313–14.

———. 1976e. The case for extreme educational acceleration of intellectually brilliant youths. *Gifted Child Quarterly* 20 (1, Spring): 66–75, 41.

———. 1976f. Concern for intellectually talented youths: How it originated and fluctuated. *Journal of Clinical Child Psychology* 5(3): 38–42.

———, Keating, D. P., and Fox, L. H. (eds.). 1974. *Mathematical talent: Discovery, description, and development.* Baltimore, Md.: The Johns Hopkins University Press.

Terman, L. M. 1925. Mental and physical traits of a thousand gifted children. *Genetic studies of genius,* vol. I. Stanford, Calif.: Stanford University Press.

———, and Oden, M. H. 1947. The gifted child grows up. *Genetic studies of genius,* vol. IV. Stanford, Calif.: Stanford University Press.

———. 1959. The gifted group at mid-life: Thirty-five years' follow-up of the superior child. *Genetic studies of genius,* vol. V. Stanford, Calif.: Stanford University Press.

Viernstein, M. C., and Hogan, R. 1975. Parental personality factors and achievement motivation in talented adolescents. *Journal of Youth and Adolescence* 4(2): 183–90.

Viernstein, M. C., McGinn, P. V., and Hogan, R. 1977. The personality correlates of differential verbal and mathematical ability in talented adolescents. *Journal of Youth and Adolescence* 6(2): 169–78.

Watson, J. D. 1968. *The double helix: A personal account of the discovery of the structure of DNA.* New York: Atheneum.

Webb, R. A. 1974. Concrete and formal operations in very bright six- to eleven-year-olds. *Human Development* 17: 292–300.

Wiener, N. 1953. *Ex-prodigy.* Cambridge, Mass.: Massachusetts Institute of Technology Press.

———. 1956. *I am a mathematician.* Cambridge, Mass.: Massachusetts Institute of Technology Press.

Worcester, D. A. 1956. *The education of children of* above-average *mentality.* Lincoln, Nebr.: University of Nebraska Press.

Young, P. 1972. The transistor's coinventor makes history with a super-cold superprize. *National Observer* 11(50): 1, 22.

ADDITIONAL REFERENCES, NOT CITED

Fox, L. H. 1976. Career education for gifted pre-adolescents. *Gifted Child Quarterly* 20(3): 262–70.

George, W. C. (Chairman). 1977. Negative attitudes and behaviors: Barriers to education of the gifted. *Talents and Gifts* 19(4): 2–15, 21–26. Papers by S. J. Cohn, L. H. Fox, M.C. Pyryt, and C. H. Solano. Discussion by George.

Keating, D. P., and Stanley, J. C. 1972. Extreme measures for the exceptionally gifted in mathematics and science. *Educational Researcher* 1(9): 3–7.

Maeroff, G. I. 1977. The unfavored gifted few. *New York Times Magazine,* Aug. 21, pp. 30–32, 72ff.

Montour, K. M. 1976. Three precocious boys: What happened to them. *Gifted Child Quarterly* 20(2): 173–79.

Stanley, J. C. 1976. Identifying and nurturing the intellectually talented. *Phi Delta Kappan* 58:(3): 234–37.

Time. 1977. Smorgasbord for an IQ of 150. 109(23): 64. Also see the October 1977 (Vol. 8, No. 7) issue of the *Smithsonian.*

6

SEX DIFFERENCES: IMPLICATIONS FOR PROGRAM PLANNING FOR THE ACADEMICALLY GIFTED

Lynn H. Fox

ABSTRACT

Studies of gifted children have typically ignored sex differences, yet in the past gifted women have achieved far less than men. This paper reviews the research on sex differences in intellectual abilities, achievement, values, and interests that have relevance to educational planning for gifted children. Early admission to kindergarten or first grade, and early college entrance both appear to be valuable for gifted boys and girls. Grade skipping, subject-matter acceleration, and advanced placement programs in mathematics and the sciences in the junior high school years, however, are more effective for gifted boys than for gifted girls. Homogeneously grouped accelerated programs in mathematics can promote achievement of gifted girls as well as gifted boys in some classroom environments but not in others. Part of the differential academic success of the sexes in subjects like mathematics is a result of the sex-role stereotyping activities in early childhood and adolescence. The reduction of sex-role stereotyping should increase both male and female creativity and achievement in many areas. Early identification of children and counseling of parents is needed. Career education and early planned intervention are particularly crucial for gifted girls. Teachers need to help gifted students, especially girls, become better intellectual risk takers.

In recent years the failure of women to achieve eminence in many aspects of life, especially in academic and scientific areas, has been noted quite often. Therefore, in this year, which is both International Woman's Year and the fiftieth anniversary of the publication of the first volume of

Terman's *Genetic Studies of Genius* (1925), it appeared that some attention to the plight of gifted females is desirable.

Although I decided not to entitle this paper "The Gifted Female," I wondered how many written articles or presented papers on the topic "The Gifted Child" would have been more realistically entitled "The Gifted Male." The failure of many educators and researchers to consider that the sex difference in achievements of gifted adults was a serious educational problem is somewhat understandable in light of our society's expectations for women in the past. Today, however, the issue of the fulfillment of promise for gifted females as well as males must be considered. We should not ignore psychological and biological differences between males and females that relate to their achievements in the classroom, their sense of personal worth, and their successful adjustment to adult life. A major premise of this paper is that research findings and suggestions for program planning for the gifted child should be reexamined to determine their relevance for both sexes.

Unfortunately, this task will be difficult. Many studies in the past did not treat the sex of subject as a variable. Past findings related to sex differences may be less relevant for people of today than for the populations studied ten or more years ago. Also, we should exercise some caution in generalizing from findings of studies of sex differences in the general population to gifted and talented youth.

One further caution is indicated. The concepts of masculinity and femininity are complex. Sex-role appropriate behavior results from a combination of biological and psychological factors. In a discussion of sex as a psychological variable, it is important to keep individuals as well as groups in mind. Not all the seeming correlates to gender identity apply uniformly to the individual.

With these limitations and constraints in mind, let us examine what is known about sex differences and the gifted child. First, we shall consider a brief summary of sex differences in the cognitive and affective domain. Second, we shall review some of the general types of accelerative and nonaccelerative educational strategies for the gifted with respect to their usefulness for males and females. Third and last, we shall consider what modifications and innovations are needed in both research and program planning efforts for the gifted and talented child.

SEX DIFFERENCES: A BRIEF REVIEW

The psychology of sex differences has recently been rather thoroughly researched (Maccoby and Jacklin 1975). The following section briefly summarizes some points from this research that seem relevant to the discussion of the gifted child. Where possible, these findings are supplemented with specific studies of sex differences in gifted populations.

Intellectual Ability

Men and women do not appear to differ on measures of global intelligence. As Maccoby (1963) pointed out, this is less meaningful than it first appears. In the process of constructing standardized intelligence tests, items that seem biased in favor of one sex or the other are often eliminated or balanced. Although men and women are probably about equal in general intellectual ability, they do appear to differ with respect to some specific abilities.

In mathematical ability sex differences are not consistently found until the end of the elementary school years. A recent National Assessment report (Mullis 1975), however, found sex differences in geometry skills as early as age nine. By the end of the secondary school years, young men are quite superior to young women with respect to mathematical reasoning ability. Among very gifted seventh and eighth graders the gap at the higher levels of mathematical reasoning ability is quite large. In three years of testing mathematically gifted students, the Study of Mathematically Precocious Youth (SMPY)[1] found 167 boys but only 19 girls who, as seventh and eighth graders, scored 640 or above on the Scholastic Aptitude Test—Mathematics (SAT-M).[2] The mean-score difference between boys and girls in the three contests has been at least 35 points in favor of the boys (Stanley 1973). Although attempts at The Johns Hopkins University to intervene to raise the level of achievement in mathematics of gifted girls have been somewhat successful, intervention efforts have not yet been able to improve the basic mathematical reasoning ability of gifted girls to equal that of the ablest boys (Fox 1974*a*).

Males in general are superior to females on tests of spatial relationships from adolescence to adulthood (Anastasi 1958). Sex differences in

[1]The Study of Mathematically Precocious Youth (SMPY) was begun at The Johns Hopkins University by Julian C. Stanley in 1971 and is supported by grants from the Spencer Foundation of Chicago and the Robert Sterling Clark Foundation. The rationale of this program is discussed in chapter 5. Detailed reports of the three mathematics contests are reported in *Mathematical talent: Discovery, description, and development* and *Intellectual talent: Research and development* which are volumes I and II, respectively, of the Studies of Intellectual Precocity series published by The Johns Hopkins University Press.

[2]The Scholastic Aptitude Test is administered under the direction of the College Entrance Examination Board in cooperation with The Educational Testing Service, Princeton, N.J.

spatial-visualization ability do appear to be innate (Bock and Kolakowski 1973).[3] The extent to which sex differences in mathematical ability are related to sex differences in spatial-visualization ability is not yet known. In a study of a small group of seventh graders (thirteen boys and eight girls) who participated in a special accelerated mathematics class on Saturday mornings, the expected sex differences on the Revised Minnesota Paper Form Board Test[4] were not found (Fox 1974*b*). The highest score was earned by a girl, and five of the thirteen boys scored lower than the lowest-scoring girl. The mean score for the boys was about equal to the mean for the twelfth-grade boys reported in the manual. The eight girls scored significantly higher than the mean for twelfth-grade boys and girls. Perhaps girls who have superior spatial abilities are better candidates for special mathematical enrichment than girls with less of this ability. The relationship of spatial abilities to interest and talent in mathematics should be studied further.

Although males seem to be superior to females on measures of quantitative skills, females are generally found to be superior to males on measures of verbal ability before age three and after age eleven (Maccoby and Jacklin 1975). Clearly, more boys than girls are found to have reading problems. In a verbal contest for gifted seventh and eighth graders conducted by the Study of Verbally Gifted Youth (SVGY)[5] at The Johns Hopkins University (McGinn 1976), the expected female superiority was not found. Although fewer boys than girls entered the contest, there were no sex differences in performance on the Scholastic Aptitude Test—Verbal (SAT-V). Some of the highest scorers were boys. In 1973, the girls and boys who entered the mathematics talent search sponsored by SMPY were also tested on the SAT-V. Although the boys outnumbered the girls, they scored as well on the SAT-V as the girls but better on the SAT-M. It is interesting that sex differences in cognitive abilities found in general adolescent populations are found in gifted samples in the quantitative area but not the verbal.

Whether or not these sex differences in performance on tests of specific abilities are innate or a result of differential learning experiences and socialization, or a combination of the two, is not entirely clear. Talent in mathematics, for example, does appear to be related to masculine

---

[3]A test of spatial-visualizing ability was administered to parents and offspring in a sample of 167 families. The results were consistent with the hypothesis that spatial ability depends in part upon a recessive, sex-linked gene. The magnitude of the familial correlations suggested that about 46 percent of score variance is attributable to genetic variation.

[4]The Revised Minnesota Paper Form Board Test is published by the Psychological Corporation, New York.

[5]The Study of Verbally Gifted Youth (SVGY) was begun in 1972 by Robert Hogan, Catherine Garvey, and Roger Webb at The Johns Hopkins University and is supported by a grant from the Spencer Foundation of Chicago.

interests and values (Aiken 1970; Astin 1974; Carey 1958; Milton 1957). Many educators do believe that sex differences in interests in mathematics and science result, at least in part, from differential childhood experiences and reinforcements of sex-role-appropriate interests (Fox 1977).

The absence of a father in early childhood has been shown to be related to a discrepancy between mathematical and verbal abilities for boys. Father-absent boys have lower mathematical aptitude relative to verbal aptitude than do their father-present cohorts (Carlsmith 1964). It has been hypothesized that this difference is related to a learned conceptual style or approach to problem solving. In general, boys learn an "analytic approach" while girls learn a "global approach." Thus, boys in father-absent homes may learn a more global or feminine approach and thus tend to perform relatively less well on quantitative measures than verbal ones with respect to male norms.

Studies of productive and creative female mathematicians found that these women tended to come from homes where the fathers were professional men and very dominant in the family (Helson 1971). These women tended to be eldest daughters who had no brothers. Significantly more of the creative than the less creative female mathematicians had identified primarily with their fathers and not their mothers. Although these women did not score low on measures of femininity, perhaps they had developed a more analytic than global cognitive style.

Clearly, problem-solving skill is correlated with sex-role identity for both males and females (Milton 1957). Early identification with a father, particularly an intellectual and analytic father, is related to quantitative interests and ability for both sexes.

Early interest in mathematics is likely to be noticed and supported more by parents of boys than parents of girls. Astin (1974) studied the family background questionnaires of a sample of highly mathematically precocious children. Parents of boys far more than parents of girls had noticed their children's mathematical gifts in the preschool years. Parents of girls were far less likely than parents of boys to have bought toys and games of a scientific and mathematical nature for their children.

Gifted girls who took advanced placement courses in science and mathematics in high school reported their early frustrations in trying to get chemistry or construction sets as toys (Casserly 1975). Girls lamented the fact that parents seemed to fear that the girls would hurt themselves with a chemistry set, yet did not fear the girls would hurt themselves in the kitchen.

Gifted boys, too, may suffer from sex-role expectations of parents. This is likely to be particularly true for gifted boys from lower class backgrounds where literary and artistic pursuits are not valued. Some segments of the population do not consider reading to be a masculine endeavor. Even in families where education is highly valued, boys may be rewarded for physical and aggressive activities rather than for more passive intellectual ones.

Achievement

With respect to grades earned in high school and college, women are more academically predictable than men (Seashore 1962; Stanley 1967). This seems ironic in light of the relatively lower levels of achievement of women in graduate school and beyond. In a study of graduate students in psychology, the single best predictor of success was sex (Educational Testing Service 1972). Females were less likely than males to attain the doctorate.

Women may be less predictable than men with respect to achievement as measured by standardized tests in situations where masculine interests and motivation are important. In a study of gifted junior high school students in a special accelerated after-school algebra class, mathematical aptitude as assessed by the SAT-M correlated with algebra achievement of boys but not of girls (Fox 1976a).

Recent results of the National Assessment testing program indicate that by age seventeen, boys score as well or higher than girls on achievement tests in all areas except writing (Mullis 1975). In the areas of mathematics and science, sex differences in achievement are related in part to differential course taking in high school. Many girls with high mathematical aptitude elect not to take advanced courses such as calculus (Haven 1972). (Differential course taking does not account, however, for sex differences in geometry skills found at age nine.)

Differential course taking of girls in high school is related to girls' perceptions of the value of such courses for their future, and differential encouragement by teachers, parents, and peers. There is some controversy as to whether or not girls have less achievement motivation than boys. Maccoby and Jacklin (1975) say there are no consistent sex differences, whereas Horner (1968) says girls fear success. In the case of advanced mathematics and science courses it seems more likely that girls fear failure and poor grades on the one hand and possible peer rejection on the other. Teachers and peers may reinforce expectations for failure at the high school level.

Although boys and girls in elementary school both believe their own sex-peer group to be superior in all subjects, by high school their expectations have changed. Then both sexes believe that girls are better at English but poorer in science than boys (Ernest 1975).

A study of elementary school teachers found that 41 percent felt boys did better in science and mathematics and 63 percent felt girls did better in

English (Ernest 1975). Although these attitudes may reflect real differences these teachers have observed in their classrooms, such expectations are likely to influence teacher behaviors and thus reinforce the differences.

Casserly (1975) reports that gifted girls felt that their teachers, both male and female, reinforced stereotypes even when they were obviously inappropriate. For example, it often happens that some girls in eighth grade are taller than all the boys in their classes, yet teachers may overlook the real differences and ask for tall, strong boys to help get materials from the cupboard. Girls were told in science class that the next few remarks were only for the boys; the teacher then discussed the applications of the unit studied to repairing bicycles.

Creativity

Studies of children and adults on measures of creative potential do not systematically favor either sex (Maccoby and Jacklin 1975). Yet, as with general intellectual achievement, men and women differ with respect to creative accomplishments in life in most areas of human endeavor. This is at least partly so because women in the past have not seriously aspired to professional levels of excellence. As more women move into professional roles on a full-time basis, the numbers of those judged creative and productive should increase.

Studies of creative people find that such persons have certain masculine and feminine interests and characteristics. A certain openness to all experiences seems necessary for creative productivity (MacKinnon 1962). Thus, persons who struggle to suppress their opposite sex traits and interests may stifle some of their creativity as well.

Women need to develop their capacities for independence and intellectual aggressiveness. Men are more likely than women to need to develop their aesthetic sensitivity and openness to emotional experiences. The reduction of sex-role stereotypic thinking and behavior is likely to be as necessary for fostering creative thinking as the introduction of divergent thinking games and activities into the classroom.

Other Talents and Gifts

At present we are unable to assess potential talent effectively in most nonacademic areas. It is impossible to say whether or not men and women differ significantly in artistic, musical, or leadership potential. Artistic and literary interests are typically considered feminine. Women tend to score higher than men on measures of artistic interest. Yet there are far more men than women who have won acclaim as professional artists and writers.

Success in the arts is based upon judgments by one's peers. It seems likely that such judgments are influenced by the greater status of men in society. Studies have shown that paintings and written essays receive higher ratings from adults and college students when these products are designated as the products of males rather than females (Goldberg 1968; Pheterson, Kiesler, and Goldberg 1971). There are occasional exceptions when essays on such feminine topics as cooking or child care are rated equally for authors Jane or John Doe. Perhaps women should be encouraged to sign their creative works with initials or, like George Eliot, adopt a masculine pen name.

While women may face great barriers to achieving eminence as adults, men may have difficulties developing their interests in artistic pursuits as children. Artistic sensitivity should be encouraged in both sexes in childhood and adulthood. Sex-role stereotyping and prejudice work against men and women in the arts. For example, parents are often quite upset if their sons score high on femininity scales of personality measures. These scores often reflect not homosexual tendencies, as the parents fear, but artistic sensitivity.

Educational programs for the gifted must deal with two problems: first, sex-role appropriate behavior stereotypes which may inhibit male participation in the arts; and second, barriers to the adult achievement of women.

Values and Interests

Interests, values, and personality factors as well as cognitive abilities help determine an individual's achievement in school and life. Sex differences in the affective domain appear greater than those in cognitive areas. Men and women differ markedly with respect to interests and values that relate to achievement and creativity.

Adults, college students, and high school students differ consistently with respect to value scores on the Allport–Vernon–Lindzey *Study of Values* (SV).[6] Males score higher than females on the theoretical, economic, and political scales and score lower in the social, aesthetic, and religious values (Allport, Vernon, and Lindzey 1970).

In studies of the values of gifted youth, these same patterns of sex differences were found (Fox and Denham 1974; Fox 1976b). Gifted boys

[6]The Allport-Vernon-Lindzey *Study of Values* is published by the Houghton Mifflin Company, Boston.

scored higher than girls on the theoretical, political, and economic scales and lower on the social, aesthetic, and religious scales. Even when samples of gifted boys and girls were matched on verbal and quantitative aptitude and socioeconomic background, the sex differences in theoretical, aesthetic, and social values were still highly significant.

The pattern of value ordering for gifted boys closely resembled that of a normative high school sample described in the manual. Gifted girls did differ, however, from the normative high school sample of girls. For gifted girls the theoretical value was their third highest score while the religious value was fifth. In the normative high school sample the theoretical value was sixth and the religious value was first.

MacKinnon (1962) and others (Southern and Plant 1968; Warren and Herst 1960) have found that high scores on the theoretical and aesthetic value scales are associated with creativity. Studies of gifted adolescents at The Johns Hopkins University have found many males, but few females, who scored highest on the theoretical value scale. Few males or females score highest on the aesthetic value.

Of 240 gifted females and 416 gifted males tested on the SV in 1973, 37 percent of the boys but only 15 percent of the girls scored highest on the theoretical scale. Only 13 and 5 percent of the girls and boys, respectively, scored highest on the aesthetic scale. Over 55 percent of 135 very mathematically gifted boys scored highest on the theoretical value. Thus, theoretical interests appear to be correlated to mathematical talent. Boys and girls who scored highest on the theoretical value scale also had the highest mean score on the SAT-M in the 1973 contest (Fox 1976*b*).

Boys who have high theoretical values and mathematical talent are far more interested in accelerating their educational progress in mathematics than boys or girls who have the talent but score higher on social value measures. Differential values and interests appear to be a major factor in the sex differences in mathematical achievement at the high level of ability. Although gifted girls are more likely to have high theoretical interests associated with scientific pursuits than average-ability girls, they are still less theoretically oriented than their gifted male cohorts.

Further evidence that gifted girls have stronger academic interests than less gifted girls comes from a study of career interests of gifted youth (Fox, Pasternak, and Peiser 1976). Gifted seventh-grade boys and girls were compared with a normative sample of ninth graders on the fourteen basic interest scales of the Strong–Campbell Interest Inventory (SCII).[7]

Gifted girls and boys scored significantly higher than their respective normative counterparts on the scales of writing, mathematics, science,

[7]The Strong-Campbell Interest Inventory (SCII) is published by the Psychological Corporation, New York.

public speaking, and medical science. These scales clearly reflect a greater interest in intellectual pursuits. Gifted girls also scored higher than the normative group on the scales of law and politics and mechanical activities. Although the normative sample of girls scored higher than the gifted girls on scales of social and conventional interest, such as domestic arts and office practice, these differences were not statistically significant. Thus, gifted girls are not less interested in the more traditional female areas than average girls, simply more interested in the more masculine areas, such as science, mathematics, and mechanical activities.

Average boys differed from gifted boys in that they had lower scores on the more intellective scales, as noted above, and significantly higher scores on the adventure scale. The latter scale, according to Campbell (1974), reflects vocational immaturity. Gifted boys scored higher than the normative group on all three artistic scales, but only the difference in the writing scale reached significance.

Thus, both gifted girls and boys differ from their less-gifted cohorts on measures of intellectual interests. For boys, this does not seem to involve a real difference with respect to the masculine stereotype. For gifted girls, however, there appears to be a source of sex-role conflict. Girls have both masculine and feminine interests.

For a number of reasons gifted girls probably experience more conflict than boys in making career choices. First, they must decide whether or not to seek a career instead of, or in addition to, a role of wife and mother. Second, if they elect to pursue a career, they must choose between a traditionally accepted female one or a more intellectual, but masculine one.

Gifted girls are less likely than gifted boys to exhibit sex-role stereotype in naming occupational choices. For example, girls are far more likely to name physician as a career choice than boys are to name nurse. Of course, job status and pay are also tied to career aspirations. Most occupations designated female have less status and monetary reward than more masculine occupations.

On a semantic differential measure, gifted boys and girls matched on measures of ability and socioeconomic background were asked to rate their self-perceptions in eight occupations. Gifted girls perceived themselves favorably in both masculine and feminine careers, whereas boys had negative perceptions of themselves as nurse, homemaker, or professor of English. Elementary school teacher was rated somewhat favorably by boys, but far less so than the occupations of mathematician, physician, professor of science, or computer programmer.

For girls career aspirations as early as grade seven or eight appear to be related to achievement in some subject-matter areas. Girls who see mathematics as useful for their future careers are more likely to take advanced courses and maintain high levels of achievement in mathematics during the high school years (Astin 1968; Astin and Myint 1971; Haven 1972). Gifted girls who are interested in careers of a scientific or mathematical nature are more likely to persist in special mathematics courses and accelerate their achievement than girls who have social, artistic, or enterprising career aspirations (Fox 1974a, 1975b). A study of 161 girls who took advanced placement courses in mathematics, chemistry, and/or the physical sciences found that 80 percent of these girls were interested in careers in science (Casserly 1975).

In brief, gifted boys and girls do differ significantly with respect to interests and values. These differences, in turn, seem related to differential achievement of the sexes in school and life. Let us now consider how these differences relate to special types of programs for gifted children.

FACILITATING THE DEVELOPMENT OF TALENT

A great variety of educational alternatives and teaching strategies have been advocated for enriching the education of gifted children in academic areas. Some of these methods are clearly accelerative in nature. Others are less specifically designed to promote rapid learning and precocious achievement. Not all educators agree on the relative merits of each method; however, few researchers have systematically analyzed the advantages of these strategies separately for girls and boys. We shall now try to address this problem. We will first consider methods that have clear accelerative components.

Accelerative Enrichment

Studies of children who enter school early have, in general, found early admission to be a viable method for gifted children (Worcester 1956). In most such studies girls have outnumbered boys. In a study by Hobson (1963) of early entrants in 1946 and 1947 in a Boston suburb, girls outnumbered boys by about two to one. Very gifted boys and girls are likely to be ready for the intellectual experiences and demands of first grade a year or more before the standard entering age. Birch (1954) suggested that girls' early verbal superiority might make them more visible to their parents at an early age. To the extent that girls are developmentally ahead of boys in the early childhood years, we might expect that early admission to kindergarten or first grade would be even more effective for girls than boys. Research is needed to determine whether or not this is, in fact, true. If so, parents of gifted girls should be alterted to this because, as we shall see, attempts to foster accelerated achievement among gifted students at older ages appear more difficult for girls than boys.

In a report to Congress, the Commissioner of the U.S. Office of Education (Marland 1971) noted that grade skipping of one or two years has generally been found to be a successful alternative for gifted children. To be most effective, however, grade skipping needs to be well planned to avoid unnecessary adjustment problems for the child. Grade skipping that takes place at natural transition points in the school process is likely to be least disruptive for the child. The ages at which acceleration is least traumatic may differ for the sexes.

Although moderate grade skipping in the elementary school years may be equally successful for boys and girls, grade skipping at the secondary school level does not appear currently to have equal appeal to both sexes. A sample of gifted seventh- and eighth-grade boys and girls who entered a mathematics contest at The Johns Hopkins University were canvassed as to their attitudes toward acceleration. Girls were significantly less favorable than boys toward acceleration for themselves (Fox 1976a). Only 54 percent of the girls as compared with 73 percent of the boys expressed a willingness to accelerate. Significantly more girls than boys felt their parents would disapprove of acceleration.

These findings support the observations by the SMPY staff of mathematically gifted adolescents and their parents in counseling situations. Girls appear to be more fearful than boys of possible peer rejection for academic acceleration. Adolescent girls appear more fearful than boys of trying something different because they might not succeed (Fox 1974b). Girls who have high self-esteem, as measured by expectations for success in the contest, were significantly more likely to favor acceleration than girls who predicted they would score average or poor relative to the other girls in the contest. Expectations for success, however, were not correlated with actual performance. Thus, the most able girls were not necessarily high on self-esteem or eagerness to accelerate. Girls may or may not truly fear success, but they do appear to be, as adolescents, less confident than boys about their ability to succeed in unknown situations. Perhaps girls are more willing than boys to suffer intellectual boredom to ensure their social standing in the peer group.[8] This, again, would seem to argue that girls are likely to benefit from accelerative experiences in the

---

[8]Occasionally girls who were reluctant to accelerate in grades 7 or 8 express an interest in acceleration in grade 11. They appear to become "fed up" with high school, both intellectually and socially, and want to go to college early. Unfortunately, they often have not planned their high school programs well for this goal. Therefore, they lack courses like calculus, physics, and chemistry in addition to senior-year English. This makes it difficult for them to go to college early.

early elementary school years before they become socialized against acceleration and intellectual pursuits.

Since double promotions appear to have some drawbacks, SMPY has investigated some alternative acceleration strategies for meeting the needs of mathematically talented students. Let us consider how well some of these strategies meet the needs of gifted boys and girls.

Subject-matter acceleration by advanced placement is a rather straightforward idea but has not been noted in the literature until recently (Fox 1974c). In this scheme, students would be placed in classes appropriate for them in specific content areas. Thus, a twelve-year-old who is mathematically gifted might be in homeroom, physical education, English, and social studies with age peers in a junior high school, but be placed in geometry and chemistry with tenth and eleventh graders at a high school. Subject-matter acceleration of this type works well in situations where elementary, junior, and senior high schools are physically nearby or where transportation from school to school can be arranged.

The extreme of this model is having junior and senior high school students take college courses in those areas in which they are most gifted, and yet remain in the secondary school for most of the school day. This method has many advantages at present. A very mathematically gifted youth may easily learn all the precollege mathematics and science available in the public secondary school one or two years before he or she is ready for full-time entrance to a college or university.

College course work can be taken during the day, at night, in summer or by correspondence in the appropriate subject areas. SMPY has well documented the fact that very gifted adolescents can succeed in college courses (Keating, Wiegand, and Fox 1974; Solano and George 1976).

These methods of subject-matter acceleration all appear to be very effective for gifted males. Gifted adolescent girls, however, are far less likely than boys to take advantage of these options. Gifted girls have been known to actually repeat a course to avoid this type of acceleration. It is not completely clear whether or not girls are actually less successful than boys in these types of accelerative programs because so few girls have tried them.

The rejection of subject-matter acceleration by girls seems to be in part a sex-by-subject-area interaction. At present, mathematics and science lend themselves best to this type of acceleration. Although girls apparently report liking math as much as boys do (Ernest 1975), there is considerable evidence when mathematics and science courses are optional, gifted girls elect not to take them in far greater numbers than boys do (Haven 1972).

Differential course taking for the sexes at advanced levels is very clear in the case of the Advanced Placement Program (APP).[9] The APP allows students to earn advanced standing in college courses, college credit, or both for courses studied in high school. These courses were specifically designed for the academically talented student.

Gifted girls take fewer of these courses than boys, particularly in mathematics and science. In 1974, only 17.2 percent of the APP candidates in chemistry were girls. Only 12.9 percent of the students who took the physics B-level examination and 6.8 percent of those who took the physics C-level examination were girls. In mathematics, only 27.9 percent of those who took the calculus AB-level examination were girls, while only 21 percent of those who took the BC-level calculus examination were girls (Casserly 1975).

In 1975, 50,384 exams were taken by boys and 35,402 were taken by girls. Of the nineteen different exams given, girls outnumber boys in only six: art history, studio art, English, French language, French literature, and Spanish. Boys outnumber girls in American history, European history, the classics, German, and all the science and mathematics courses, including biology (CEEB 1975).

Casserly (1975) did an extensive study of twelve American high schools which enrolled over twice the national percentage of girls in their APP courses in mathematics and science. Her findings are very enlightening.

Schools that enroll sizable numbers of girls in these APP courses tend to have one or both of the following characteristics:

1. Teachers of such courses who actively recruit girls for the classes. These teachers exhibit few signs of sex-role stereotyping in their thinking or in their classroom behavior. They expect high-level performance from the girls as well as the boys, and they demand it from both.
2. Students who were tracked as early as the fourth grade into homogeneously grouped and sometimes accelerative programs. Thus, the taking of APP courses is a natural sequence in a special program for superior students.

It is interesting to note that interviews with counselors in these schools indicated that these counselors were not always supportive of APP courses for the gifted girls. Both male and female counselors admitted that they often discouraged girls from taking these courses. The reasons for such counseling differed by sex. Female counselors tended to project their own dislike or fear of science and mathematics in their counseling strategies. Some said that the girls needed time for social activities, which would be lost if they had to work hard on APP courses. Others said they hated to put girls in situations where they could not

[9]The Advanced Placement Program (APP) is operated by The Educational Testing Service, Princeton, N.J.

succeed, where they might make low grades and thus hurt their otherwise excellent academic records.

The concern for good grades is particularly interesting because interviews with the girls enrolled in APP courses at those schools indicate that the girls earned high grades in these courses. This seemed to conflict with the girls' self-estimates of their actual abilities and performance in the classes. The girls thought themselves to be in the bottom of their classes, yet their grades and achievements indicated they were not. Only 3 of the 161 girls studied were in danger of making poor grades.

Male counselors had a somewhat different argument for counseling girls out of the APP courses. They felt it would be "unfair to the girls" because the job market was so tight in the physical sciences and the jobs should *of course* go to the men.

If these attitudes are found among counselors at schools that have the greatest female enrollments in APP courses in mathematics and science, what must be the attitudes and counseling strategies in schools that have much lower rates of female participation? These findings are staggering. Recall, this study was done in 1974–75. It reflects the kinds of barriers that still exist today for gifted girls. How intrepid the girls must be to pursue the development of their talents.

Advanced placement courses appear to be an excellent model for the types of programs that we might wish for the academically talented child. Alas, these programs do not have a true counterpart at the junior high school or elementary level. Stanley, Keating, and Fox recently created a model for the upper elementary and junior high school grades in mathematics which parallels the APP (Fox 1974*b*; Fox 1975*a*; George and Denham 1976; Stanley 1976). This model is the provision of fast-paced homogeneously grouped classes for fifth through eighth, ninth, or tenth graders.

The first experimental class was conducted on the campus of The Johns Hopkins University for two hours a week on Saturday mornings from the summer of 1972 until 1973. A teacher, well trained in mathematics, paced the best of the students (eight boys and one girl) through four and one-half years of precalculus mathematics in a year's time. The least ambitious students (mostly girls) learned two years of mathematics in a year. Most of the students had only completed the sixth grade when they entered the program.

The boys who completed the precalculus mathematics in a year went on to take calculus in a high school the following year. All but one were successful. The single girl, however, chose to repeat plane geometry in a self-paced course the following two years to avoid acceleration.

By the end of the school year 1974–75, twelve accelerated mathematics classes had been conducted at Hopkins or in public and private schools and school systems in Maryland. These classes have all been successful in promoting high-level achievement at a rapid rate. There have been, however, notable sex differences. Boys and girls do not achieve equally well under all conditions.

Girls are far more likely to participate in such classes if they are conducted as part of the regular school program rather than as extracurricular activities. Girls apparently are less likely to give up a Saturday morning to study math beyond their regular school program than are boys. Thus, the more closely the program is tied to the school, the more likely girls will participate.

Girls are more likely to achieve as well as or better than boys in these types of classes if they are taught by women in all-girl classes or classes where there is at least a sizable number of girls relative to the boys. When classes are taught by men and the number of girls is very small relative to the boys, the girls often drop out. (There are, of course, exceptions. One girl chose to be in an otherwise all-boy class taught by a male and was highly successful.) In general, the presence of a female role model and other girls seem to be helpful in promoting achievement of girls in accelerated classes.

Hawley (1972) found that women who majored in mathematics and science in college tended to view these areas as less antithetical to femaleness than did college women in other fields. Perhaps the presence of a woman teacher and other girls help dispel the feeling that mathematics is a masculine domain. Since girls appear to be somewhat concerned about establishing their feminine identity in early adolescence, the sex-role appropriateness of the task is apparently a psychologically relevant factor.

Since boys should experience no sex-identity conflict about being accelerated in mathematics, the sex of the teacher should be less important for them. Only three of the twelve classes of students to date have had female teachers for boys. An all-male class taught by a woman was extremely successful. Boys in mixed-sex classes taught by women did not do quite as well as expected. Perhaps if classes become too "feminized" or social, boys will enjoy them less.

The analysis of the twelve classes has not been in any way a true experiment. Therefore, conclusions cannot be drawn, only tentative hypotheses suggested. What needs to be studied explicitly is the differential performance of gifted males and females in educational experiences which are congruent and incongruent with sex-role stereotypes.

I do not mean to suggest that we as educators should try to reinforce sex-role stereotypes, but I would like to argue that we cannot ignore them. What we need to do is examine them critically and unemotionally to determine their significance as classroom environmental variables that need to be considered in educational planning.

For example, what, if any, benefits can arise from explicitly planning for sex differences in educating the gifted? In the summer of 1973, this author taught twenty-six seventh-grade girls algebra I. Eighteen of the girls persisted in the program and were highly successful. The class was specifically designed to foster interest in mathematics and achievement (Fox 1974a). By the end of the ninth grade about half of the girls who had initially come for the class had managed to become accelerated in mathematics by at least one year.

Although this is not as impressive as the acceleration accomplished by many boys in the SMPY program, it was a substantial gain for girls. The girls had been matched on a number of cognitive and social variables with two control groups. The control boys and girls did not participate in the classes but did receive counseling by mail as to the advantages of subject-matter acceleration. Only 20 percent of the control boys and 16 percent of the control girls had become accelerated in mathematics. All three groups were equally gifted in mathematics. Thus, attempts to intervene to encourage girls to develop their mathematical talent can be successful.

Prior to the program, both groups of girls were alike with respect to interests in careers in science and mathematics and considerably less interested than their male counterparts. Two years later, the girls who had accelerated were significantly more interested in these career areas than the control boys or girls. Now it is true that the girls who benefited most from the program were those who initially had investigative career interests. The effect of participation in the program was to help reinforce and maintain that interest (Fox 1976a).

Early admission to college is the final accelerative experience for consideration. Radical early admission to college, as studied by SMPY (Stanley 1974), does indeed appear to be a male domain. To date, SMPY has not in general found girls who appear to be ready for college full-time at age fourteen. This is, at least in part, because most radical accelerates are extremely gifted in the quantitative areas. Such extreme precocity in the quantitative area appears less frequently among females.

Early admission to college by one year, however, does appear to be as effective for gifted young women as men. The studies of the early entrants by Flesher and Pressey (1955) did not find women to be less able than men to succeed in college early. Early admission to college by one year or even two does not seem to be limited to those gifted in the quantitative areas. It is too soon to say whether or not this method of acceleration will be widely used by both sexes.

Counseling efforts by SMPY suggest that some girls who in the seventh and eighth grades were not eager to accelerate are giving serious consideration to graduating from high school a year early or entering college at the end of the eleventh grade. Until early admissions programs gain wider acceptance, it will be difficult to evaluate their effectiveness for both sexes.

There is no direct evidence that any of the aforementioned accelerative strategies are truly less effective for educating gifted girls than boys, only that they are less likely to be tried by gifted girls. Since acceleration is clearly more feasible in mathematics and science, the reluctance of girls to attempt acceleration may be, in some cases, a form of mathematics-avoidance behavior.

Nonaccelerative Strategies

There are a number of educational strategies recommended for the gifted which do not necessarily lead to advanced grade placement. Homogeneously grouped classes for the purpose of enrichment are an example. What may be accomplished under this type of program is so situation-specific as to make any evaluation of benefits of such programs for either sex difficult, if not impossible.

Self-paced independent study projects, like enriched classes, are difficult to evaluate. It seems likely that success in these activities is related to interest in the subject area, motivation, and the work and study skills of the students. Informal observations suggest that, at least in mathematics, girls achieve more in classes than by self-paced, independent study. Perhaps one reason some girls drop out of accelerated programs is because these classes require more outside independent study of the textbook than do slower-paced classes. It is doubtful that in general girls have poorer study skills and habits than boys. More likely, differential motivations account for the differences. Apparently, the greater theoretical orientation of boys helps them enjoy learning on their own in mathematics. Girls who score high in social interest measures probably dislike solitary learning situations and prefer more interaction with teachers and peers.

Harold C. Lyon, former Director of The Office of Gifted and Talented in the U.S. Office of Education, has spoken repeatedly of the value of mentorship programs for gifted students (Lyon 1975). Adolescents would be placed into close working relationships with adults who have similar interests. Epstein (1970) and Robin (1975) caution that women can have various difficulties in the mentor–mentee relationship if the mentor is a male. Although they are speaking of young adult women, the problem may be true for younger girls as well. Intellectual development may be better fostered for girls if the mentor is female. Mentor relationships that place young girls in contact with successful women models who have not rejected their femininity in their struggle to achieve would seem to be a particularly desirable program for gifted girls.

Internship and work-study programs that allow students to work in offices, laboratories, hospitals, and so forth, have excellent value for the gifted. Care should be taken, however, to ensure that gifted girls are not placed in situations that will reinforce harmful sex stereotypes.

The whole area of career education for the gifted is a relatively new one. There is perhaps no other single program which has so much potential for helping gifted female and minority students.

CONCLUSION

On the basis of the existing evidence concerning educational aptitudes, interests, and achievement of the gifted, five major areas of concern for future research and program planning can be identified.

The first area is that of sex-role stereotypes. Creative and productive behavior of both males and females in school and in life is likely to increase as unrealistic sex-role stereotyping of activities gives way. The ideas that smocks in art classes or aprons in cooking class threaten the sexual identity of males while aprons in shop class cause the loss of femininity of females are no more absurd than the ideas that science is a male domain and poetry is for sissies.

Gifted boys and girls both need moral and intellectual role models who exhibit the heights that gifted persons can achieve. For girls the exposure to women who utilize the full range of their talents and gifts seems particularly crucial.

Career counseling is important for both sexes. At present not enough is known about the career counseling needs of gifted women. Models need to be developed and tested. At present the choice of a career as homemaker is still generally limited to women. Therefore, the career counseling needs of women will not be identical to those of men. Since some women may not wish to begin a career outside the home until they are forty or older, consideration should be given to providing continuing educational and career development programs for them. Efforts are needed to encourage women not to eliminate later career possibilities by failing to develop their talents in adolescence and young adulthood.

Counselors and teachers need to become more aware of the special needs of the gifted learner, as well as the general problems of sex-role stereotyping. If teachers are to prepare children for the future, they must themselves be helped to understand social change and adjust to it.

Parents as well as educators need to become aware of the negative outcomes of early sex-role stereotyping. Parents of gifted children should be counseled about the talents of their offspring as early as possible. Parents of girls may need urging about the values of certain so-called boys' toys and games for their daughters. Parents of gifted boys may need encouragement to be tolerant of their sons' aesthetic and verbal interests. Perhaps groups such as the National Association for Gifted Children could experiment with counseling centers for parents of the gifted.

A second issue is that of homogeneous grouping. At present that concept is too often limited to grouping on the basis of an IQ score. Children with the same overall intelligence score can be very different with respect to specific abilities and interests. Perhaps ability grouping with respect to interests and specific skills would be more beneficial to all.

Whether or not students are actually segregated into special classes or dealt with in teamed class situations, some attention to interest should be considered. Perhaps students with mathematical talents and interests would enjoy language classes more if they read and wrote articles related to mathematics and science. What would be the result of offering a course in mathematics or science taught in German or Russian? Perhaps students with strong social interests would appreciate mathematics more if the course was interlaced with applied problems of a social nature. Courses in statistics and mathematical psychology could be developed which also taught the basic mathematics of algebra through calculus.

Perhaps children would become more creative if educators and parents set better examples in their approaches to teaching. In life, skills are far less compartmentalized than in school. In life, ability, interests, and experience play greater roles in work situations and assignments than age. Yet in schools chronological age is the major factor that determines what child learns what topic at a given level. Gifted boys and girls would both probably benefit if attention to readiness and interest for learning were more important than age.

This leads to the third area of concern: the acceleration of learning and appropriate content for the gifted. At the first World Conference on Gifted, Gallagher (1975) stressed quite eloquently that the major need for progress in educating the gifted is the development of appropriate content to be studied. In mathematics and science such content has been well developed. The problem for gifted learners is one of allowing them to study the mathematics and science content at the most appropriate time and pace. For example, SMPY has clearly demonstrated that some sixth and seventh graders can easily master the content of algebra and geometry at a high level. The problem is how to adjust the school program to allow the natural transition from computational skills to abstract mathematics to occur at the right time for the gifted learner. In the case of girls this problem is particularly difficult because to learn this material at the appropriate time often requires some type of acceleration of grade placement, either in the subject or overall.

Gifted students, particularly girls, would benefit from changes in school environments that create greater flexibility in the content presented to a given student at any age. The concept of the ungraded school is to be lauded. But, unfortunately, this concept is too often more limited in practice than in theory. Self-pacing independent study is also less than ideal. Talented children need to interact with their intellectual peers and can benefit from the guidance of good teachers.

The acceleration of learning of appropriate content is the major issue. At present some form of grade skipping, or at least subject acceleration, is all that is available to most gifted students. Although these methods do work, they are unattractive to many, especially gifted girls. The ultimate solution for the gifted child, as well as the slow learner, is the abolishment of age–grade segregation.

Stanley (1959) has proposed longitudinal teaching teams in various subject-matter areas. This concept needs to be expanded and tested. It is possible that the creation of learning centers with specialists in subject areas who develop long-range curriculum programs for students might eliminate some of the problems of desegregation as well as problems of the "deviant learner." Major changes in educational strategies come slowly. Thus, while on the one hand educators should experiment with innovation, on the other hand they must deal with today's gifted children, who exist in less than ideal situations.

This leads to the fourth critical issue: the need for early identification and planning for the child who is gifted. Some parents recognize early that their child is exceptional. The extremely precocious child who learns to read at age three or four is not likely to go unnoticed. In some families, however, the gifted child may not be recognized.

Given the present educational process, early entrance to first grade would seem to be desirable for most very bright students. Early entrance is particularly desirable for girls since later acceleration is less appealing to them. Early entrance to school is also likely to benefit the child from the educationally disadvantaged background. Yet few school systems encourage early entrance. Clearly, better screening procedures would seem to be needed in order to identify children who should enter school early. Research is needed to devise ways of finding talented students early to foster advanced school registration. The concept of Head Start seems to be truly needed for gifted girls and the children from educationally disadvantaged homes.

Early identification and admission to kindergarten or first grade by itself is not enough. Program planning for the advanced learner needs to be started early and continued through college. For girls, early tracking into academic programs that lead to AP courses and early high school graduation seems imperative. The gifted learner will need the level and stimulation of advanced course work earlier than others. College-level work may be necessary for the very bright learners when they are only ten to fifteen years old. Exactly how this is handled will vary with each child. There is no single solution to fit all gifted students.

This leads to the fifth and final issue of concern: counseling for the gifted learner. Since there can be no single plan for all children, there is a real need for early educational counseling and planning services for the gifted child. Gifted children and their parents must be alerted to the various alternative strategies that exist in order to plan a program. Girls, in particular, need early counseling about the value of advanced placement courses, early college admission, and studying mathematics and science. Sensitive counselors are needed who will stimulate, not discourage, the intellectual interests and achievement of gifted girls and boys.

America needs talented scientists, artists, gifted leaders, and informed, concerned citizens. All children today need educational programs that prepare them for the demands of the future. Gifted learners are too often frustrated rather than helped to fulfill their promise by the unnecessary rigidity of our present educational system. The gifted child, especially the female child, is often discouraged from seeking intellectual challenge. In the year that we honor both women and Terman's impressive study of the gifted child, educators and parents should make a strong commitment to quality educational programs that lead to the realization of potential for all children, including gifted and talented boys and girls.

REFERENCES

Aiken, L. R. 1970. Attitudes toward mathematics. *Review of Educational Research* 40(4): 551–96.

Allport, G. W., Vernon, P. E., and Lindzey, G. 1970. *Manual for the study of values: A scale for measuring the dominant interests in personality.* Boston: Houghton Mifflin.

Anastasi, A. 1958. *Differential psychology: Individual and group differences in behavior.* New York: Macmillan.

Astin, H. S. 1968. Career development of girls during the high school years. *Journal of Counseling Psychology* 15(6): 536–40.

———. 1974. Sex differences in mathematical and scientific precocity. In J. C. Stanley, D. P. Keating, and L. H. Fox (eds.), *Mathematical talent: Discovery, description, and development.* Baltimore, Md.: The Johns Hopkins University Press, pp. 70–86.

————, and Myint, T. 1971. Career development and stability of young women during the post high school years. *Journal of Counseling Psychology* 19(4): 369–94.

Birch, J. W. 1954. Early school admission for mentally advanced children. *Exceptional Children* 21(3): 84–87.

Bock, R. D., and Kolakowski, D. 1973. Further evidence of sex-linked major-gene influence on human spatial visualizing ability. *American Journal of Human Genetics* 25: 1–14.

Campbell, D. P. 1974. *Manual for the Strong-Campbell Interest Inventory.* Stanford, Calif.: Stanford University Press.

Carey, G. L. 1958. Sex differences in problem-solving performance as a function of attitude differences. *Journal of Abnormal and Social Psychology* 56: 256–60.

Carlsmith, L. 1964. Effect of early father absence on scholastic aptitude. *Harvard Educational Review* 34: 3–21.

Casserly, P. L. 1975. An assessment of factors affecting female participation in advanced placement programs in mathematics, chemistry and physics. Report of National Science Foundation Grant GY-11325.

College Entrance Examination Board. 1975. *Summary Report of 1975 Advanced Placement Examinations.* Princeton, N.J.: College Entrance Examination Board.

Educational Testing Service. 1972. *The prediction of doctorate attainment in psychology, mathematics, and chemistry: Preliminary Report.* Princeton, N.J.: Educational Testing Service Preliminary Report.

Epstein, C. F. 1970. Encountering the male establishment. Sex status limits on women's careers in the professions. *American Journal of Sociology* 75(6): 965–82.

Ernest, J. 1975. *Mathematics and sex.* Santa Barbara, Calif.: Mathematics Department, University of California.

Flesher, M., and Pressey, S. L. 1955. War-time accelerates ten years after. *Journal of Educational Psychology* 46: 228–38.

Fox, L. H. 1974a. Facilitating the development of mathematical talent in young women. Unpublished doctoral dissertation in psychology, The Johns Hopkins University. *Dissertation Abstracts International,* 1974, 35, 3553B. (University Microfilms No. 74-29027.)

————. 1974b. A mathematics program for fostering precocious achievement. In J. C. Stanley, D. P. Keating, and L. H. Fox (eds.), *Mathematical talent: Discovery, description, and development.* Baltimore, Md.: The Johns Hopkins University Press, pp. 101–25.

————. 1974c. Facilitating the educational development of mathematically precocious youth. In J. C. Stanley, D. P. Keating, and L. H. Fox (eds.), *Mathematical talent: Discovery, description, and development.* Baltimore, Md.: The Johns Hopkins University Press, pp. 47–69.

————. 1975a. *Annual Report to the Spencer Foundation.* Baltimore, Md.: Intellectually Gifted Child Study Group, Evening College and Summer Session, The Johns Hopkins University.

———. 1975*b*. Career interests and mathematical acceleration for girls. Paper presented at the 1975 annual meeting of the American Psychological Association, Chicago, August 1975.

———. 1976*a*. Sex differences in mathematical precocity: bridging the gap. In D. P. Keating (ed.), *Intellectual talent: Research and development*. Baltimore, Md.: The Johns Hopkins University Press, pp. 183–314.

———. 1976*b*. The values of gifted youth. In D. P. Keating (ed.), *Intellectual talent: Research and development*. Baltimore, Md.: The Johns Hopkins University Press, pp. 273–84.

———. 1977. The effects of sex role socialization on mathematics participation and achievement. Paper prepared for Education and Work Group, Career Awareness Division, National Institute of Education, U.S. Department of Health, Education and Welfare, Contract Number FN17 400-76-0114. Washington, D.C.: U.S. Government Printing Office, 1977 (in press).

———, and Denham, S. A. 1974. Values and career interests of mathematically and scientifically precocious youth. In J. C. Stanley, D. P. Keating, and L. H. Fox (eds.), *Mathematical talent: Discovery, description, and development*. Baltimore, Md.: The Johns Hopkins University Press, pp. 140–75.

———, Pasternak, S. R., and Peiser, N. L. 1976. Career related interests of adolescent boys and girls. In D. P. Keating (ed.) *Intellectual talent: Research and development*. Baltimore, Md.: The Johns Hopkins University Press, pp. 242–61.

Gallagher, J. J. 1975. Design and organization of special curricula for gifted children. Paper presented at first World Conference on Gifted Children, London, September 1975.

George, W. C., and Denham, S. A. 1976. Curriculum experimentation for the mathematically talented. In D. P. Keating (ed.), *Intellectual talent: Research and development*. Baltimore, Md.: The Johns Hopkins University Press, pp. 103–31.

Goldberg, P. 1968. Are women prejudiced against women? *Trans-Action* 5: 28–30.

Haven, E. W. 1972. Factors associated with the selection of advanced academic mathematics courses by girls in high school. *Research Bulletin* 72: 12. Princeton, N.J.: Educational Testing Service.

Hawley, P. 1972. Perceptions of male models of femininity related to career choice. *Journal of Counseling Psychology* 19(4): 308–13.

Helson, R. 1971. Women mathematicians and the creative personality. *Journal of Counseling and Clinical Psychology* 36(2): 210–20.

Hobson, J. R. 1963. High school performance of underage pupils initially admitted to kindergarten on the basis of physical and psychological examinations. *Educational and Psychological Measurement* 23(1): 159–70.

Horner, M. 1968. Sex differences in achievement motivation and performance in competitive and non-competitive situations. Unpublished doctoral dissertation, University of Michigan.

Keating, D. P., Wiegand, S. J., and Fox, L. H. 1974. Behavior of mathematically precocious boys in a college course. In J. C. Stanley, D. P. Keating, and L. H. Fox (eds.), *Mathematical talent: Discovery, description, and development*. Baltimore, Md.: The Johns Hopkins University Press, pp. 176–85.

Lyon, H. C. 1975. REAL-ising potential: A rational report on the education of the gifted and talented in the USA. Paper presented at first World Conference on Gifted Children, London, September 1975.

Maccoby, E. E. 1963. Women's intellect. In S. M. Farber and R. H. L. Wilson (eds.), *The potential of woman.* New York: McGraw-Hill, pp. 24–39.

————, and Jacklin, C. N. 1975. *The psychology of sex differences.* Stanford, Calif.: Stanford University Press.

MacKinnon, D. W. 1962. The nature and nurture of creative talent. *American Psychologist* 17(7): 484–95.

Marland, S. P., Jr. 1971. Education of the gifted and talented. Vol. I: Report to the Congress of the United States by the U.S. Commissioner of Education. Washington, D.C.: Department of Health, Education, and Welfare.

McGinn, P. V. 1976. Verbally gifted youth: Selection and description. In D. P. Keating (ed.), *Intellectual talent: Research and development.* Baltimore, Md.: The Johns Hopkins University Press, pp. 160–82.

Milton, G. A. 1957. The effects of sex-role identification upon problem-solving skill. *Journal of Abnormal and Social Psychology* 55: 208–12.

Mullis, I. V. S. 1975. *Educational achievement and sex discrimination.* Denver, Colo.: National Assessment of Educational Progress.

Pheterson, G. I., Kiesler, S. B., and Goldberg, P. 1971. Evaluation of the performance of women as a function of their sex, achievement, and personal history. *Journal of Personality and Social Psychology* 19(1): 114–18.

Robin, E. P. 1975. Some social factors in career choice. Research issues in the employment of women: Proceedings of a workshop. Washington, D.C.: Commission on Human Resources and The National Research Council.

Seashore, H. G. 1962. Women are more predictable than men. *Journal of Counseling Psychology* 9(3): 261–70.

Solano, C. H., and George, W. C. 1976. College courses for the gifted. *Gifted Child Quarterly,* 20(3, Fall): 274–85.

Southern, M. L., and Plant, W. T. 1968. Personality characteristics of very bright adults. *Journal of Personality and Social Psychology* 75(1): 119–26.

Stanley, J. C. 1959. Enriching high-school subjects for intellectually gifted students. *School and Society* 87 (2151): 170–71.

————. 1967. Further evidence via the analysis of variance that women are more predictable academically than men. *Ontario Journal of Educational Research* 10: 49–55.

————. 1973. Accelerating the educational progress of intellectually gifted youths. *Educational Psychologist* 10(3): 133–46.

————. 1974. Intellectual precocity. In J. C. Stanley, D. P. Keating, and L. H. Fox (eds.), *Mathematical talent: Discovery, description, and development.* Baltimore, Md.: The Johns Hopkins University Press, pp. 1–22.

————. 1976. Special fast-mathematics classes taught by college professors to fourth- through twelfth-graders. In D. P. Keating (ed.), *Intellectual talent: Research and development.* Baltimore, Md.: The Johns Hopkins University Press, pp. 132–59.

Terman, L. M. 1925. Mental and physical traits of a thousand gifted children. *Genetic studies of genius,* vol. 1. Stanford, Calif.: Stanford University Press.

Warren, J. R., and Herst, P. A. 1960. Personality attributes of gifted college students. *Science* 132: 330–37.

Worcester, D. A. 1956. *The education of children of above-average mentality.* Lincoln, Nebr.: University of Nebraska Press.

III
THREE MAJOR
APPROACHES
TO CREATIVITY

7

COGNITIVE AND AFFECTIVE COMPONENTS OF CREATIVITY IN MATHEMATICS AND THE PHYSICAL SCIENCES

William B. Michael

ABSTRACT

On the basis of data provided by biographical and assessment studies, personality characteristics as well as salient features on demographic and home-related variables were identified and summarized for samples of creative and/or eminent physical scientists and mathematicians. Differences in these characteristics were also delineated between groups of mathematicians and physical scientists judged to be creative or noncreative. Although both creative physical scientists and mathematicians tend to be highly intelligent, intuitive, introverted, autonomous, individualistic, flexible and open-minded in working styles, and emotionally stable, creative scientists differ from creative mathematicians in being more self-assertive, dominant, striving, and hard working, but somewhat less oriented toward humanitarian concerns and toward a need for order. To explain the nature of intellectual functions involved in the creative process and in the steps required in creative problem solving, Guilford's structure-of-intellect (SOI) model and his information-processing structure-of-intellect problem-solving (SIPS) model were described. The constructs of these two models were related to Rossman's seven-step paradigm for invention, which also provides a useful description of the sequence of steps for creative production and problem solving. Implications of the two Guilford models for teaching for creative endeavor in mathematics and the physical sciences were set forth and illustrated.

The Study of Mathematically (and Scientifically) Precocious Youth (SMPY) within the Department of Psychology at The Johns Hopkins University indeed offers a unique opportunity for psychologists to

141

identify the extent to which each of its gifted student participants possesses measurable components of affective and cognitive behaviors previously shown to be related to creative productivity of recognized physical scientists and mathematicians. It also affords many high school and college teachers directly or indirectly associated with SMPY a chance to devise individualized instructional strategies that can facilitate creative problem solving on the part of its mathematically and scientifically precocious youth. In harmony with these two possible activities among a host of many others in the SMPY effort, the three major purposes of this paper were (1) to describe personality and background characteristics of eminent and presumably creative scientists and mathematicians (although admittedly in some situations eminence might be confounded with clever promotional or manipulative efforts reflecting a high level of political social intelligence rather than creative achievement) on the basis of biographical, longitudinal, and assessment studies that have identified affective and cognitive components as well as demographic and home-related factors associated with creative performance; (2) to offer a partial and at best tentative explanation of the nature of the creative process in problem-solving endeavors primarily in terms of the constructs within the comprehensive theoretical framework of the structure-of-intellect (SOI) model developed by Guilford (1967a, 1968, 1970) and of the subsequent operational information-processing model for problem solving referred to as the structure-of-intellect problem-solving (SIPS) model (Guilford 1967a, 1970; Guilford and Tenopyr 1968); and (3) to suggest some possible ways of teaching for creative endeavor, particularly in science and mathematics, largely in terms of implications of the SOI and SIPS models for effective teaching strategies.

Although Guilford's models, which took their beginnings from a presidential address to the American Psychological Association (Guilford 1950), furnish a comprehensive basis for the conceptualization of creativity, at this point creative endeavor, or simply creativity, may be defined as representing "an effort on the part of a student to generate or bring about new information, a novel idea, or a unique product previously nonexistent in his conscious experience" (Michael 1968, p. 238). Not incompatible with this orientation to creativity are alternative definitions such as "any mental process or set of processes in which an individual generates information he did not have before" (Guilford and Tenopyr 1968, p. 30), "the ability to solve problems by original and useful methods" (Fox 1963, p. 141), or "a purposive psychological process leading to novel behavior" (Blade 1963, p. 197). Detailed attempts to conceptualize and to describe creativity in terms of products, their properties, and processes reflecting personal qualities and cognitive styles have been developed at length by Jackson and Messick (1967) and to some extent by Roe (1963) and Kagan

(1967). Efforts to understand the nature of the creative process within the context of the history of scientific discovery have been undertaken by Brush (1974), Kuhn (1963, 1970), Libby (1971), and Watson (1968); and within the context of the long and exciting history of mathematical invention and discovery, described by Bell (1937) and Hadamard (1945). The implications of these several ways of defining and conceptualizing the creative process to teaching for creative endeavor in an educational or school setting have been discussed and illustrated in a number of different sources (Guilford 1967a, 1968, 1970; Guilford and Tenopyr 1968; Meeker 1969; Michael 1968; Polya 1954, 1957; Torrance 1962).

PERSONALITY AND BACKGROUND CHARACTERISTICS

Biographical and Longitudinal Studies of Creative or Eminent Scientists

In her intensive investigation of the life histories of 22 eminent physical scientists nominated by their peers, Roe (1951, 1953, 1956) noted within the context of personal and family backgrounds several rather distinctive behavior patterns which reflect identifiable affective and cognitive characteristics as follows:

1. The depth of absorption in their work manifested by a driving persistence and an insatiable curiosity was probably as important as any other factor in the level of achievement of physical scientists. In fact, work was tantamount to leisure.

2. From an early age they were avid and voracious readers who enjoyed school and studying.

3. As a group these scientists tended to be highly autonomous, self-sufficient, and independent.

4. They expressed a high degree of respect if not affection for their fathers, who tended to be professional men in homes in which there was a sincere love of learning for its own sake, as well as considerable stability in the marriages of the parents (as revealed by an almost absence of divorce).

5. Most of the physical scientists (as well as biologists whom Roe studied) were slow in social development, shy, and withdrawing in their relationships with the opposite sex, as indicated in part by relatively late marriages.

6. As introverts or "loners," most scientists avoided association or identification with gangs or socially (recreationally) oriented groups, but instead had one or two close friends with interests and values similar to their own.

7. In general, physical scientists exhibited little interest in religion or in church-related activities. This indifference was not necessarily a reflection of antagonistic feelings toward religion.

8. Among the experimental physicists in particular, there had been a long-time interest in gadgets and hardware.

9. As in other groups of scientists studied, an initial research experience often encouraged or facilitated by a single highly perceptive and nonauthoritarian teacher decisively influenced them to pursue a career as a research scientist. In fact, once the men studied had learned that they could do research and once they had experienced the joy of satisfying their curiosity by accomplishing successfully a task on their own, the choice was made to become a scientist even though many had to forbear incompetent and dull teachers.

10. On the average, the physical scientists did receive their doctorates at an earlier age (mean age, 24.6) than did the biologists or social scientists (mean ages, 26.0 and 26.8, respectively).

11. Although the physical scientists exhibited a high but not always an exceptionally high level of performance on tests of scholastic aptitude or intelligence, it appeared that their success was more a function of how hard they had worked at their career than of how truly bright they were.

In a well-known longitudinal investigation of scientists and non-scientists in a group of approximately 800 gifted men, Terman (1954, 1955) substantiated many of Roe's observations of twenty-two eminent scientists. Using essentially the same sample of gifted men as those who as California school children had placed in the top 1 percent of intelligence test scores in 1921 and 1922 relative to their respective ages and thus had been subjects in the well-known *Genetic Studies of Genius* (Terman 1925; Cox 1926; Burks, Jensen, and Terman 1930; Terman and Oden 1947; Terman and Oden 1959; Oden 1968), Terman retrospectively compared each of nine subgroups of men in categories of physical science research ($N = 51$); engineers ($N = 104$); medical–biological sciences ($N = 61$); physical or biological science—nonresearch ($N = 68$); social scientists ($N = 149$); lawyers ($N = 83$); humanities ($N = 95$); the noncollege group ($N = 177$), who were omitted from most comparisons; and social sciences—research ($N = 19$), who also were not included in the intergroup comparisons. Specifically, the group of fifty-one individuals in physical science research as compared with those individuals in the other groups studied tended to come from families with the largest proportion of fathers being college graduates as well as being participants in professional types of employment. Constituting the sample with the largest proportion of early readers (more than 60 percent being able to read before entering school), this group performed at the highest or nearly highest level on a measure of abstract intelligence known as the Concept Mastery Test as well as in their record of scholastic achievement in both high school and college. Relative to vocational interests, these scientists placed at the highest or second highest level in their frequency of superior scores on the Strong Vocational Interest Blank for six kinds of scientists of chemist, engineer, psychologist, physician, architect, and mathematics–science teacher. As children they most often had chosen science as being the most suitable occupation for themselves in later life. These men most often indicated that "work itself" was the single characteristic of life yielding greatest satisfaction to them and that life offered satisfactory outlets for their intellectual talents. However, they showed the smallest frequency of favorable standings in measures of social adjustment, revealed the lowest possible degree of expressed interest in religion, and contrary to Roe's interpretation, demonstrated a minimal relative incidence of affection and understanding between father and son. Thus, in general, on the basis of Terman's and Roe's observations, a rather distinctive pattern or profile of cognitive and affective characteristics of the physical scientist may be inferred, although admittedly important individual differences did exist among the gifted men.

Additional confirmatory evidence of the findings posed by Roe and Terman was apparent in Cattell and Butcher's (1968, pp. 216–80) summary of biographical characteristics of eminent research scientists as conceptualized within the framework of Cattell's factor dimensions of personality. Although introverted in the sense of being skeptical, withdrawn, restrained, solemn, unsociable, critical, and precise, the physical scientist was, nevertheless, highly resourceful, adaptable, and adventurous in his propensity to take risks in his creative endeavor. Despite the introverted tendencies of productive scientists, Cattell and Butcher have agreed with Terman that the level of ego strength and emotional stability of creative geniuses tends to be higher than that of individuals in the general population. They have also emphasized that although anxiety and excitability among scientists do occur, well-developed neuroses are quite rare. In being emotionally stable, the creative research scientists may exhibit socially rather uncongenial and somewhat "undemocratic" attitudes that are associated with their tendencies to be dominant, intellectually self-sufficient, and often critical of others who are less capable than they. Thus Cattell and Butcher have concluded that the characteristic personality pattern observed in eminent research scientists reveals both introversion and emotional stability accompanied by "high (but not necessarily exceptionally high) intelligence, dominance, desurgent taciturnity [quiet, restrained, serious, if not solemn demeanor], and self-sufficiency" (p. 280).

Consistently supported interpretations of this pattern of personality characteristics of creative research scientists have also been furnished by Goertzel and Goertzel (1962), who included several research scientists in their biographical study of 400 eminent individuals in a variety of endeavors; by Shouksmith (1970, pp. 139–41), who interpreted both historiometric and psychometric studies by Cattell and his associates; and by Eiduson (1973, pp. 3–33), who furnished a comprehensive and lengthy review of studies dealing with the psychological aspects of career choice and development in research scientists. In describing the psychodynamics of creative physical scientists, McClelland (1962) not only reiterated several of the previously reported findings of Roe, Terman, and Cattell but also cited the relatively high incidence of a background of radical Protestantism among experimental physical scientists accompanied by their lack of interest in religion, their liking of music but seeming dislike for poetry and art, their intensely masculine identification, their high level of interest early in life in analysis and structures of phenomena, and their avoidance of and disturbance by complex human emotions, particularly interpersonal aggression.

Perhaps one of the most succinct and possibly one of the most cogent summaries of the relationship of personality and biographical factors to scientific creativity was that by Chambers (1964, p. 359):

> The studies to date indicate the typical creative scientist to be an extremely strongly motivated man . . . who needs no pushing but rather is self-propelled . . . dominating others to gain his desired outcome . . . and being completely engrossed in his work to the exclusion of social and civic interests, with evidently no need for religion in his life. . . . Yet, this same man who apparently is not "well rounded" is neither insecure nor unhappy . . . but rather gains a great deal of enjoyment from his work. . . .

Integrative Summary

Finally, in integrating the information about intellectual, motivational, and personality characteristics of scientists obtained from the contributions embodied in selected papers from the Proceedings of the First, Second, and Third University of Utah Conferences that were concerned with the identification of creative scientific talent, Taylor and Barron (1963, pp. 385–86) abstracted the traits found among creative scientists in study after study as follows:

> 1. A high degree of autonomy, self-sufficiency, self-direction.
> 2. A preference for mental manipulations involving things rather than people: a somewhat distant or detached attitude in interpersonal relations, and a preference for intellectually challenging situations rather than socially challenging ones.
> 3. High ego strength and emotional stability.
> 4. A liking for method, precision, exactness.
> 5. A preference for such defense mechanisms as repression and isolation in dealing with affect and instinctual energies.
> 6. A high degree of personal dominance but a dislike of personally toned controversy.

7. A high degree of control of impulse, amounting almost to overcontrol: relatively little talkativeness, gregariousness, impulsiveness.

8. A liking for abstract thinking, with considerable tolerance of cognitive ambiguity.

9. Marked independence of judgment, rejection of group pressures toward conformity in thinking.

10. Superior general intelligence.

11. An early, very broad interest in intellectual activities.

12. A drive toward comprehensiveness and elegance in explanation.

13. A special interest in the kind of "wagering" which involves pitting oneself against uncertain circumstances in which one's own effort can be the deciding factor.

Assessment Studies

At the Institute for Personality Assessment and Research (IPAR) at the University of California in Berkeley, MacKinnon and his associates (MacKinnon 1962, 1965, 1967, 1971, 1972) largely within a psychoanalytic framework have emphasized the study of motivational and temperamental rather than cognitive characteristics of recognized creative architects, writers, scientists, and mathematicians, as they believe that manifestation of creative productivity is largely dependent upon one's personality structure, motivational patterns, enduring interests, values, cognitive styles, self-image, and whole-hearted commitment to creative endeavor. Although MacKinnon (1967) has declared that both quantitative and qualitative characteristics of intellectual processes are important to creative enterprise, his two observations that intelligence tests show relatively low correlations with measures of creative abilities and that Guilford's tests of various dimensions in creative thinking have exhibited relatively low correlations with criteria of creative performance have tended to support his position of relying upon affective and background measures as a means to identifying and describing the behaviors of creative individuals.

Creative Scientists. In the assessment at IPAR of scientists on a number of measures, scientists classified as creative in relation to those not nominated or judged to be creative tended to place higher on measures indicating identification with values on theoretical and aesthetic matters, intuition, introversion, nonconforming–individualistic–autonomous (but adaptive) tendencies, striving behaviors, assertive self-assurance, and flexibility or open mindedness in working styles (MacKinnon 1967, 1972). Although individual exceptions have occurred, these findings have been generally consistent with those derived from biographical accounts by Roe (1951, 1953) and Chambers (1964), from the longitudinal investigation by Terman (1954, 1955), from the study of young college science majors designated as Higher Creatives or Lower Creatives by Garwood (1964), and from the examination by Parloff et al. (1968) of the personality characteristics of samples both of high school science students classified as creative and of subsamples of adults who were designated as creative mathematicians, research scientists, architects, and writers. (Incidentally, Parloff et al. also found that creative high school adolescents as a group did show a higher level of disciplined self-effectiveness than did creative members of the adult samples.)

Creative Mathematicians. Although much less work has been done with creative mathematicians than with creative scientists, the psychologists at IPAR have carried out a small number of studies involving mathematicians. These investigations probably constitute the most important systematic work on the personality characteristics of creative mathematicians that has been done to date, especially after one has gained a perspective of research from Aiken's (1973) impressive review of studies that were concerned with the relationship of ability to creativity in mathematics as well as with the identification of personality correlates of creative mathematicians. In a landmark investigation involving the personality assessment of sixty-three male mathematicians with a Ph.D. degree, of whom thirty-four had been nominated as creative and twenty-nine had not been so nominated, Helson and Crutchfield (1970*b*) observed that, on the average, the group designated as creatives as compared with the sample of noncreatives had received the Ph.D. nearly three years earlier, had submitted their first published paper about five years sooner, and had published at least three times as many papers. Relative to adjustment patterns the nominated creatives in comparison with the noncreatives had exhibited on the California Personality Inventory (CPI) scales scores that were indicative of significantly lower self-control, higher flexibility, and greater lability and had demonstrated higher standing on the MMPI Hypochondriasis scale. On a variety of other measures the creatives, in relation to the noncreatives, had shown very significantly higher placement on an art-scale measure, reflecting preference for asymmetrical and somewhat disordered or complex designs; had placed higher on an originality measure; had displayed lower scores on two scales of the Strong Vocational Interest Blank (SVIB), i.e., vocational agricultural teacher and president of a manufacturing concern; and had expressed less of a value commitment to religion.

On individual clusters of items dealing with (1) neatness and orderliness in habits of work, (2) confidence and mathematical sociability, (3) initiative and inventiveness in research, and (4) role of critical leadership in one's field, the creatives placed significantly lower than did members of the comparison sample in the first cluster, but significantly higher on each of the other three item clusters, particularly on the fourth cluster. Although there were no reliable differences in average performance of the creative and comparison groups on the Wechsler Adult Intelligence Scale (WAIS), life-history variables showed that besides more often being the eldest child and more frequently being foreign-born or second-generation Americans largely of Jewish heritage, creative mathematicians in relation to noncreative mathematicians had fathers and mothers with greater educational attainments and relatively more fathers in professional occupations; more often aspired in high school to be a physicist, chemist, or engineer than a mathematician or teacher of mathematics; and more often obtained a position at an institution with a high rating for its research prestige (even though the creatives and the comparison subjects had earned doctorates at institutions of similar research status). In their home relationships, the creatives, in relation to comparison subjects, exhibited greater respect and warmth for their mothers, although no such differences relative to fathers appeared.

Comparisons between Mathematicians and Scientists.   When Helson and Crutchfield made comparisons between a sample of mathematicians (both creatives and noncreatives) and a group of research scientists and architects on personality characteristics, the mathematicians on the average appeared to be lower on the measure of Assertive Self-Assurance, higher on measures of Humanitarian Conscience and Adaptive Autonomy, but at about the same level on the measure of Disciplined Effectiveness—a set of outcomes nearly parallel to those reported for a sample of 938 talented high school science contestants by Parloff et al. (1968), who compared a subsample of 156 boys intending to become mathematicians with the other contest participants. Apparently, mathematicians as compared to the research scientists are not driven to the same extent to comprehend and to control the real world—a pragmatic concern that may motivate the research scientists of some degree of eminence to try to control the extensive resources needed for their experimental and data-gathering efforts. Other comparison data between the group of mathematicians and samples of scientists and architects revealed that the mathematicians placed higher on measures, reflecting a need for order, but far below architects in art scale reflecting preference for asymmetry and disordered designs. Whereas the mathematicians had an average IQ score on the WAIS of 135 as compared with the averages of 133 and 130, respectively, for research scientists and architects, on the highly abstract and very demanding Concept Mastery Test, which had previously been used by Terman (1954), a subsample of 12 Princeton mathematicians had a mean score of 149 relative to the means of 118 and 113, respectively, for samples of research scientists and architects.

For mathematicians as a group, the following summary statement by Helson and Crutchfield (1970*b*) is definitive:

> In sum, the mathematicians appear to be reserved, sensitive, conscientious, conventional in behavior though highly individualistic in spirit, and to have their personality concentrated, so to speak, in an intellectuality which is flexible and inquiring, but also precise and directed. They are able to find stimulation within themselves, that is, in a stable environment (p. 252).

In the comparison of the outcomes of their study of mathematicians with those of other investigators of eminent natural scientists in the United States, Helson and Crutchfield have succinctly interpreted the findings as follows:

> The results of this study of mathematicians do not coincide with findings reported by investigators of eminent natural scientists in the United States. The latter are described as predominantly Protestant, native-born, descended from British, Scottish, or German stock, and as having fathers in the professions (Roe 1953; Terman 1954; Visher 1947). They are said (by Roe) to have respected their fathers profoundly, but to derogate their mothers. Though personally withdrawn, they show marked dominance, initiative, research drive, and willingness to work long hours (Cattell 1963; Chambers 1964; Roe 1953, 1956).
>
> In contrast, parents of almost half of the mathematicians were Jewish, one-third were foreign-born—from ten different countries—and only one-third had fathers in the professions. Most of them respected their fathers but only a few "profoundly," and many had close relationships with their mothers. In personality, the creatives differed from the comparison Ss not in personal dominance but in flexibility and ego-enrichment. In their mathematics, they differed in these qualities and also in ambition, self-confidence, initiative, and professional participativeness. Finally, working a great many hours a week appears to be emphasized less by creative mathematicians than by eminent scientists (p. 256).

Differences within Groups of Creative Scientists and Mathematians. Thus far in the consideration of personality assessment data for creative scientists and mathematicians, emphasis has been placed on salient characteristics descriptive of each group and on differences between the two groups on certain life variables, affective attributes, and intellectual traits. It should be stressed, however, that individual differences within groups are usually considerably greater than are average differences between groups. Recognizing this fact, Gough (Gough and Woodworth 1960; MacKinnon 1967) extracted for a group of industrial research scientists eight "person-factors," i.e., eight stylistic types of scientific researchers, which he labeled or identified as (1) methodologist, (2) initiator, (3) zealot, (4) artificer, (5) diagnostician, (6) aesthetician, (7) independent, and (8) scholar. This particular order of enumeration corresponded to the mean score from high to low on a criterion of creativeness and general competence, which peers and superiors had assigned to their fellow workers classified as being in each of the eight categories. The rank order of values might well have been different in an academic setting.

Similarly, Helson and Crutchfield (1970a) endeavored to identify creative types within the previously cited sample of thirty-four creative mathematicians. Although the sample was small, five somewhat overlapping creative types on the basis of a Tryon cluster analysis involving Q sorts emerged. Because of the smallness of the sample, additional efforts with new groups need to be undertaken so that some basis for generalization of findings can be established. Nevertheless, the variations from one type to another were substantial and suggestive of important stylistic and affective characteristics among creative mathematicians.

Female Mathematicians. Studies about *creative* women mathematicians are rare. In her investigation of forty-five women mathematicians with the doctorate of whom eighteen had been rated by peers as creative in terms of placing at a value of 4.0 or higher on a seven-point scale and the remaining twenty-seven as comparison subjects, Helson (1971) found slight differences, if any, between the obtained measures of intelligence, cognition, and masculinity for the two subgroups. However, creative subjects as compared with those not so rated exhibited a stronger drive toward research activity, higher flexibility, more originality, and greater rejection of outside influences. The creative in relation to the comparison subjects showed on the MMPI significantly higher mean scores on scales of hypochondriasis, depression, masculinity, psychoasthenia (compulsiveness), schizophrenia, social introversion, and repression, but a significantly lower mean score on hypomania. Nearly half the creatives were foreign-born, and most of them had professional men as fathers. Interviewers perceived the creatives to identify primarily with their fathers and deduced that their interest in mathematics had evolved from a sublimation or search for autonomy in their fantasies instead of from a reaction formation or withdrawal pattern of behavior. When compared with creative male mathematicians, the creative women demonstrated less assurance, published fewer articles, and tended, if employed, to hold less prestigeful positions.

TENTATIVE EXPLANATION OF THE NATURE OF THE CREATIVE PROCESS IN PROBLEM-SOLVING ACTIVITIES IN TERMS OF CONSTRUCTS OF TWO INTERRELATED MODELS

In two sections to follow the properties of each of two models are described that furnish a partial basis for explaining the nature of creative problem solving, although it should be realized that any explanation is highly tentative and speculative.

The Guilford Structure-of-Intellect Model

To provide a systematic and comprehensive basis for the conceptualization of human intelligence as well as a means of testing hypotheses derived from his theory, Guilford (Guilford 1967*a*, pp. 60–66; Guilford and Hoepfner 1971, pp. 17–32; Guilford and Tenopyr 1968, pp. 26–29) has developed what he has termed the structure-of-intellect (SOI) model, which contains three major dimensions or parameters: *contents* (four broad classes or types of information or stimulus material in the environment which the organism discriminates), *operations* (five major types of intellectual activity that are required to process the discriminable information), and *products* (six forms that information can assume after being processed). Borrowing from the astronomer Zwicky (1957) the term *morphological*, which defines a cross-classification of intersecting categories instead of the presence (or nesting) of categories within other categories as in a hierarchical model, Guilford has devised a morphological model to organize intellectual abilities within a unitary orthogonal system in which each dimension is made up of a set of more-or-less mutually exclusive or independent categories. Actually, the categories in the content dimension can be viewed as *inputs* of given information, and the categories of the product dimension as *outputs* of new information in modified form as a consequence of the inputs having been processed through use of one or more psychological operations.

As shown in figure 7.1, the model is represented as a three-dimensional solid composed of $5 \times 4 \times 6$ or 120 different cells formed by all possible permutations of categories within the three dimensions. Each cell denotes a supposedly *independent* factor of intellectual ability, i.e., a psychological construct. From the detailed description of each of the categories within each of the three dimensions as set forth in the lower portion of figure 7.1, the definition of a factor represented by a cell can be provided. For example, verbal ability as typically measured by multiple-choice vocabulary tests with items involving a stimulus word as the stem and four or five possible response alternatives, one of which is a correct synonym, is hypothesized to be the cognition of semantic units, an expression indicating that after an examinee has become aware of (cognized) semantic content (given information) he selects a product in the form of a unit of new information (one of the alternative words).

Guilford has suggested that each factor indicated by a cell in the three-dimensional solid has been or eventually can be shown to exist from

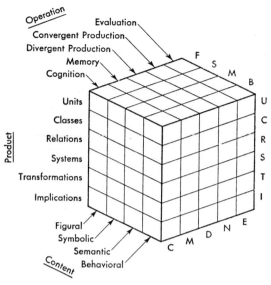

Fig. 7.1. The structure-of-intellect model and definitions of its categories

OPERATIONS

Major kinds of intellectual activities or processes; things that the organism does with the raw materials of information, information being defined as "that which the organism discriminates."

C — *Cognition.* Immediate discovery, awareness, rediscovery, or recognition of information in various forms; comprehension or understanding.

M — *Memory.* Retention or storage, with some degree of availability, of information in the same form it was committed to storage and in response to the same cues in connection with which it was learned.

D — *Divergent Production.* Generation of information from given information, where the emphasis is upon variety and quantity of output from the same source. Likely to involve what has been called transfer. This operation is most clearly involved in aptitudes of creative potential.

N — *Convergent Production.* Generation of information from given information, where the emphasis is upon achieving unique of conventionally accepted best outcomes. It is likely the given (cue) information fully determines the response.

E — *Evaluation.* Reaching decisions or making judgments concerning criterion satisfaction (correctness, suitability, adequancy, desirability, etc.) of information.

CONTENTS

Broad classes or types of information discriminable by the organism.

F — *Figural.* Information in concrete form, as preceived or as recalled possibly in the form of images. The term "figural" minimally implies figure-ground perceptual organization. Visual spatial information is figural. Different sense modalities may be involved, e.g., visual kinesthetic.

S — *Symbolic.* Information in the form of denotative signs having no significance in and of themselves, such as letters, numbers, musical notations, codes, and words, when meanings and form are not considered.

M — *Semantic.* Information in the form of meanings in which words commonly become attached, hence most notable in verbal thinking and in verbal communication but not indentical with words. Meaningful pictures also often convey semantic information.

B — *Behavioral.* Information, essentially non-verbal, involved in human interactions where the attitudes, needs, desires, moods, intentions, perceptions, thoughts, etc., of other people and of ourselves are involved.

PRODUCTS

Forms that information takes in the organism's processing of it.

U — *Units.* Relatively segregated or circumscribed items of information having "thing" character. May be close to Gestalt psychology's "figure on a ground."

C — *Classes.* Conceptions underlying sets of items of information grouped by virtue of their common properties.

R — *Relations.* Connections between items of information based upon variables or points of contact that apply to them. Relational connections are more meaningful and definable than implications.

S — *Systems.* Organized or structured aggregates of items of information; complexes of interrelated or interacting parts.

T — *Transformations.* Changes of various kinds (redefinition, shifts, or modification) of existing information or in its function.

I — *Implications.* Extrapolations of information, in the form of expectancies, predictions, known or suspected antecedents, concomitants, or consequences. The connection between the given information and that extrapolated is more general and less definable than a relational connection.

the results of carefully designed factor-analytic studies employing batteries of experimental tests for hypothesized factors and of reference or anchor tests for previously demonstrated factors (Guilford 1967a, pp. 25–41; Guilford and Hoepfner 1971, pp. 33–60). Guilford himself is quite amenable to modifying his model to whatever extent or in whatever ways future research may suggest that its dimensionality or numbers of categories within one or more dimensions may need to be consolidated or extended. Probably it is the heuristic value of the model that constitutes its greatest importance to psychological theory and research about intellectual activities.

Criticisms of the SOI Model. It would be remiss not to mention, however, that a number of psychologists have questioned whether the somewhat subjective factor-analytic methods employed by Guilford have indeed provided reliable and valid empirical evidence in support of the existence of the constructs underlying SOI theory. For example, Harris and Harris (1971) developed a set of rigorous rotational criteria for establishing the presence of comparable common factors that have been obtained from use of several factor-analytic methods on a given set of correlational data. In general, their reanalyses of Guilford's data in nine different correlational matrices failed to meet the criteria set forth for replication of common factors but yielded instead factors that suggested several alternative interpretations to those provided by the SOI model.

Likewise, in a highly convincing argument that has thrown considerable light on the subjective character of the empirical basis for validation of the SOI model, Horn and Knapp (1973, 1974) took correlated data from three SOI studies with which Guilford was associated and demonstrated that application of the same Procrustean factor-analytic methods that Guilford had used could furnish almost as compelling support for theories generated by random sampling procedures as for the SOI theory itself. Although not denying the heuristic value of the SOI model or even its explanatory merit as a theory, Horn and Knapp emphasized that their factor-analytic rotational solutions neither supported nor disconfirmed the SOI theory. Despite these criticisms regarding the level of affirmative empirical evidence for the constructs of the SOI model, SOI theory would appear to be a highly useful conceptualization of the nature of human intelligence and of the ways in which psychological processing of information in problem solving could occur.

Representation of Creative Thinking Abilities in the SOI Model. Guilford (1963, 1967a, 1967b, 1968, 1970, 1971) has concluded that many creative thinking abilities are those represented in the divergent production "slice" of the SOI model that cuts across figural, symbolic, and semantic content as well as across most of the forms of products.

These abilities emphasize the generation of a quantity and almost unrestricted variety of products which reflect (1) a *fluency of verbal expression* (divergent production of semantic units, relations, and systems); (2) *spontaneous flexibility*, a mental shifting from one class to another class of responses involving the naming of alternative uses of familiar objects (divergent production of classes and/or transformations), (3) *adaptive flexibility*, or *originality*, as in finding several clever titles for a short story (divergent production of semantic transformations), or as in making a number of new objects from given figural material such as pictures of assorted geometric forms (divergent production of figural transformations), and (4) *elaboration*, as in citing how many occupations might be associated with a given symbol, such as a bell (divergent production of semantic implications).

In addition to these divergent thinking abilities that are required in the creative efforts of writers and artists, Guilford has proposed two other sets of creative abilities that are of particular relevance to the activities of mathematicians, scientists, engineers, and inventors. The first set of abilities, reflecting a *flexibility of closure* (an ability requiring *redefinition*), embodies the convergent production of figural, symbolic, or semantic transformations; the second set, referred to as *sensitivity to problems*, involves the cognition of figural, symbolic, or semantic implications. Two examples of redefinition or flexibility of closure abilities include (1) the familiar figure–ground problems in the Sunday supplement of a few years ago in which the individual has to find hidden or obscure figures such as faces or animals in a pictorial landscape (convergent production of figural transformation), or (2) the less familiar figure–ground task of locating embedded or concealed words or numbers within a complex background of other words or numbers (convergent production of symbolic transformations). Another illustration of a redefinition ability involving flexibility of closure with semantic material would be the selection of a given object or device that is quite familiar to the observer from a number of other such objects or devices to be used for a unique purpose or for achievement of a specific requirement in a highly foreign if not totally unfamiliar context. An example would be the selection of a guitar from several other stimulus objects, such as a shoestring, Thermos bottle, wristwatch, or hammer, so as to use one of the strings to slice a cake of cheese in the absence of a knife. Such redefinition abilities necessitate a solution with marked constraints, as indicated by a very specific requirement or application. Thus an engineer might need to find the most cost-effective solution in a complex production problem in a large manufacturing concern. For the second set of abilities involving sensitivity to problems, an example requiring cognition of semantic implications would be trying to anticipate difficulties that could arise in undertaking a new assignment or in carrying out a mission with many potential risks.

A Model for Creative Problem Solving (the SIPS Model)

In essentially equating creative production to problem solving, although problem solving is considerably broader than creative thinking (Kleinmuntz 1966), Guilford (Guilford 1967a, 1968, 1970; Guilford and Tenopyr 1968) has proposed a general information-processing model, or communication system, for problem solving. In its use of the major constructs of the SOI theory, the model closely resembles many of the features of a high-speed computer (Jones 1963), a conceptualization which may be referred to as the structure-of-intellect problem-solving model (SIPS). To a limited extent Guilford has endeavored to show how several of the components in problem solving, creative production, and invention paradigms proposed by Dewey (1910), Wallas (1926, 1945), and Rossman (1931), which are detailed in table 7.1, can be conceptualized within the framework of many of the constructs from the SOI model. As indicated previously, an important goal of this paper has been to show in a step-by-step fashion how the seven stages of the Rossman paradigm can be conceptualized in terms of the SOI constructs of the SIPS model.

Although the contents and operations categories of the SOI model are shown in the SIPS model (figure 7.2) with no distinction being made between convergent or divergent production, the specifications of the six SOI products categories are implied only in terms of the form in which various types of information, having resulted as products from processing of prior information, are portrayed in an illustrative manner in the memory-storage rectangle. The two-way arrows that extend between cognition and memory storage and between production and memory storage, as well as between evaluation and cognition and between evaluation and production, reveal that both adding of information to and drawing of information from the memory storage in an interactive manner take place. In addition, the monitoring of the activity by the filtering function of evaluation occurs to facilitate appropriate testing of tentative solutions. The dynamic nature of the model actually permits an interplay of the steps of problem solving in terms of feedback loops, which in turn allow for a variation in the sequence of problem-solving steps as well as for an almost simultaneous interplay of intellectual activities. These activities do not necessarily follow the invariant orders of problem-solving steps that were suggested by Rossman (1931), Dewey (1910), or Wallas (1926) or that rather specific sequence of steps in mathematics problem solving that were offered to students by Polya

Table 7.1. Steps in invention, creative production, and problem solving as perceived by Rossman, Wallas, and Dewey

Rossman (1931) (invention)	Wallas (1926) (creative production)	Dewey (1910) (problem solving)
1. Observation of need or difficulty (problem situation, area of concern) 2. Analysis of need; problem formulated and defined 3. Survey of all available information	1. Preparation (information obtained)	1. Felt need or difficulty observed 2. Difficulty or problem situation located and problem defined (formulated)
Rudimentary incubation (unconcious work) possible, depending on problem complexity		
4. Formulation of many possible (objective) solutions 5. Critical analysis and examination of these solutions for their advantages and disadvantages		3. One or more possible solutions suggested 4. Consequences considered and evaluated
Sustained and ongoing incubation (unconscious work) probable, particularly for complex problems	2. Incubation (unconscious work occurring)	
6. Birth and formulation of new ideas, invention, or solution to problem 7. Testing of most promising solution and selection and perfection of final embodiment of solution by some or all of the previous steps; more or less final acceptance of revised solution	3. Illumination (one or more solutions emerging) 4. Verification (solutions tested, judged for appropriateness, and elaborated upon)	5. Solution accepted at least tentatively

(1957)—namely, understanding the problem, devising a plan, carrying out the plan, and examining (checking) the solution obtained.

Brief Overview of Hypothesized Psychological Operations in the SOI Model Appearing at Each of the Seven Steps of the Rossman Paradigm. Although in the next major section of this paper a detailed description of the correspondence of the geometric properties of the SIPS model to each of the seven steps in the Rossman paradigm of problem solving in invention is presented, a brief overview of the SIPS model, as shown in figure 7.2, in relation to Rossman's paradigm may be helpful. First, the model portrays the individual as recognizing a problem situation, a stage directly analogous to Rossman's first step of an observed need or difficulty, in which Guilford's operations of cognition and evaluation are substantially involved. Corresponding to Rossman's second step of

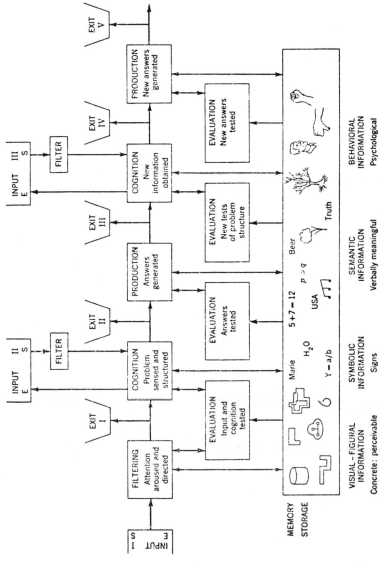

Fig. 7.2. An operational model for problem solving in general, based upon concepts provided by the structure-of-intellect model

formulating and defining the problem in conjunction with analyzing the need or difficulty posed in the first step, the SIPS model reveals that a person delineates the characteristics and parameters of the problem in relation to new information available, particularly in relation to existing information in the memory storage. This second step likewise incorporates operations of cognition and evaluation. Relative to Rossman's third step of surveying all available information, the matching activity in the SIPS model is one of devising a search model (searching strategy) with cues broadly consistent with the problem requirements. The cues are essential for acquiring information to resolve the problem, an activity that necessitates convergent and/or divergent production of new information from existing information in the memory storage as well as from any additional information provided by the external and internal (somatic) environment of the organism. During this third step considerable evaluation of the evolving information for its relevance to the problem occurs.

It is this simultaneous process of evaluation in association with use of the search model that carries the problem solver to Rossman's fourth step of formulating one or more tentative solutions. Correspondingly, in Guilford's model the subject selectively delves into his memory storage in pursuit of information pertinent to the requirements of the problem, as well as explores to the extent necessary the external and internal environment for additional inputs. It is at this point that a crucial step takes place in reaching a tentative solution to a problem through a transfer process involving the recall of information from memory storage to be used in the convergent and/or divergent production of new information that may constitute at least a tentative solution to a problem, a process that Guilford terms *transfer recall*. Viewed somewhat negatively, transfer recall is retrieval of information instigated by cues in relation to which the information had not been committed previously to memory storage or had not been assimilated as part of those cues. Viewed positively, transfer recall is the retrieving of information from a partial set of cues in the memory storage and the using of this information in a new context and in novel ways. This transformed use of retrieved information is effected largely by flexibly reclassifying, reinterpreting, or redefining well-organized information within the memory storage in relation to the demands of a clearly defined problem. In contrast to *replicative recall* in an associational learning context that necessitates the retrieval of previously stored information in its original or essentially original form, as in recalling the capitals of states as the states are enumerated in alphabetical order, transfer recall in a cognitivist learning context embodies and requires active use of a search model scanning the realm of a rich memory storage to select the kinds of information necessary to fit the requirements of a carefully defined problem.

In Guilford's SIPS model the evaluation of the tentative solution to a problem in light of available criteria corresponds to Rossman's fifth step of a critical examination of the advantages and disadvantages of a proposed solution. In the instance of complex problem solving, a period of seemingly suspended and nonapparent intellectual activity termed *incubation* may occur after the concerted evaluative activity associated with Rossman's fifth step has ceased. During this incubation period intellectual processes of which the organism is unaware are hypothesized to take place. Such activities sometimes result later in Rossman's sixth step: (1) the occurrence of a more-or-less sudden and illuminating birth or formulation of a new idea or modified solution to the problem, or (2) substantial incremental steps in its solution. Guilford has hypothesized that during incubation a number of transformations in products occurs —transformations involving use of the psychological operations of both convergent and divergent production, reflecting the manifestation of different kinds of flexibility.

In the seventh and last step of Rossman's formulation the most promising solutions are further evaluated until a more-or-less final acceptance of a revised solution is realized. Actually, the sixth step in Rossman's paradigm constitutes a successive reiteration or replication of its first four steps that already have been reviewed in relation to Guilford's SIPS model, and the seventh step is a revisitation of the fifth step. Finally, as indicated previously, it should be emphasized that the order or sequence of steps in problem solving is *not* invariant. There is much jumping about from one step to another, particularly in the later stages of refining initial tentative solutions to a problem.

Detailed Description of the Correspondence of SIPS Model to Each of the Seven Steps in the Rossman Paradigm. The purpose of this portion of the presentation is to show in an expanded and detailed manner how each of the previously outlined seven steps or stages of the Rossman paradigm can be related to and integrated with the SIPS model. Since incubation may represent a condition in the organism of apparent relaxation of effort in problem solving or creative production—at least an unobservable phenomenon—whereas the other stages constitute activities, insertion of incubation within the paradigm may not be altogether appropriate. Nevertheless, many psychologists in introductory textbooks have indicated the importance of some form of unconscious or intuitive process underlying the problem-solving process (which they have elected to call incubation), much like the eminent late French mathematician Poincaré (Bell 1937; Hadamard 1945).

First Step. As shown in figure 7.2, inputs of information, which must necessarily provide some form of challenge, incongruity, or source of tension to the organism if a problem situation is to be sensed, arise both from the external environment (E) and from the internal environment or soma (S) of the organism. The soma reflects important motivational, emotional, and temperamental dispositions and tendencies both necessary to energize, sustain, and direct efforts of the individual and essential to indicate how much effort an individual will expend in problem solving. These initial sensory inputs are filtered in a manner that arises and directs attention of the organism to retrieve almost simultaneously and selectively one or more of the four kinds of figural, symbolic, semantic, and behavioral information from memory storage and to evaluate it in relation to sensory inputs. This new information is integrated with old information to permit the *first stage* of the problem-solving endeavor to evolve, *an initial cognition of a possible problem situation or felt difficulty* which may be evaluated either as being of little or trivial interest or slight importance, with the result that further activity is terminated (exit 1) or as a promising or interesting enough situation for additional cognition to take place.

Second, Third, and Fourth Steps. Such additional cognition provides the *second stage* of problem solving, as the problem may be *perceived and structured* (that is, formulated and defined) in relation again both to information in storage and to new information subject to filtering and evaluation (input II). At this point the individual may give up or fall victim to distracting influences which prevent his continuing with the problem-solving endeavor (exit II), or he may elect to continue his productive efforts. If so, once the difficulty has been located and defined, or equivalently once the problem has been formulated (sensed and structured), a preparatory stage of indeterminant duration occurs for the *accumulation and survey of information*, the *third step* of the problem-solving process. During this third stage, the organism develops a search model for acquisition of information from the memory storage as well as from the external and internal environment. This *third step*, which involves some evaluative activity, blends almost imperceptibly into the *fourth step*, during which the individual generates through convergent and/or divergent production possible answers to the problem which are tested (evaluated). If the answer is judged appropriate, there is an exit from the problem-solving situation (exit III). Thus the *fourth stage* has been consummated, particularly if the problem is *simple*.

Incubation. For a *complex* problem, however, a period of seeming inactivity may occur. This incubation period, about which more is to be said shortly in terms of an hypothesized production of transformations of information, is often followed by the sudden appearance of a promising solution or by the occurrence of substantial increments of progress toward a solution—an outcome referred to as *insight* or as an *intuitive flash* or as *illumination*. This condition of suspended activity could arise between the third and fourth steps just cited or very likely between the *fifth step*, during which a proposed solution has been *critically examined* and found wanting, and the *sixth step*, during which a *new solution* or *new idea* has been formulated. This new solution would be subsequently evaluated (tested) and quite possibly accepted as being satisfactory (*seventh step*).

Fifth Step. In such complex problem solving, in which the initial or tentative solution arrived at in the fourth step is judged (evaluated) to be inappropriate, the SIPS model would next involve a second block of cognition of new information, that is, newly sought inputs that come from new sources of data (input III). This new information is filtered and evaluated along with information from the memory storage in relation to the possible *restructuring* or *reconceptualization* of the former problem (*fifth step*), a process that is prerequisite to the formulation of a *new solution* to the problem (*sixth step*). If the individual either has tired of the problem itself or has become discouraged with his rate of progress toward its solution, he might permanently or temporarily terminate his efforts (exit IV). If, however, he cannot afford to spend any more time, he might cease further active or conscious effort (also noted as leaving the field through exit IV), although he would quite possibly continue to work at an unconscious level (incubate) for minutes, hours, days, weeks, or even months to come.

Sixth and Seventh Steps. On the other hand, if he generates or produces a new answer or new solution to the initial problem or to its *reconceptualization* (*sixth step*) and if he finds that his evaluation of it is favorable so that the *solution can be accepted* (*seventh step*), then he can cease activity (exit V). Of course, if the new solution still has shortcomings, then a third cognition block involving the acquisition and evaluation of information from new inputs in conjunction with information in the memory storage occurs and the process of problem solving continues in the manner as previously described. In other words, the process as pictured in figure 7.2 can repeat itself indefinitely.

Importance of Memory Storage and Systems to the First Three Steps of Problem Solving. In the first three steps of problem solving as related to the first cognition block and even to the achievement of a tentative solution (fourth step), Guilford first has stressed the importance of a vast memory storage of neatly classified and well-organized information as a necessary resource to creative problem solving—information that has been conceptualized in terms of products of broad rather than narrow or highly specific classes to effect transfer recall (the process of an individual's retrieving stored information and using it in a new context and in novel ways largely by flexibly reinterpreting or redefining previously learned information in a new context or by flexibly reclassifying well-organized information within the memory storage into new classes or subsets of knowledge). Second, Guilford has stressed the roles of systems or schemata as evidenced in the production of a drawing of the figural components of a mechanical device, in the formation of a complex semantic structure of a philosophical essay, in the generation of a systematic organized sequence of symbolic elements encountered in solving a differential equation, or in the development of selected combinations of semantic or symbolic components as evidenced by a grid or taxonomy in model or theory building in the social sciences.

Hypothesized Importance of Transformations During Incubation. During the incubation period, Guilford has hypothesized that transformation of information from one form to another—possibly among stored products interacting with one another and with new inputs from the external or internal environments—may account for what occurs in intellectual operations. Thus insight would constitute the culmination or near-culmination of the transformation process involved in the evolution of a problem solution. Supportive evidence for such a statement was found in a survey of the perceptions of scientists regarding which intellectual resources were most valued. They ranked abilities involving convergent and divergent production of transformations as well as cognition of transformations among the most highly significant (Guilford 1963).

Hypothesized Importance of Flexibility Factors During Incubation. Important to the manifestation of transformation in incubation are two kinds of flexibility: (1) *adaptive flexibility or originality* requiring numerous changes in strategy underlying the divergent production of transformations, as in the match problems test, in which an examinee is asked to remove a specified number of matches from an intricate design to leave a designated number of complete squares or triangles; and (2) *redefinition*, a form of *flexibility* falling in the category of convergent production of transformations. Such transformations occur when objects or information from a familiar context must be employed for a specific purpose in a literally new or foreign context, as in the use of a blanket to smother a small but potentially dangerous fire, the ability that inventors and applied scientists so often manifest in discovering new uses for familiar objects or devices in almost entirely new settings. Whereas measures of *adaptive flexibility* or *originality* tend to be negatively correlated with those of persistence, tests embodying *redefinition factors* are antithetical to measures of *functional fixedness*, a *rigidity* phenomenon preventing the use of familiar objects in new ways or the application of familiar knowledge or information in new contexts. This circumstance often occurs when one cannot change a mental set or perspective as in trying to find a new strategy to solve a novel mathematics word problem when the ten previous word problems have required use of the same rule or algorithm for their solution.

One additional type of flexibility which Guilford has proposed as occurring in the thinking processes during incubation is *spontaneous flexibility*. This ability requires a *readiness to shift rapidly from class to class* in searching for information as in the divergent production of semantic classes, a task necessitating a perceptual reorganization of the field of information. On the basis of studies he reviewed, Guilford (1967*a*) suggested that the problem solver needs to have a broad, highly generalized conceptualization (all-inclusive classification) of knowledge so that he can have a powerful search model for moving rapidly from one subclass to another within the large class and thus for finding a relatively quick and workable solution to his problem.

Hypothesized Importance of Evaluation and Implications During the Fifth Step.   At the *fifth step* of problem solving or creative production, which corresponds to Wallas' verification step, in which solutions are tested and elaborated upon or to Rossman's critical examination of solutions, it would appear that the operation of evaluation and the product of implications would be particularly important. Thus implications, which really represent forms of elaboration, inferences, or extrapolative activities, provide a means for deducing additional information suggested by the problem statement (second step) as well as possible cues for invention of new tactics or strategies to solve a given problem. In fact, even in the first and second steps of problem solving involving observations of a need or difficulty and the formulation or definition of a problem, cognition of implications of symbolic and semantic information would seem to be important to the mathematician or scientist who needs to be sensitive to identifying and defining problems, whereas cognition of figural implications could be important to problem formulation in architecture and certain branches of engineering.

Sixth and Seventh Steps as Reiteration of First Five Steps. Usually the sixth and seventh steps in the problem-solving paradigm involve operations and products that are a reiteration of those outlined in the first five stages, as the last two steps constitute replications of basic activities already described in relation to the SIPS model. In particular, the operation of evaluation and the product-reflecting implications would be important, as newly devised transformations are modified or adjusted in refining problem solutions.

It may be appropriate at this point also to hypothesize, particularly during the last three of Rossman's seven steps in problem solving, that the operation of evaluation may mediate between the processes of convergent production and divergent production. Although convergent production in relation to a problem formulation that is overdetermined in its constraints or in the redundance of its cues might produce an acceptable but cumbersome solution, divergent production in relation to somewhat mild constraints or to sets of incomplete cues in the problem statement might facilitate the use of those psychological processes in transfer recall that are required to generate several alternative solutions. One of these solutions might well be evaluated deductively or inductively as the most nearly general in its applicability, pragmatically as the most efficient, or aesthetically as the most elegant.

SOME IMPLICATIONS OF THE SOI AND SIPS MODELS FOR TEACHING FOR CREATIVE ENDEAVOR

Several suggestions may be formulated regarding how the teacher, whom Brandwein (1955) in his extensive report of his involvement with gifted adolescents in experimental and innovative science programs has so eloquently described as the key agent in discovering and nurturing the future scientists or mathematicians, can facilitate the development of problem solving or creative productivity in their students (the first two not being directly related to the SOI and SIPS models) as follows:

1. Encourage and reward, that is reinforce, manifestations of creative behaviors and imaginative, original ideas *with respect* to ensure that creative problem solving becomes an intrinsically satisfying, pleasant, and valued experience to be sought for its own sake. If redirection of efforts seems appropriate, make use of tactful suggestions in the form of constructive evaluative feedback so that the self-esteem of the student is preserved and his motivation or love for learning is not impaired or destroyed.

2. Once a profile of baseline data from the testing of several creative abilities has been established, undertake formal training on an individual basis of those abilities identified as being associated with problem solving and creative production. Ample opportunities need to be afforded for practice in problem solving in a wide variety of settings, so that external inputs can be monitored to allow for individual differences and to provide for an individualized and potentially rewarding experience for each student. Generous allotments of time in class assignments and in examinations must be provided to allow for the emergence of creative and ingenious solutions to problems.

3. Within the framework furnished by the constructs of the SOI and SIPS models, take steps to develop each of the five major SOI psychological operations through a variety of sound teaching approaches based on the psychology of learning and directed toward the active participation and involvement of the student, as in discovery learning or in self-initiated research activities. For each of the five SOI operations a separate set of suggestions is offered as follows:

a. In the instance of developing cognition, the teacher needs to emphasize approaches that encourage understanding through showing relationships (similarities and differences) among units of information, through describing classes (concepts) to which these units belong, and through organizing relationships and integrating sequential properties of units and classes of information into systems. Both positive and negative instances of membership of objects in a class need to be enumerated. The place and function of a unit of information or concept (class of information) within a system needs to be illustrated. Special efforts should be directed toward developing a student's cognition or awareness of implications so that the learner becomes sensitive to the identification of a problem situation and to the desirability of a clear definition of the problem prior to an attempted solution.

b. Since a large, well-organized memory storage is essential for effective information retrieval in transfer recall that is central to problem solving, the teacher desirous of improving memory abilities in problem solving is probably well advised not only to classify and organize information in the teaching-learning process in the way described for development of cognitive abilities but also to avoid units of instruction which interfere with one another in terms of an unfavorable degree of similarity so that negative transfer or interference can be minimized. Admittedly overlearning of information can often minimize confusion of one instructional unit with another. Care must be taken, however, that *overlearning* and the resulting completeness and specificity of the cues in the newly processed information as well as the *recency* of exposure to new information in turn neither jeopardizes a flexibility to perceive new classes of information nor generates a mental set or rigidity (functional fixedness) against the redefinition or reinterpretation in new contexts of the overly learned information or of other previously acquired information. A period of relaxation in the recall process might permit differential forgetting of the cues inappropriate to the context of a new problem to occur as well as a period of suspended judgment to take place as suggested by Osborn (1963), so that an overly critical evaluation process can subside. That is, a relaxed state or condition perhaps akin to that found in incubation can occur to facilitate quantitative output of tentative solutions or answers, one of which might be judged later as appropriate. Of course, a clearcut statement of the problem and a well-defined search model with a pattern or cues that are carefully anchored to the goal or objective (end product) of learning sought would also facilitate the instigation of transfer recall of a correspondingly harmonious but not identical pattern of cues from the memory storage. The resulting convergent or divergent production of information afforded by transfer recall provides a potential or tentative solution that can be subsequently evaluated for goodness of fit to the requirements posed by the problem.

c. To promote convergent production in problem solving, a teacher needs to provide a variety of approaches that allow the attainment of a desired or specified unique outcome or answer in a number of different ways. In addition to the employment of models or algorithms and the use of numerous illustrative examples both arranged in an appropriate sequence of difficulty level and grouped in meaningful classifications, teaching for convergent production necessitates an acquisition of an understanding of concepts as well as the development of a memory storage with well-encoded information so that the search model can be devised to effect transfer recall. A carefully designed search model permits a selective survey of the memory storage subject to the action of an evaluative filter to exclude competitors to the required information. Such selectivity can be quite helpful in mathematics, logic, and the sciences, where customarily only one or a few alternative forms of newly generated information (i.e., answers) are acceptable.

d. Although divergent production abilities, which emphasize the generation of a quantity and variety of new information from given information, are more apparent in creative writing, speech and artistic endeavors than they are in the solution of science and mathematics problems, which typically require one or two acceptable answers as found in convergent production, opportunities for divergent production of transformations embodying transfer recall do exist for the engineer who wishes to find new uses for familiar mechanical or electrical devices, for the scientist who needs to generate alternative hypotheses to account for the outcomes in a given set of data, or for the applied mathematician who is charged with the task of devising several computer programs to meet numerous divergencies in the exceptional or corollary cases that can arise as in the instance of several subroutines in multivariate data analyses. In recent research efforts that have highly important implications for the development of divergent thinking abilities of scientists, Frederiksen and Evans (1974) have developed promising training models that have improved both the number and quality of hypotheses college students could furnish to explain research findings as set forth in a test entitled Formulating Hypotheses. In an expanded long-term effort, Frederiksen, Evans, and Ward (1975) have reported on preliminary results obtained from a battery of new tests with high face validity currently being prepared that provide criteria for sampling several aspects of a scientist's productive thinking efforts. Frederiksen and Evans (1974) also have presented evidence indicating that the quantitative score (number of hypotheses written) represented an ideational fluency construct akin to the divergent production of semantic units and that the qualitative score for hypotheses generated reflected divergent production of semantic transformations as well as a positive correlate of verbal ability. The efforts of Frederiksen and associates should furnish an important supplementary if not complementary contribution to (1) the often-used classroom exercise requiring students to state some consequences to be expected if some unusual hypothetical event such as the early exhaustion of oil as an energy source should occur, (2) the brainstorming question-asking technique devised by Osborn (1963) to provide a wide range of information in a nonevaluative atmosphere that can be used to generate productive ideas and potential transformations of information, and (3) Crawford's (1954) method of attribute listing. This method includes first a detailed citing of the properties of a familiar object, device, or situation, second an examination of a problem situation existing in a different context, and third the application or transfer of a salient attribute in the prepared list to the partial resolution of the problem situation in the foreign context with the possibly resulting improvements, alterations, or modifications having to be evaluated for appropriateness.

e. Since the practice of evaluation is involved almost continuously in carrying out each of the previously cited operations in problem-solving endeavors, it should be evident that the accuracy and usefulness of criteria upon which the evaluation of information rests depend on how an individual cognizes a problem and upon how he proceeds to set up his search model to retrieve information from the memory storage. Thus the previously mentioned approach of teaching for understanding in relation to the operations of cognition and memory is essential for establishing correct concepts upon which criteria for evaluation can be based at each of the major steps of the problem-solving endeavor. Attention also needs to be directed toward making students aware of several of the constraints or conditions applicable to criteria such as their continuous rather than discrete nature, toward recognizing differences in the value systems of individuals as sources for the generation of diverse if not contradictory sets of evaluative criteria, toward taking into account the maturity level of the student so that an appropriate norm or expectation of level and quality of creative effort can be established, and toward making allowances for a student's selective sensitivities in identifying classes of problems and in applying differential sets of criteria for evaluation of the appropriateness of their solutions. Use of training models for evaluation of problem solutions should also be helpful in developing competencies in the evaluation process and in critical thinking.

CONCLUDING STATEMENT

The demonstrated existence of important differences in the personality characteristics between mathematicians and physical scientists nominated or classified to be creative and those not so designated would suggest that early identification of those precocious youth who are most likely to be productive in later years is possible with probably a higher-than-chance expectation. Even though a few of the affective characteristics associated with creative scientists and mathematicians might be judged as not entirely sociably desirable relative to the norms of certain subcultures in American society, tolerance for the behavior patterns of highly intelligent individuals with creative potential is important in a democracy that stands to gain so much from the significant contributions of so few. It is incumbent upon the teachers of precocious youth to facilitate in an emotionally supportive and rewarding environment the manifestation of creative endeavor through a variety of individualized teaching approaches that can be conceptualized within a workable theory of intellectual function and creative problem solving.

REFERENCES

Aiken, L. R., Jr. 1973. Ability and creativity in mathematics. *Review of Educational Research* 43(4): 405–32.

Bell, E. T. 1937. *Men of mathematics.* New York: Simon and Schuster.

Blade, E. 1963. Creative science. In M. A. Coler (ed.), *Essays on creativity in the sciences.* New York: New York University Press, pp. 183–206.

Brandwein, P. F. 1955. *The gifted student as future scientist: The high school student and his commitment to science.* New York: Harcourt, Brace.

Brush, S. G. 1974. Should the history of science be rated X? *Science* 183 (4130): 1164–72.

Burks, B. S., Jensen, D. W., and Terman, L. M. 1930. The promise of youth: Follow-up studies of a thousand gifted children. *Genetic studies of genius,* vol. 3. Stanford, Calif: Stanford University Press.

Cattell, R. B. 1963. The personality and motivation of the researcher from measurements of contemporaries and from biography. In C. W. Taylor and F. Barron (eds.), *Scientific creativity: Its recognition and development.* New York: Wiley, pp. 119–31.

————, and Butcher, H. J. 1968. *The prediction of achievement and creativity.* Indianapolis, Ind.: Bobbs-Merrill.

Chambers, J. A. 1964. Relating personality and biographical factors to scientific creativity. *Psychological Monographs: General and Applied* 78(7): 1–20 (Whole No. 584).

Cox, C. M. 1926. The early mental traits of three hundred geniuses. *Genetic studies of genius,* vol. 2. Stanford, Calif.: Stanford University Press.

Crawford, R. P. 1954. *The techniques of creative thinking: How to use your ideas to achieve success.* New York: Hawthorn Books.

Dewey, J. 1910. *How we think.* Boston: D.C. Heath.

Eiduson, B. T. 1973. Psychological aspects of career choice and development in the research scientist. In B. T. Eiduson and L. Beckman (eds.), *Science as a career choice: Theoretical and empirical studies.* New York: Russell Sage Foundation, pp. 3–33.

Fox, H. H. 1963. A critique on creativity in science. In M. A. Coler (ed.), *Essays on creativity in the sciences.* New York: New York University Press, pp. 123–52.

Frederiksen, N., and Evans, F. R. 1974. Effects of models of creative performance on ability to formulate hypotheses. *Journal of Educational Psychology* 66(1): 67–82.

———, Evans, F. R., and Ward, W. C. 1975. Development of provisional criteria for the study of scientific creativity. *Gifted Child Quarterly* 19(1): 60–65.

Garwood, D. S. 1964. Personality factors related to creativity in young scientists. *Journal of Abnormal and Social Psychology* 68(4): 413–19.

Goertzel, V., and Goertzel, M. C. 1962. *Cradles of eminence.* Boston: Little, Brown.

Gough, H. G., and Woodworth, D. G. 1960. Stylistic variations among professional research scientists. *Journal of Psychology* 49(1): 87–98.

Guilford, J. P. 1950. Creativity. *American Psychologist* 5(9): 444–54.

——— 1963. Intellectual resources and their values as seen by scientists. In C. W. Taylor and F. Barron (eds.), *Scientific creativity: Its recognition and development.* New York: Wiley, pp. 101–18.

———. 1967a. *The nature of human intelligence.* New York: McGraw-Hill.

———. 1967b. Creativity: Yesterday, today, and tomorrow. *Journal of Creative Behavior* 1(1): 3–21.

———. 1968. *Intelligence, creativity, and their educational implications.* San Diego, Calif.: Robert R. Knapp.

———. 1970. Creativity: Retrospect and prospect. *Journal of Creative Behavior* 4(3): 149–68.

———. 1971. Some misconceptions regarding measurement of creative talents. *Journal of Creative Behavior* 5(2): 77–87.

———, and Hoepfner, R. 1971. *The analysis of intelligence.* New York: McGraw-Hill.

———, and Tenopyr, M. L. 1968. Implications of the structure-of-intellect model for high school and college students. In W. B. Michael (ed.), *Teaching for creative endeavor.* Bloomington, Ind.: Indiana University Press, pp. 25–45.

Hadamard, J. 1945. *An essay on the psychology of invention in the mathematical field.* Princeton, N.J.: Princeton University Press.

Harris, M. L., and Harris, C. W. 1971. A factor analytic interpretation strategy. *Educational and Psychological Measurement* 31(3): 589–606.

Helson, R. 1971. Women mathematicians and the creative personality. *Journal of Consulting and Clinical Psychology* 36(2): 210–20.

———, and Crutchfield, R. S. 1970a. Creative types in mathematics. *Journal of Personality* 38(2): 177–97.

———, and Crutchfield, R. S. 1970b. Mathematicians: The creative researcher and the average Ph.D. *Journal of Consulting and Clinical Psychology* 34(2): 250–57.

Horn, J. L., and Knapp, J. R. 1973. On the subjective character of the empirical base of Guilford's structure-of-intellect model. *Psychological Bulletin* 80(1): 33–43.

———, and Knapp, J. R. 1974. Thirty wrongs do not make a right: Reply to Guilford. *Psychological Bulletin* 81(8): 502–04.

Jackson, P. W., and Messick, S. 1967. The person, the product, and the response: Conceptual problems in the assessment of creativity. In J. Kagan (ed.), *Creativity and learning.* Boston: Beacon Press, pp. 1–19.

Jones, L. V. 1963. Beyond Babbage. *Psychometrika* 28(4): 315–31.

Kagan, J. 1967. Personality and the learning process. In J. Kagan (ed.), *Creativity and learning*. Boston: Beacon Press, pp. 153–63.

Kleinmuntz, B. (ed.). 1966. *Problem solving: Research, method, and theory*. New York: Wiley.

Kuhn, T. S. 1963. The essential tension: Tradition and innovation in scientific research. In C. W. Taylor and F. Barron (eds.), *Scientific creativity: Its recognition and development*. New York: Wiley, pp. 341–54.

––––––. 1970. *The structure of scientific revolutions* (2nd ed.). (International Encyclopedia of Unified Science, vol. 2, no. 2.) Chicago: University of Chicago Press.

Libby, W. F. Creativity in science. 1971. In J. D. Roslansky (ed.), *Creativity*. Amsterdam: North-Holland, pp. 33–52. (Reproduced by National Technical Information Services, Springfield, Va.)

McClelland, D.C. 1962. On the psychodynamics of creative physical scientists. In H. E. Gruber, G. Terrell, and M. Wertheimer (eds.), *Contemporary approaches to creative thinking*. New York: Atherton Press, pp. 141–74.

MacKinnon, D. W. 1962. The nature and nurture of creative talent. *American Psychologist* 17(7): 484–95.

––––––. 1965. Personality and the realization of creative potential. *American Psychologist* 20(4): 273–81.

––––––. 1967. The study of creative persons: A method and some results. In J. Kagan (ed.), *Creativity and learning*. Boston: Beacon Press, pp. 20–35.

––––––. 1971. Creativity and transliminal experience. *Journal of Creative Behavior* 5(4): 227–41.

––––––. 1972. The role of personality traits in the development of scientific abilities. In A. Rosca (chm.), Symposium 18: The detection and training of scientific talent. *Proceedings, 17th International Congress of Applied Psychology, Liege, Belgium, 25–30 July 1971*. Brussels: EDITEST. Vol. 1, pp. 515–18.

Meeker, M. N. 1969. *The structure of intellect: Its interpretation and uses*. Columbus, Ohio: Charles E. Merrill.

Michael, W. B. 1968. The college and university. In W. B. Michael (ed.), *Teaching for creative endeavor*. Bloomington, Ind.: Indiana University Press, pp. 237–60.

Oden, M. H. 1968. The fulfillment of promise: 40-year follow-up of the Terman gifted group. *Genetic Psychology Monographs* 77(1): 3–93.

Osborn, A. F. 1963. *Applied imagination: Principles and procedures of creative problem-solving* (3rd ed.). New York: Scribner's.

Parloff, M. B., Datta, L., Kleman, M., and Handlon, J. H. 1968. Personality characteristics which differentiate creative male adolescents and adults. *Journal of Personality* 36(4): 528–52.

Polya, G. 1954. Patterns of plausible inference. *Mathematics and plausible reasoning*, vol. 2. Princeton, N.J.: Princeton University Press.

––––––. 1957. *How to solve it: A new aspect of mathematical method* (2nd ed.). Princeton, N.J.: Princeton University Press.

Roe, A. 1951. A psychological study of physical scientists. *Genetic Psychology Monographs* 43(2): 121–235.

––––––. 1953. *The making of a scientist*. New York: Dodd, Mead.

————. 1956. *The psychology of occupations.* New York: Wiley.

————. 1963. Psychological approaches to creativity in science. In M. A. Coler (ed.), *Essays on creativity in the sciences.* New York: New York University Press, pp. 153–82.

Rossman, J. 1931. *The psychology of the inventor: A study of the patentee.* Washington, D.C.: Inventors Publishing Co.

Shouksmith, G. 1970. *Intelligence, creativity, and cognitive style.* London: B. T. Batsford.

Taylor, C. W., and Barron, F. 1963. A look ahead: Reflections of the conference participants and the editors. In C. W. Taylor and F. Barron (eds.), *Scientific creativity: Its recognition and development.* New York: Wiley, pp. 372–89.

Terman, L. M. 1925. Mental and physical traits of a thousand gifted children. *Genetic studies of genius,* vol. 1. Stanford, Calif.: Stanford University Press.

————. 1954. Scientists and nonscientists in a group of 800 gifted men. *Psychological Monographs: General and Applied* 68(7): 1–44 (Whole No. 378).

————. 1955. Are scientists different? *Scientific American* 192(1): 25–29.

————, and Oden, M. H. 1947. The gifted child grows up: Twenty-five years' follow-up of a superior group. *Genetic studies of genius,* vol. 4. Stanford, Calif.: Stanford University Press.

————, and Oden, M. H. 1959. The gifted group at mid-life: Thirty-five years' follow-up of the superior child. *Genetic studies of genius,* vol. 5. Stanford, Calif.: Stanford University Press.

Torrance, E. P. 1962. *Guiding creative talent.* Englewood Cliffs, N.J.: Prentice-Hall.

Visher, S. S. 1947. *Scientists starred, 1903–1943, in "American Men of Science": A study of collegiate and doctoral training, birthplace, distribution, backgrounds, and developmental influences.* Baltimore, Md.: The Johns Hopkins Press.

Wallas, G. 1926, 1945. *The art of thought.* New York: Harcourt, Brace.

Watson, J. D. 1968. *The double helix: A personal account of the discovery of the structure of DNA.* New York: Atheneum.

Zwicky, F. 1957. *Morphological analysis.* Berlin: Springer.

8

CREATIVELY
GIFTED AND DISADVANTAGED
GIFTED STUDENTS[1]

E. Paul Torrance

ABSTRACT

Three gaps in Terman's research on gifted students have been of interest to the author: (1) the careers of creatively gifted students, (2) the origins and careers of students outside of mathematics and physical science, and (3) the identification and nurturance of giftedness among disadvantaged and culturally different groups, especially blacks.

A variety of longitudinal studies initiated in the late 1950s and early 1960s are still in progress. One of these involving a twelve-year follow-up is summarized. In 1959, 392 students (grades seven to twelve) enrolled in the University of Minnesota High School were administered the Torrance Tests of Creative Thinking, *individual and/or group intelligence tests, and the* Iowa Tests of Educational Development. *In 1971, 254 of them responded to a follow-up questionnaire through which they reported their creative achievements and described their three most creative achievements and aspirations for the future. The measures of creative thinking ability yielded consistently higher validity coefficients in predicting the creative achievement criteria than did the measures of intelligence and educational achievement. Through canonical correlation methods, the combined creativity predictors yielded coefficients of correlation of .51 for the total group, .59 for men, and .46 for women in predicting the combined criteria.*

Based on rather extensive experiences with disadvantaged black students, the author makes a case for searching for those kinds of giftedness that are encouraged by the specific culture and socioeconomic group of a student. His thesis is that the greatest strengths of disadvan-

---

[1]This paper was not presented at the Terman Memorial Symposium. Instead, it was commissioned to supplement chapter 7, which dealt with mathematics and science only.

taged and culturally different students are their creative skills and motivations and that these should be given priority consideration in developing curricula and career plans for disadvantaged and culturally different gifted students. Studies showing that the Torrance Tests of Creative Thinking *and the creativity score of the* Alpha Biographical Inventory *have little or no racial or socioeconomic bias and studies showing little or no heritability of creative thinking abilities provide preliminary support for this thesis.*

William B. Michael has provided an excellent review of the state of knowledge concerning the cognitive and affective components of creativity in mathematics and physical sciences. However, it largely ignores what to me are three important gaps that Lewis M. Terman's great work also ignored. The first of these gaps concerns the careers of creatively gifted students and calls for long-range, Terman-like studies of creatively gifted students. The second gap concerns the origins and careers of gifted students outside of mathematics and physical science—those who excel in the social sciences, the arts, literature, and unconventional occupations. The third gap concerns the identification and nurturance of giftedness among disadvantaged and culturally different groups, especially blacks. Since these three concerns have more or less dominated my work since 1958, I shall describe some of the things that I have done in an effort to provide information about these gaps.

Two statements made during the First Minnesota Conference on the Gifted held in 1958 (Torrance 1960) influenced me greatly. One of these statements was made by Catharine Cox Miles, one of Terman's associates. She stated that Terman had challenged "educators, sociologists, and psychologists to produce *if they can* another concept as effective as the IQ for delimiting a group of talent to include the most successful students, the best achievers in the academic world, and, as he believed, in the world of human relationships and human endeavor generally" (Miles 1960, p. 51). Already, I was interested in studying creatively gifted students and was experimenting with new measures for assessing this kind of giftedness. In reexamining Terman's work, I found that he had recognized the existence of "creative intelligence," stating that creative intelligence had been faintly glimpsed but never adequately measured (Terman 1925, 1954). It was then that I resolved to conduct some Terman-like studies of creatively gifted children and initiated such studies the following September.

The second statement made in the First Minnesota Conference on the Gifted that continued to haunt me came from my colleague John E.

Anderson (1960). He pointed out that high levels of ability are found in some degree within all levels of our population and that the search for high talent must be wide in scope and opportunities must be provided at all levels. Anderson also assumed the position that a good and universal program of education for children between the ages of five and seventeen years offers the best opportunity for the systematic exploration of talent. He believed that stimulation, encouragement, and opportunities were necessary prerequisites for effective identification of talent. Anderson believed that giftedness was far rarer among economically disadvantaged groups than among more affluent groups but that it was essential to search for such talent. It was not until I moved from the University of Minnesota to the University of Georgia in 1966 that I was able to initiate investigations to respond to this tension. In 1958, I had not really questioned Anderson's conclusion that giftedness was far rarer among economically disadvantaged groups than among affluent ones. It was a logical one. Gradually, as I worked with disadvantaged children, especially those who were black, I began to understand that there was just as much giftedness among such children as among affluent children in our dominant culture. The problem was that different kinds of giftedness are required for survival and success in different cultures. Their giftedness was simply of a different type.

Few children from low socioeconomic classes, particularly blacks, appeared in Terman's gifted groups. Neither do they appear with much frequency in today's programs for gifted students. As with Terman's sample, tests that place a high premium on verbal comprehension, speed of response, sequential and logical processing of information, and ability to select the one and only correct response have played determining roles in the identification of such groups. Such tests are loaded with bias against culturally different students. In a reevaluation of the Terman studies on their fiftieth anniversary Fincher (1973) pointed out that there were few lower-class children of any kind in Terman's sample; 80 percent of their fathers came from the professions, semiprofessions, and business. Terman limited his sample largely to urban areas, so there were few blacks or Mexicans in the schools from which he drew his subjects.

It has been a highly publicized fact that the children in Terman's sample tended to be bigger, stronger, faster-maturing sexually, more successful all-around in school, and better developed ethically than children in general. Much less highly publicized is the fact that there were few children in the Terman sample who later excelled in art, literature, drama, athletics, and the like. In a 1954 paper, Terman recognized the importance of giftedness outside of mathematics and science, but even then he believed that "the spirit of the times" was not favorable to "the discovery and encouragement of potential poets, prose writers, artists, statesmen, and social leaders." (It is encouraging that current programming in the Office of Gifted and Talented in the U.S. Office of Education recognizes all of these types of giftedness.)

While both "the spirit of the times" and limitations of time and finances have prevented my doing any definitive studies in either of these three neglected areas, I have continued to work at them and have several relevant studies in process and others planned and awaiting the first available opportunity for execution. I shall try to sketch briefly what I have done and what I have thus far learned about these three gaps in information.

LONG-RANGE STUDIES OF CREATIVELY GIFTED STUDENTS

Concerns about longitudinal studies of creatively gifted students go even beyond the concerns of studies such as those of Terman. Few people now doubt the social value of the kind of giftedness Terman dealt with. This has not been true with respect to creative giftedness. As a fairly clear profile of the creative child unfolded during the early 1960s, there arose widespread skepticism and opposition to concerns about the more humane treatment of creative children and about a more creative educational experience in general. The skeptics (MacKinnon 1966; McNemar 1964; Martinson 1961; Martinson and Seagoe 1967; Newland 1963; Taylor and Holland 1964) expressed doubts that the children we had identified as highly creative would produce useful creative achievements as adults. Although few people question the conclusion that creativity (however defined) was a common characteristic of those who have made important breakthroughs in science, medicine, invention, and the arts, many people argued that creative children such as those identified in our research are a menace to society.

I believed that only long-range predictive validity studies and longitudinal developmental studies could answer the serious charges of these critics. My associates and I recognized this need when we initiated our studies in 1959. Unfortunately, it is still too early to obtain adequate follow-up data on the elementary children tested in 1959 and the years that followed. However, I do have plans for following up approximately 1,000 such children. Negotiations are also underway for following up approximately 1,000 children tested in 1961 in New Delhi, India. I have similar sets of data for children in Western Australia, Western Samoa, Norway, West Germany, and Singapore. I also have such data on a sample of black children tested in 1960 in a segregated school. If "the spirit of the times" continues to change, it may be possible to find financial support for some of these studies.

I do have results of the twelve-year follow-up of the high school students tested in 1959 and shall try to summarize the highlights concerning their career patterns and achievements (Torrance 1972*b*). First, I shall describe the basic study and then present data concerning the following questions:

1. Do young people identified as highly creative during their high school years become productive, creative adults?

2. Is seven years after high school graduation or twelve years after high school graduation a better time to obtain predictive validity data?

3. Do the unusual career choices of creative high school students persist and become realities?

4. What are the most common career routes of creatively gifted young people?

5. In what fields do students identified as highly creative on the basis of a test of general creative thinking ability achieve creatively as adults?

6. How does the nature of the peak creative achievements of the more creative students differ from that of their less creative peers twelve years later?

The Basic Study

The basic study was initiated in September, 1959. The total enrollment of the University of Minnesota High School (grades seven to twelve) were administered the Torrance Tests of Creative Thinking (1966, 1972*b*, 1974). A majority of the 392 subjects were sons and daughters of professional and business people. At this time, however, the enrollment also included a block of students from a less affluent school district lacking a school building. The mean intelligence quotient of the total sample as assessed by the Lorge–Thorndike test was 118, and the mean percentile rank on the Iowa Tests of Educational Development was 84 on national high school norms.

The test battery consisted of the following tasks: Ask Questions, Guess Causes, Guess Consequences, Product Improvement, Unusual Uses, and Circles. Test booklets were scored in 1959 according to the scoring guides then in use for the following variables: fluency (number of relevant responses), flexibility (variety of categories of responses), inventive level (following the criteria of the U.S. Patent Office), and elaboration (amount of detail used to describe how ideas would be implemented). In 1961, all test booklets were rescored for originality according to a guide developed at that time. The interscorer reliability of each of the scorers was in excess of .90 for all variables. Test–retest reliabilities had also been found to be satisfactory (Torrance, 1966, 1974).

Near the end of the senior year, the subjects were asked to make three nominations of students in their respective classes on the basis of each of the following creativity criteria:

1. Who in your class come up with the most ideas?
2. Who have the most original or unusual ideas?
3. If a situation changed or if a solution to a problem wouldn't work, who would be the first ones to find a new way of meeting the problem?
4. Who do the most inventing and developing of new ideas, gadgets, and the like?
5. Who are best at thinking of all the details involved in working out a new idea and thinking of all the consequences?

Seven-Year Follow-Up

The first follow-up of this study was with the class of 1960 and was executed in 1966. The follow-up questionnaire requested information concerning the subject's marital status, number of children, occupation, spouse's occupation, highest level of education attained, undergraduate and graduate universities attended, honors, employment experiences, post-high school creative achievements, descriptions of peak creative achievements, and a statement of aspirations.

Responses were received from forty-six of the original sixty-nine subjects. Although the nonrespondents tended to have slightly higher creativity scores than the respondents, there were no statistically significant differences between the creativity, intelligence, and achievement scores of these two groups.

An index of Quantity of Creative Achievements was developed from self-reports based on responses to checklists of creative achievements in the following categories: poems, stories, songs written/published; books written/published; radio and television scripts/performances; music compositions produced/published; original research designs developed /executed; in-service training for coworkers created/executed; research grants received/completed; scientific papers presented/published; business enterprises initiated; patentable devices invented/produced; awards or prizes for creative writing, musical composition, art, leadership, research, etc.

An index of Quality of Creative Achievement was obtained by having five judges (all advanced students of creativity) rate on a 10-point scale the originality/creativeness of the most creative achievements described. The judges had no information about the high school creativity, intelligence, and achievement scores of any of the subjects. An index of Quantity of Creative Behavior was obtained by assigning a weight of one for each achievement attained once or twice and a weight of two for each achievement attained three or more times and then adding the weights. The five judges also rated the degree of originality/creativeness necessary to realize each subject's aspirations for the future.

Pearson product-moment coefficients of correlation for flexibility and the criteria were .48 (quality of creative achievements), .44 (quantity of creative achievements), and .46 (creativeness of aspirations). For originality, the coefficients of correlation with the criteria were .43 (quality of creative achievements), .40 (quantity of creative achievements), and .42 (creativeness of aspirations). For fluency and elaboration, the coefficients of correlation were somewhat lower, ranging from .25 for elaboration and creativeness of Aspirations to .44 for fluency and quantity of creative achievements.

Twelve-Year Follow-Up

A twelve-year follow-up of the 1959 high school sample (N = 392) was conducted in 1971. Completed questionnaires were obtained from 254 (126 males and 125 females) of the subjects. The questionnaire was similar to the one used in 1966 but in addition requested descriptions of the subject's three most creative or peak post-high school achievements. Again, slightly more of the high creative than the low creative subjects failed to respond. However, there were no significant differences between the creativity, intelligence, and achievement scores of the respondents and nonrespondents. Most subjects supplied rather complete information.

The criterion measures were obtained in essentially the same way as those obtained in the 1966 study. The mean reliability coefficient of the five judges was .91.

Combining the scores of the creativity test battery to predict the combined creative achievement criteria, a canonical correlation of .51 was obtained for the full sample. A first canonical correlation coefficient of .59 was obtained for the men alone and one of .46 for women alone. Actually, the canonical correlations do not increase greatly the magnitude of the relationship between the predictor and criterion variables over those found for specific predictors such as originality and inventivlevel. The product-moment coefficients of correlation for originality were .40 (quantity of creative achievements), .43 (quality of creative achievements), and .39 (creativeness of aspirations). For inventivlevel, the coefficients of correlation were .36 (quantity), .41 (quality), and .35 (aspirations). For 254 subjects, all of these coefficients are significant at the .01 level or better, as are those for fluency and flexibility. When the data are analyzed separately for males and females (Torrance 1972c), the coefficients for males are consistently slightly higher than those given above and those for women are consistently somewhat lower.

Time and Predictability of Creative Achievement

At the time I analyzed the data from the 1966 follow-up, there was much to suggest that the differences between the high and low creatives would in time be increased. Follow-up data from forty-six members of this class were obtained in 1966 and from fifty-two in 1971. Table 8.1 presents the product-moment coefficients of correlation between the predictors and criterion measures for both studies. It will be noted that there is a completely consistent trend for the validity coefficients to increase, as predicted. The most startling increase is noted for the sociometric or peer nomination predictors. The coefficients increased from .13, .13, and .18 to .34, .39, and .38, or from insignificant relationships to relationships significant at the .01 level. Intelligence quotient and achievement test scores also show better prediction. However, the creativity measures of flexibility, originality, and fluency still have a slight edge over them.

Unusual Occupational Choices

Critics of the Getzels and Jackson (1962) study have deplored the finding that highly creative students tend to choose unusual occupations. Counselors have pointed out that such choices are unrealistic and that such goals can lead only to failure and disillusionment. To determine

Table 8.1. Product-moment coefficients of correlation between creativity predictors established in 1959 and criterion variables established in 1966 and 1971 ($N = 46$ for 1966 and 52 for 1971)

| | Criterion variables | | | | | |
| | Quality | | Quantity | | Motivation | |
Predictors	1966	1971	1966	1971	1966	1971
Flexibility (TTCT)	.48*	.59*	.44*	.58*	.46*	.54*
Originality (TTCT)	.43*	.49*	.40*	.54*	.42*	.51*
Fluency (TTCT)	.39*	.53*	.44*	.54*	.34	.49*
Intelligence test	.37*	.45*	.22	.46*	.32	.41*
Elaboration (TTCT)	.32	.40*	.37*	.43*	.25	.41*
Achievement (ITED)	.20	.47*	.09	.38*	.15	.46*
Peer nominations	.13	.34*	.13	.39*	.18	.38*

*Significant at the .01 level.

whether highly creative students actually find fulfillment in unusual occupations, the responses of the 254 subjects of this study were analyzed according to the same criteria Getzels and Jackson used. Unusual combinations of occupations were also classified as unconventional (Torrance 1972*a*).

Both the present and projected occupations were classified according to these criteria. The high- and low-creativity groups were determined by a median split by sex within each grade on the basis of composite scores on the 1959 creativity test battery. Data were available for 116 of the high creatives and 138 of the lows.

It was found that 55 percent of the high creatives and 9 percent of the low creatives are currently in unconventional occupations. The difference in proportions yields a chi square of 66.48, significant at better than the .001 level. When future aspirations or projected occupations were classified, 71 percent of the high creatives and 32 percent of the low creatives expressed a preference for unusual or unconventional occupations. This difference in proportions yields a chi square of 37.63, significant at better than the .001 level.

Foreign Study or Work Experience

For fifty-three of the subjects of this study, foreign study or work experience was mentioned as a part of their career preparation or development. Thirty-four (or 30 percent) of the high creatives and 19 (or 14 percent) of the low creatives reported foreign educational and/or work experiences. The resulting difference in proportions yielded a chi square of 9.00, significant at the .005 level.

Fields of Creative Achievement

The Torrance Tests of Creative Thinking are designed to provide measures of general creative ability, and the choice of test tasks represents a deliberate attempt to include an optimum sample of ways of thinking creatively.

To explore the role of the predictors in creative achievements in specific fields, each subject was given a rating in each of the following areas: visual arts, music, creative writing, science–medicine, business–industry, and leadership–politics. A rating of 1 was given those reporting no creative achievements in the area in question; a rating of 2 was given if the subject reported one or two creative achievements in an area or a larger number of moderate achievements in the area; a rating of 3 was given if the subject reported a large number (three or more) of achievements of high quality in the area. These ratings and the number of areas in which each subject reported creative achievements were correlated with each of the predictor variables.

These analyses are too complex for detailed presentation, but gross trends can be noted. Creative achievements in writing were more easily predicted than in any other field, followed by creative achievement in science and medicine and in leadership. Only figural fluency, figural elaboration, consequences flexibility, and product improvement flexibility yielded positive and significant relationships in the visual arts. Only sociometric originality, unusual-uses-of-tin-cans fluency, and flexibility yielded significant relationships in music. For achievement in business and industry, there were significant positive relationships for inventiveness, ask-questions originality, and guess-causes originality. For creative writing, twenty-nine of the thirty-three coefficients of correlation with the creativity predictors were significant at the .05 level and ranged as high as .62 for consequences flexibility, .60 for inventiveness, .58 for verbal originality, .57 for verbal flexibility, and .55 for both guess-causes originality and guess-consequences originality. Twenty-seven of the thirty-three creativity predictors yielded statistically significant correlations with the number of different areas in which subjects reported creative achievement. Thus it seems that the highly creative students in adulthood used their creative abilities not just in one field but in varied fields.

As might be expected, the predictors functioned differently in numerous instances for men and women. These results, however, are too complex for presentation here but are available elsewhere (Torrance 1972*c*).

Peak Creative Achievements

At a rather gross level, we may ask whether the young adults who had been identified as highly creative in 1959 reported more peak creative achievements than the low creatives. It was found that 68 percent of the high creatives compared to 37 percent of the low creatives reported three or more such experiences. Thirty-five per cent of the low creatives and 10 percent of the high creatives reported no such experiences. When the distributions for the high and low creatives are compared, a chi square of 31.28 was obtained (significant at the .001 level).

These differences become more impressive and meaningful when the nature of the peak creative achievements are examined. Many of the achievements described by the low creatives might be classified as "cop-out" experiences. For example, one of the men in this group ranked his most important creative achievements as follows:

1. Dodging the draft.
2. Dropping out of college.
3. Taking LSD.

Some high creatives also cited withdrawal experiences, but their experiences were of a different type from those that seemed to be typical of the low creatives. The following are examples.

One of the high creative women "quit working for [a large stock-brokerage firm] not because they were bad but because they were silly." At the time of the follow-up she was in Spain, had written three novels, compiled a volume of poetry, and written and performed songs for the guitar.

Another of the high creative women ranked her most creative achievement as helping her husband design and build a home in an inaccessible piece of mountain property. In addition to the three experiences or achievements requested, she added, "learning that you can do more things and in more satisfying ways by breaking with U.S. customs. To travel is to hitchhike with tent and sleeping bag, home is where you are, and food is not just in small packages and cans."

One of the younger highly creative men ranked as his second most creative achievement the planning and construction of a cabin in northern Minnesota. His top achievement, however, was in the area of his work, "research in enzymology of human lactate dehydrogenase and development of an electrophoretic assay system for quantification from serum." His third-ranked creative achievement was in the area of his hobby, oil painting.

A common note in the accounts of the high creative group was the desire to escape for renewal temporarily from society's "rat race," but to continue contributing to society in some unique, creative way.

The high and low creative groups were compared by means of chi-square analysis concerning the more common categories of peak achievements. The most striking and statistically significant differences in favor of the high creatives were for: writing such as poetry, novels, dramas, etc.; medical and surgical discovery; musical composition; and human relations and organization.

Conclusions

From the results cited, it seems reasonable to conclude that:

1. Young people identified as creative during the high school years tend to become productive, creative achievers.

2. At least 12 years after high school graduation appears to be a more advantageous time than seven years for a follow-up of creative adults.

3. The unusual occupations expressed as choices by highly creative high school students tend to become realities.

4. Highly creative high school students tend to develop careers that involve detours for relevant but unusual combinations of training and/or experience. A larger proportion of them include study or work in foreign countries as a part of their career development than do their less creative peers.

5. Creative achievements in writing, science, medicine, and leadership are more easily predicted by creativity tests administered in high school than are creative achievements in music, the visual arts, business, and industry. (This is also true of the other predictors.)

6. Young adults identified as highly creative in high school more frequently than their less creative peers attained their peak creative achievements in writing, medical and surgical discovery, dissertation research, musical composition, style of teaching, and human relations and organization. The low creatives tended to report "cop-out" or "drop-out" experiences unaccompanied by constructive action, while many of their more creative peers reported withdrawal experiences either for periods of renewal or for creating a new and (in their opinion) more humane life style.

In interpreting the results of this study, it must be remembered that most of these young people have had reasonably good opportunities to achieve their potentialities. It would not be reasonable to expect such positive findings from a disadvantaged population with limited opportunities. However, studies of disadvantaged and culturally different groups should be made. This problem will be discussed in a later section of this paper.

What Will They Become?

In 1966, I had a strong intuitive feeling that the differences between those identified as high creatives in 1959 and those identified as low creatives would become greater with the passage of time. This hypothesis was supported strongly by higher correlations between the creativity and criterion variables. Now, this impression is even stronger than it was in 1966. The high creatives seemed to be still searching and were still in the process of "becoming," of "creating themselves." By contrast, many low creatives seemed to be happy that they had "made it" and were virtually ready for retirement, glad that they can "take it easier."

To check this impression, I analyzed the responses of each of the 254 subjects as to whether they are still searching and pressing to new goals or are satisfied with what they have attained.

As I had suspected, a far greater proportion of the high creatives than of the low creatives are still searching for new goals and see themselves still in the process of creating themselves and their careers. Almost four times as many of the low creatives as of the high creatives indicated satisfaction with what they had already attained as their life work.

Different Patterns of Searching

The raw data were reexamined to identify the different patterns of searching suggested by responses to the questionnaire. The following four major patterns emerged:

1. New vistas in present career but no real discontinuity with present career.

2. New vistas through a genuine discontinuity with the past and present.

3. Openness to multiple future alternatives.

4. Moving from an unproductive life without goals to definite goals for productive living.

Looking to Future Studies

It is quite clear that the story of the 254 subjects of this study is far from complete. I would predict that any future follow-up of these 254 young adults will show a somewhat higher level of predictive validity for the creativity predictors than has the study described herein. Today's atmosphere is unquestionably more creative than it was in 1959, and this may bring into existence new ways of looking at creative behavior. One of the women who was in the seventh grade in 1959 suggested this possibility in response to my summary of the findings of the twelve-year follow-up:

> Your study covers a change in attitudes that really took place. I like the idea of your study and I think it must have been exciting for you to see in your findings that something really was changing, something really important, and that you are able to observe pretty minutely what was happening, or at least a part of what was happening.
>
> But more important things are happening. Vast changes in people's states of mind, very little is taken for granted either by twelve-year-olds or middle-aged gentlemen. I think these changes are so great and the vistas are

opening up so suddenly that the "creativity" concept no longer applies to life in quite the same way. The background is changing. Perhaps what I am trying to share with you is my impression that a very highly creative attitude is becoming so prevalent that it soon may be the background against which more extraordinary states of mind will be seen.

These comments provide a challenging perspective against which to conduct the future follow-up studies of the elementary school children tested in Minnesota and India in 1959 and 1961 and the black children tested in a segregated school in Georgia in 1960.

What Happened to Those Gifted in Mathematics and Natural Science?

Since Michael's paper as well as the Johns Hopkins project (SMPY) are concerned primarily with giftedness in mathematics and the natural sciences, I was stimulated to reexamine some of the longitudinal data for those who might have been identified as gifted in this respect in 1959. For those who were in grades nine to twelve, scores on the Iowa Tests of Educational Development were available. Subjects were classified as gifted in mathematics and science if they scored at or above the 95th percentile on the following three tests on national norms: background in the natural sciences, ability to do quantitative thinking, and ability to interpret reading materials in the natural sciences. Of the 185 subjects for which I have complete data in grades nine to twelve, fifty-one (28 percent) had scores that placed them in the upper 5 percent on these tests and their responses were studied and compared with those of their peers less gifted in mathematics and science.

It was found that only twelve (23.5 percent) of these fifty-one mathematically and scientifically superior students were women, compared with 53 percent of their less-gifted peers (chi square = 12.96, significant at the .01 level).

Thirty-six (70.6 percent) of them attained creativity scores that placed them in the upper half of their respective classes compared with 45.5 percent of their less-gifted peers (chi square = 9.31, significant at the .01 level).

Thirty-three (64.7 percent) of them were awarded some kind of scholarship, fellowship, or assistantship for postsecondary education compared to 29.1 percent of their less-gifted peers (chi square = 19.70, significant at the .01 level).

Twenty-six of these mathematically and scientifically gifted young people (50.9 percent) had completed their doctorates by 1971 while only 14.18 percent of their less-gifted peers had attained this distinction (chi square = 27.18, significant at the .001 level).

Fifteen (29.4 percent) of this exceptional group had devoted time to foreign study or work compared to 20.9 percent of their less-gifted peers (chi square = 1.50, not significant at the .05 level).

In table 8.2, the mathematically and scientifically gifted group is compared with the rest of the group from which they were drawn on number of honors, number of jobs held, inventiveness, originality, composite creativity, and the three criterion measures of creative achievement. It will be noted that the gifted group exceeded the total group on each of these variables, including number of different jobs held.

At the time of the follow-up in 1971, twenty-four (47 percent) of the mathematically and scientifically gifted group held college or university teaching and/or research positions. However, only four of them were in mathematics or physical sciences. Nine were in the social sciences, eight were in the medical sciences, and three were in other fields. It should be noted, however, that some of the social scientists have emphasized the quantitative aspects of their disciplines. One of the economists and one of the sociologists had obtained graduate fellowships in quantitative economics and quantitative sociology. The economist indicated that if he were free to choose what he wanted to do in the future, he would work in "pure mathematics."

Even some of those in the humanities have maintained their interests in science and mathematics. For example, one of the women who was completing her doctorate in literature had written scripts for "Star Trek" and writes science fiction. The twenty-seven nonacademics were distributed as follows: writing, editing, etc., 5; film making, 2; developing new products, 2; business and industry, 2; music, 2; law, 2; teaching, 2;

Table 8.2. Comparison of means of mathematically/scientifically gifted students with the rest of the respondents (grades nine to twelve) on major predictor and criterion variables

Measure	Math/science gifted (N = 51)		Peers math/science gifted (N = 134)		t
	Means	St. dev.	Means	St. dev.	
Number honors	2.08	2.01	0.64	1.33	4.743†
Number jobs	4.67	2.85	3.57	2.29	2.470*
Inventiveness	47.84	17.25	39.69	15.99	2.929*
Originality	133.78	54.03	103.86	37.65	3.633†
Total creativity	265.71	78.18	234.89	61.54	2.532*
Creative achievement: quantity	20.57	12.38	14.85	15.35	2.621*
Creative achievement: quality	32.82	7.82	25.72	9.52	5.185†
Creative aspirations	32.94	7.36	26.66	9.07	4.851†

*Significant at the .01 level.
†Significant at the .001 level.

engineering, 1; claims adjustment, 1; military aviation, 1; costume designing, 1; museum curator, 1; truck driver, 1; social worker, 1; printing, 1;
unemployed, 1; and deceased, 1. A characteristic of many of these young
people is that they have combined their giftedness in mathematics and
science with the arts and social welfare interests. One of the film makers
works only in the field of medical films. The museum curator, the product
developers, the writers, and the businessmen similarly synthesize their
multitalents and multi-interests in their occupations.

It is especially interesting that so few of these young people gifted in
mathematics and science actually went into careers designated as science,
mathematics, engineering, etc. It will be recalled that at the time they were
in high school there was great pressure on young people to enter such
careers. It was the immediate Post-Sputnik era. This is in keeping with the
values of a free society in which people are free to use or not use their
talents. As I was writing this paper (November 2, 1975), John W. Oswald,
president of the Pennsylvania State University, made an important
statement to the press on this issue. He had just returned from a two-week
study tour of the Soviet Union. He stated that Russian educators are
puzzled that students in the United States are permitted to decide their life
plans without government intervention. He pointed out that closed
societies are convinced that central planning and decision making is the
best method for societal service and full employment, and yet they
observe that the accomplishments of free societies are great. Oswald's
concluding statement is especially pertinent to this issue in gifted education: "No one can or should really dictate to you in a free society that you
must use your talents nor direct just how you should use them. . . ."

It is quite likely that the particular young people in this gifted group
could have had the chance to do advanced study and find careers in
mathematics and science had they chosen to do so. I shall now direct
attention to those groups of gifted young people who frequently do not
have this chance—disadvantaged and culturally different youths.

Disadvantaged and Culturally Different Gifted Students

Although I have studied giftedness in a variety of different cultures
both in the United States and other countries (Torrance 1967, 1968,
1969), the emergent concepts that express my conclusions concerning
disadvantaged and culturally different gifted children are largely the
product of my work with economically disadvantaged black children.
This work involves both the culture of poverty and black culture. The
research literature makes it difficult at times to distinguish between
findings concerning disadvantaged blacks and affluent blacks as well as
between disadvantaged whites and disadvantaged blacks. Although the

research literature yields many important insights, my most important teachers have been disadvantaged black children.

Culturally Valued Kinds of Giftedness

It was not until I began working with disadvantaged black children that I began to see how important it is to stop trying to identify a universal type of giftedness and begin looking for kinds of giftedness that are valued by the particular culture in which a child has been reared. Thus, I have urged that we no longer insist on identifying and cultivating *only* those kinds of talent that the dominant, affluent culture values. We should look for and cultivate the types that are valued in the various disadvantaged subcultures. Since children tend to develop along the lines that are encouraged, the gifted children of a subculture are likely to be the ones who have developed to a high level those talents valued by that particular subculture.

By the end of the 1960s it had become clear that overall there was no racial or socioeconomic bias in the open-ended tests of creative thinking. In 1971, I summarized the results of sixteen different studies conducted in different localities to study racial and/or socioeconomic status differences on the Torrance Tests of Creative Thinking (1966, 1974). In some studies, there were no racial or socioeconomic differences. In others, black children excelled white children on certain tasks and white children excelled the black on others. The same was true where socioeconomic status differences were studied. For example, disadvantaged children usually excel affluent children on the unusual uses tests, while the reverse is true of the guess-causes tests. A major reason for this is that open-ended test tasks permit children to respond in terms of their experiences, whatever these have been rather than in terms of the one best answer based on experiences of children in the dominant, affluent subculture.

Since my 1971 review, the number of studies on racial and/or socioeconomic bias has about doubled, with essentially the same verdict of no racial or socioeconomic bias. Curiously, the single study dealing with an identified gifted population (Frierson 1965) shows bias in favor of the upper status gifted child on creativity tests. All of the subjects of this study, including the lower status ones, had been identified as gifted according to criteria valued by the dominant, affluent subculture and not those of the subcultures of the lower class subjects. My hypothesis is that these lower-status gifted students had sacrificed their creativity in order to gain acceptance in such a group.

In current debates concerning the heritability of intelligence (Jensen 1969, 1973; Kamin 1974), such findings have gone virtually unnoticed. A number of the classical monozygotic/dizygotic twin studies (Barron 1972;

Davenport 1967; Pezzullo, Thorsen, and Madaus 1972; Richmond 1968) bear directly upon the problem. Those that have used the Torrance Tests of Creative Thinking have found no evidence of hereditary variation in either the figural or verbal measures. The study reported by Pezzullo, Thorsen, and Madaus (1972) is perhaps the most definitive as it included also Jensen's level I and II abilities. The subjects were thirty-seven pairs of dizygotic and twenty-eight pairs of monozygotic twins carefully selected. It was found that short-term memory (Jensen's level I abilities) had a moderate index of heritability, .54; the general intelligence factor (Jensen's level II abilities) had a relatively high index of heritability, .85. The heritability index of the abilities assessed by the Torrance Tests of Creative Thinking approaches zero.

Studies by Bruch (1971, 1975), Houston (1972), and Taylor and Ellison (Institute of Behavioral Research in Creativity 1968) have supplied evidence of other measures lacking in racial and/or socioeconomic bias. These studies have provided growing support of the concept of the creative positives or strengths of disadvantaged children.

Creative Positives of Disadvantaged

Building upon Frank Riessman's (1962) suggestions concerning the "hidden" talents of disadvantaged children, I have concentrated for the past eight years on the identification, recognition, and nurturance of what I have called the creative positives of disadvantaged children (Torrance 1973). I have demonstrated that these creative positives can be observed without the use of tests by engaging children in challenging activities in science, creative writing, visual arts, music, dance, dramatics, psychology, and the like. Furthermore, these positives seem to occur as frequently or more frequently among disadvantaged children than among more affluent ones. In fact, I found (Torrance 1974) that affluent gifted children were unable to compete successfully with disadvantaged children in brainstorming and creative problem solving.

The creative positives that seem to be the best supported by research and observation and to be most useful in developing intervention programs include:

1. Ability to express feelings and emotions in communication through creative writing, music, creative movement, interpersonal relations, etc.

2. Ability to improvise with commonplace materials.

3. Articulateness in role playing, sociodrama, and storytelling.

4. Enjoyment of and ability in the visual arts—drawing, painting, sculpture, etc.

5. Enjoyment of and ability in creative movement, dance, dramatics, etc.

6. Enjoyment of and ability in music, rhythm, etc.

7. Expressiveness of speech, richness of imagery, colorfulness of language, etc.

8. Fluency and flexibility in nonverbal media (figural, motor, etc.).

9. Enjoyment of and skills in small-group activities, problem solving, etc.

10. Responsiveness to the concrete.

11. Responsiveness to the kinesthetic.

12. Expressiveness of gestures, "body language," etc., and ability to "read body language" and nonverbal communication.

13. Humor and ability to create surprise.

14. Originality of ideas in problem solving.

15. Problem centeredness and persistence in problem solving.

16. Emotional responsiveness and responsiveness to emotion.

17. Quickness of physical and emotional warm-up.

Our evidence (Torrance 1970, 1971, 1973; Torrance and Torrance 1972) indicates that these creative positives can be observed with high degrees of frequency among black disadvantaged children when they are engaged in challenging and exciting learning activities that give them a chance to use such abilities.

Since funding agencies have thus far been willing to support only compensatory programs for disadvantaged children, there have been few systematic demonstrations to support these conclusions. One such program was conducted by George Witt (1971) in New Haven, Connecticut. This program (Witt 1968) involved sixteen highly creative lower-class black children in a ghetto setting. They were selected in 1965 solely on the basis of tests of creative thinking (the Torrance figural tests and one test task developed by Witt). Twelve of them continued in this program, which continued to change to meet the children's changing needs. As truly high-level talents were manifested, opportunities were provided for them to have music, art, ballet, and other kinds of lessons from excellent teachers. Many of the children's parents were assisted in upgrading their job skills. Sponsors were arranged both for the children and their families. Fellowships were arranged for participation in science and arts camps, and scholarships were obtained for some of them in private schools. These children have competed successfully with affluent gifted children in both types of settings. The competencies with which they have succeeded in such competition were attained as an outgrowth of activities that made use of their creative positives rather than as a direct result of deliberate attempts to develop these competencies.

Although far fewer successful programs in science and mathematics are being reported than in the arts, there are even now a number of examples of both individual and group successes among disadvantaged, black, gifted youngsters. In the history of mathematical and scientific discovery, there are a number of notables among disadvantaged blacks. Included are such notables in science and mathematics as George Washington Carver, agricultural chemist; Percy L. Julian, soybean chemist; Ernest E. Just, marine biologist; Daniel H. Williams, pioneer in heart surgery; Louis T. Wright, pioneer in clinical antibiotic research; Charles L. Drew, pioneer in blood plasma, and David H. Blackwell, former president of the Institute of Mathematical Statistics. Among inventors, there are such pioneers as Benjamin Banneker, a prolific inventor, surveyor, and mathematician in the early history of the United States; Norbert Rillieux, whose invention of the vacuum-pan evaporator revolutionized the world's sugar industry; Jan E. Matzeliger, whose inventions revolutionized the shoe industry; Elijah McCoy, known as the "father of lubrication"; Granville T. Woods, whose inventions in the field of electricity have won him the label of the "Black Edison"; and Garrett A. Morgan, a pioneer in inventions related to mining safety (Haber 1970).

A present-day success story is that of Bracie Watson (*Ebony* Staff 1969), a black youth from Alabama who won top place in the 1968 International Science Fair. A promising group project in the medical science area has been described by Shepherd (1972). This experiment has been known as the High School Education Program at the University of Pennsylvania, shortened to HEP-UP. The initial program involved thirty students, ten each from three large high schools near the university. These students were selected on the basis of high motivation but not necessarily high achievement. The project directors, however, were looking for students who might have high science grades or who might be "turned on" to science. Many surprising successes followed, even though some of them were "too filled with tension and hatred to work in the situation." In the 1972 evaluation of the project, the evidence described by Shepherd indicated that some black disadvantaged students compete well with more affluent students in medical schools and graduate schools.

Rationale of Special Programs for Disadvantaged Gifted Students

The problem of providing adequately for disadvantaged gifted students is far more than one of ignoring the existence of talent from different environments. It cannot be solved simply by identifying and inserting them into existing programs for gifted and talented children. To avoid a new kind of segregation, however, it may be necessary to do some of this. For success, some kind of preceding or concurrent developmental program may be necessary. The Witt project already described provides one model for doing this. After an intensive summer program and a year-long after-school and week-end program, it was possible for these black disadvantaged children to hold their own in science and arts camps with children from wealthy and highly educated families. After about two more years it was possible for them to compete with such youngsters in the best private schools in the area. If these students had been inserted into these programs when they were first identified in 1965, they would have failed miserably. The HEP-UP program, which enabled black, disadvantaged youths to compete in medical and graduate schools, shared many of these same features. It is inconceivable that these youngsters could have succeeded in medical and graduate schools without the intervening development through the HEP-UP program.

Considering the fact that students can be gifted in so many different ways and that every culture has so many different facets, it would be impossible to specify the ways in which special programs for culturally different and disadvantaged gifted children should be special. Certainly, successful programs will have to be special to some degree in content of the curriculum, methods of instruction, and the learning environment to be used. On the basis of my experiences with disadvantaged black groups, I shall suggest some of the more obvious ways that programs for gifted children in these groups should be special.

1. The particular strengths of disadvantaged black students should be used in designing the content of the curriculum and making decisions about methods of instruction. The learning environment would have those special characteristics that would be congenial to this kind of curriculum and the accompanying methods.

2. Unreasonable economic demands should be avoided. Stress should be placed upon improvisation with commonplace materials, the use of natural phenomena, and getting free access to such public facilities as libraries, zoos, playgrounds, parks, and public buildings. There should be opportunities for purchasing books, art materials, music instruments, music lessons, and so on.

3. Activities, administrative procedures, classroom management practices, and the like should be so planned and executed so as to help the disadvantaged gifted child cope with and grow out of feelings of alienation. Basically, this will involve the development of pride in these special strengths and opportunities for sharing these special strengths with others.

4. Some provisions must be made for resources for study and getting information. Some schools will not permit disadvantaged black children to take home their textbooks or check out library books. My graduate students have to argue long and hard to persuade public librarians to permit disadvantaged black children to check out books. Librarians

cannot understand why the children's parents cannot bring them and sign their cards.

5. One characteristic of programs for disadvantaged gifted children would be a heavy reliance upon work in teams or small groups. In small groups of peers, disadvantaged black children are amazingly verbal and articulate. Repeatedly I have seen a disadvantaged black child teach another somewhat younger child quite successfully where teacher after teacher had failed completely. I have also seen them teach adults just as adroitly, using teaching skills that any professional pedagogue would have envied.

6. Disadvantaged gifted black children need sponsors who can encourage and protect their rights when they are discouraged and/or abused. They need someone special to them who can see that they "get a chance." The purpose would not be to "give them something for nothing," but rather that they have a "chance to work for it."

Just as there are needs for a bold Terman-like study of giftedness among disadvantaged students, there are needs for bold experiments to give such students "a chance to work for it."

REFERENCES

Anderson, J. E. 1960. The nature of abilities. In E. P. Torrance (ed.), *Talent and education*. Minneapolis, Minn.: University of Minnesota Press, pp. 9–31.

Barron, F. 1972. Travels in search of new latitudes for innovation. In C. W. Taylor (ed.), *Climate for creativity*. New York: Pergamon Press, pp. 49–62.

Bruch, C. B. 1971. Modification of procedures for identification of disadvantaged gifted. *Gifted Child Quarterly* 15: 267–72.

―――. 1975. Assessment of creativity in culturally different children. *Gifted Child Quarterly* 19: 164–74.

Davenport, J. D. 1967. A study of monozygotic and dizygotic twins and siblings on measures of scholastic aptitude, creativity, achievement motivation, and academic achievement. Unpublished doctoral dissertation, University of Maryland. (University Microfilms Order No. 68–3350.)

Ebony Staff. 1969. Teen scientist. *Ebony* 24(8): 96–104.

Fincher, J. 1973. The Terman study is fifty years old. *Human Behavior* 2(3): 8–15.

Frierson, E. C. 1965. Upper and lower status gifted children: A study of differences. *Exceptional Children* 32: 83–90.

Getzels, J. W., and Jackson, P. W. 1962. *Creativity and intelligence*. New York: Wiley.

Haber, L. 1970. *Black pioneers of science and invention*. New York: Harcourt Brace Jovanovich.

Houston, S. H. 1973. Black English. *Psychology Today* 6(10): 45–48.

Institute for Behavioral Research in Creativity, 1968. *Manual for Alpha Biographical Inventory.* Salt Lake City, Utah: Prediction Press.

Jensen, A. R. 1969. How much can we boost IQ and scholastic achievement? *Harvard Educational Review* 39: 1–123.

_____. 1973. *Educability and group differences.* New York: Harper & Row.

Kamin, L. J. 1974. *The science and politics of I.Q.* New York: Wiley.

MacKinnon, D. W. 1966. Instructional media in the nurturing of creativity. In C. W. Taylor and F. E. Williams (eds.), *Instructional media and creativity.* New York: Wiley, pp. 179–216.

McNemar, Q. 1964. Lost: Our intelligence? Why? *American Psychologist* 18: 871–82.

Martinson, R. 1961. *Educational programs for gifted pupils.* Sacramento, Calif.: California State Department of Education.

_____, and Seagoe, M. V. 1967. *The abilities of young children.* Washington, D.C.: Council for Exceptional Children.

Miles, C. C. 1960. Crucial factors in the life history of talent. In E. P. Torrance (ed.), *Talent and education.* Minneapolis, Minn.: University of Minnesota Press, pp. 51–65.

Newland, T. E. 1963. A critique of research on the gifted. *Exceptional Children* 29: 391–99.

Pezzullo, T. R., Thorsen, E. E., and Madaus, G. F. 1972. The heritability of Jensen's level I and II and divergent thinking. *American Educational Research Journal* 9: 539–46.

Richmond, B. O. 1968. Creativity in monozygotic and dizygotic twins. Paper presented at the annual meetings of the American Personnel and Guidance Association, Detroit, April.

Riessman, F. 1962. *The culturally deprived child.* New York: Harper & Row.

Shepherd, J. 1972. Black lab power. *Saturday Review* 55: 32–39.

Taylor, C. W., and Holland, J. 1964. Predictors of creative performance. In C. W. Taylor (ed.), *Creativity: Progress and potential.* New York: McGraw-Hill.

Terman, L. M. 1925. Mental and physical traits of a thousand gifted children. *Genetic studies of genius,* vol. I. Stanford, Calif.: Stanford University Press.

_____. 1954. The discovery and encouragement of exceptional talent. *American Psychologist* 9: 221–30.

Torrance, E. P. (ed.) 1960. *Talent and education.* Minneapolis, Minn.: University of Minnesota Press.

_____. 1966. *The Torrance Tests of Creative Thinking: Technical-norms manual.* Lexington, Mass.: Personnel Press. (Revised, 1974.)

_____. 1967. *Understanding the fourth grade slump in creative thinking.* Final report on Cooperative Research Project 995. Washington, D.C.: U.S. Office of Education, Department of Health, Education, and Welfare. (Available only from ERIC.)

_____. 1968. Testing the educational and psychological development of students from other cultures and subcultures. *Review of Educational Research* 38: 71–76.

_____. 1969. Prediction of adult creative achievement among high school seniors. *Gifted Child Quarterly* 13: 71–81.

————. 1970. *Encouraging creativity in the classroom.* Dubuque, Iowa: William C. Brown.

———— 1971. Are the Torrance tests of creative thinking biased against or in favor of disadvantaged groups? *Gifted Child Quarterly* 15: 75–81.

————. 1972a. Career patterns and peak creative achievements of creative high school students twelve years later. *Gifted Child Quarterly* 16: 75–88.

————. 1972b. Predictive validity of the Torrance Tests of Creative Thinking. *Journal of Creative Behavior* 6: 236–52.

————. 1972c. Creative young women in today's world. *Exceptional Children* 38: 597–603.

————. 1973. Non-test indicators of creative talent among disadvantaged children. *Gifted Child Quarterly* 17: 3–9.

————. 1974. Interscholastic brainstorming and creative problem solving competition for the creatively gifted. *Gifted Child Quarterly* 18: 3–7.

————, and Torrance, J. P. 1972. Combining creative problem-solving with creative expressive activities in the education of disadvantaged young people *Journal of Creative Behavior* 6: 1–10.

Witt, G. 1968. *The Life Enrichment Activity Program: A brief history.* New Haven, Conn.: LEAP, Inc., 363 Dixwell Avenue. (Mimeographed.)

————. 1971. The Life Enrichment Activity Program Inc.: A continuing program for creative, disadvantaged children. *Journal of Research and Development in Education* 4(3): 67–73.

9

PERSONALITY CORRELATES OF INTELLIGENCE AND CREATIVITY IN GIFTED ADOLESCENTS

George S. Welsh

ABSTRACT

Two independent dimensions of personality are proposed for use in theoretical and practical research on intelligence and creativity. One, intellectence, differentiates subjects interested in concrete and pragmatic matters from those preferring abstract and theoretical approaches to problems; the other, origence, contrasts preference for regular and structured situations with predilection for open-ended and unstructured experiences. Four basic types are generated by these dimensions and characterized descriptively as: (1) imaginative (high origence/low intellectence), (2) intuitive (high origence/high intellectence), (3) industrious (low origence/low intellectence), and (4) intellective (low origence/high intellectence). Data from gifted adolescents illustrate personality characteristics associated with these dimensions and with intelligence scores from Terman's Concept Mastery Test (CMT) and a nonverbal test (D-48), and with a figure-preference art scale. Relationships are shown to scales from the Minnesota Multiphasic Personality Inventory (MMPI), Allport–Vernon–Lindzey Study of Values (AVL), Strong Vocational Interest Blank (SVIB), and ratings by teachers. The argument is advanced that gifted adolescents high on both origence and intellectence resemble creative adults and may have creative potential; therefore, they may be identified by special scales on objective personality tests.

The question of the relationship between intelligence and creativity was studied in more than a thousand highly gifted and talented adolescents attending the Governor's School of North Carolina.[1] An opera-

[1]For a description of the program at the Governor's School, see a report by Welsh (1969); see also Lewis (1969) for an extensive discussion of the theory of the school.

tional approach based on psychometrics and utilizing easily administered standard tests was adopted so that objectivity in analysis of the original data could be maintained, and also to afford the opportunity for replication of the research design and the analytic results. Two tests from the battery administered were used for this purpose.

Intelligence was defined by scores on Terman's Concept Mastery Test (CMT), originally developed for follow-up work in his well-known study of intellectually gifted children (Terman 1954, 1956; Bayley and Oden 1955).[2] *Creative potential* was defined by scores on the Revised Art Scale (RA) of the Welsh Figure Preference Test (WFPT), a nonverbal personality instrument (Welsh 1959). Scores on RA, or the earlier Barron–Welsh Art Scale (Barron and Welsh 1952), have differentiated within and between more and less creative groups of artists, architects, mathematicians, musicians, scientists, and writers (Rosen 1955; MacKinnon 1962; Helson 1961; Raychaudhuri 1966; Gough 1961; Getzels and Jackson 1962; Barron 1961).

The two tests are statistically independent because CMT and RA scores have proved to be uncorrelated for adults (MacKinnon 1961), graduate students (Adair 1969), community college students (Saunders 1968), undergraduates in the present writer's tests and measurements courses, and gifted adolescents from the Governor's School (Welsh 1966). Thus, it was possible to plot the test scores on two orthogonal axes and to select four groups of Governor's School subjects falling in the "corners" of the bivariate display:

1. high on RA, low on CMT   2. high on both
3. low on both   4. low on RA, high on CMT

The actual cutting scores employed in the selection procedures and other technical details have been presented in full elsewhere (see Welsh 1975, chap. 5).

Since the students were highly selected in terms of general intelligence as well as for special talents, it was assumed that they would differ less along ability variables than they would in personality traits and temperament. Personality characteristics differentiating the four groups were inferred from an item analysis of three widely used standard tests included in the battery: the Adjective Check List (ACL) (Gough and Heilbrun 1965); the Minnesota Multiphasic Personality Inventory (MMPI) (Dahlstrom, Welsh, and Dahlstrom 1972, 1975); and the Strong Vocational Interest Blank (SVIB) (Strong 1959). First, the pool of items in each test was examined to locate subsets of items that each group answered

[2]Reports on the utility of the CMT in studies of mathematically precocious youths may be found in Stanley, Keating, and Fox (1974) and Keating (1976b). Other descriptive material and statistics on various groups of adult subjects may be found in Welsh (1975).

differently from the other three groups when in conjunction. Then features common to each group across the different tests were used for a psychological interpretation of the basic typology. A summary of these personality characteristics is given in table 9.1. Finally, two hypothetical personality dimensions were proposed to account for the fourfold typology generated from the item analysis (see Welsh 1975, pp. 78–80).

For the vertical dimension the term "origence" (ORIG) is employed because of its relation to *originality* as determined in early studies employing the art scale (Barron 1955). A counterpart term was coined for the horizontal dimension, "intellectence" (INT), to indicate the source of its psychometric inception. These dimensions are construed as independent in the conceptual model just as the uncorrelated test scores could be arrayed on orthogonal axes for the initial psychometric analysis.

Intellectence is related to personality characteristics, temperamental dispositions, and interests associated with a dimension conceptualized as extending from the concrete to the abstract. That is, at the low end of intellectence emphasis is placed on literal and specific events which may be expressed in concrete terms and that may have practical or pragmatic applications for the usual experiences of life.

At the high end of intellectence, on the other hand, an abstract attitude is evident, leading to concern with figurative or symbolic expression and generalized principles of comprehension. This attitude is also manifested in differences between the ends of the dimension regarding social behavior. The high end seems more impersonal and unsocial while the low end is much more directly personal in outlook and more socially participative.

It must be emphasized that this personality dimension has to be kept separate from the concept of general intelligence. Persons at the low end of intellectence may be just as intelligent as those at the high end and may be just as successful in dealing with ordinary problems of life. It is likely, however, that there is a positive relationship between scores on conventional intelligence tests and the dimension of intellectence because these tests are loaded with the kind of content requiring abstractions for correct response. Such tests are biased against the person who expresses his intelligence and ability in practical ways. Furthermore, these tests have been developed for the most part to predict academic achievement rather than success in the pragmatic world of everyday affairs.

Origence, by contrast, is not directly related to intellectual performance either in terms of conventional intelligence tests or academic achievement per se. The dimension seems to distinguish those at the low end who prefer and are more at home in an explicit and well-defined world which can be grasped by the application of objective rules. This is in contrast to those at the high end, who find congenial an implicit and

Table 9.1. Summary of characteristics associated with dimensional types[a]

Intrapersonal Orientation

1. *Extraversive* exhibitionistic acting out	2. *Introverted* withdrawing ruminative
3. *Extraverted* outward-directed responsive	4. *Introversive* inward-directed speculative

Direction of Activity

1. *Interactive* interdependent responder	2. *Proactive* autonomous detached viewer
3. *Reactive* dependent follower	4. *Active* independent leader

Cognitive Style

1. *Imaginative* fantasy improvisation simile	2. *Intuitive* insight meditation metaphor
3. *Customary* industry persistence allegory	4. *Rational* logic deliberation analogy

Attitudes and Beliefs

1. *Irregular* uncommon "don't conform"	2. *Unorthodox* unconventional "take risks"
3. *Orthodox* common "play safe"	4. *Regular* conventional "follow rules"

1, High origence/low intellectence; 2, high origence/high intellectence; 3, low origence/low intellectence; 4, low origence/high intellectence.

Table 9.1. (*Continued*)

Interpersonal Conduct

1. *Sociable* outgoing many acquaintances amicable	2. *Asocial* isolative few friends impersonal
3. *Social* friendly indiscriminate sociality benevolent	4. *Unsocial* shy guarded sociality humanitarian

Nature of Self Concept

1. *Self-seeking* egocentric	2. *Self-centered* egotistic
3. *Self-effacing* allocentric	4. *Self-confident* egoistic

Cognitive Development

1. *Proto-integration*
    without differen-
    tiation
diffuse
global
imprecise
	2. *Integration with*
	    differentiation
	synthesis
	organization
	composition

3. *Proto-differentiation*
    without integration
fragmented
detailed
unrelated
	4. *Differentiation with*
	    integration
	analysis
	specification
	resolution

Vocational Interests

1. *Histrionic*
action
performing and
    dramatic arts
sales occupations
	2. *Intellectual*
	ideas
	arts and humanities
	related occupations
	    (e.g., journalism)

3. *Pragmatic*
practical problems
commerce and
    business
service occupations
	4. *Scientific*
	concepts
	sciences and mathe-
	    matics
	related occupations
	    (e.g., statistician)

open universe which they can structure and order in their own subjective way. The high-origent person resists conventional approaches that have been predetermined by others and would rather do things his own way, even if it is unpopular or seems rebellious or nonconforming. He is often interested in artistic, literary, and aesthetic matters that do not have a "correct" answer agreed upon by consensus, because these matters allow him more individualized interpretation and expression.

At the low end of origence are those who are more at ease in an orderly, structured, and regular environment where problems can be solved by conventional methods and by conforming to the status quo. In academic settings that stress rote memory and course content oriented to facts and figures, these individuals may seem to achieve more than those at the upper end of the dimension. Some success in grade getting may also accrue to them because of stylistic features related to persistence and planfulness as well as personal characteristics of deference to authority and self-effacement. This seeming advantage is probably countered in courses requiring initiative and imagination, where the high-origent person would be rewarded for atypical or unusual performance and for independent study. Although uncorrelated with scores on conventional intelligence tests, origence is positively related to measures of fantasy, divergent thinking, and originality.

ANALYSIS OF RESULTS

Two basic methods of analyzing results in this study have been followed. The first is a correlational analysis based on composite scores for origence (ORIG) and for intellectence (INT) derived from the initial item analysis of the ACL, MMPI, and SVIB.[3] The emphasis here is on the relationship of the two hypothetical personality *dimensions* to other variables.

The second method of analysis emphasizes the *typology* generated by these dimensions. Rather than the fourfold typology based on extreme scores alone utilized initially, a method was developed so that medium-scoring groups could be studied as well. A scatter plot was made with orthogonal axes for the dimensions. Each student was located in terms of his or her scores on ORIG and INT. Cutting scores were then established to divide each dimension into three equal parts—low, medium, and high. Since dimensional scores were considered conjointly, it was necessary that the scatter plot be partitioned into nine sections or "novants." Ideally, each novant (assuming zero correlation) would contain exactly one ninth

---

[3]Computation of the composite scores is described in Welsh (1975, pp. 85–86).

of the cases—11.11 percent. Although this distribution was not obtained precisely, table 9.2 shows that it was closely approximated and is considered satisfactory for analytic purposes. To maintain continuity in nomenclature with the original analysis the four extreme groups are designated by the numerals 1, 2, 3, and 4, with composite numerals 1-2, 1-3, 2-4, and 3-4 employed for medium groups, while the numeral 0 for the middle group suggests its novant location at the center of both dimensions.

Nonverbal Intelligence

In addition to the CMT, which is essentially verbal in nature, a nonverbal test was given at the Governor's School for two of the three sessions covered by the present research. The test is known as the D-48 and comprises items in the form of dominoes in which the subject has to discern the principle in a sequence of dots to arrive at the correct answer. The D-48 was originally developed in Europe and was modified and adapted for use in this country by Black (1963). Although it is positively correlated with conventional verbal intelligence tests, factor-analytic studies of batteries including the D-48 have been interpreted as reflecting a source of variance different from verbal intelligence (Boyd and Ward 1966; Horn and Bramble 1967). For the Governor's School subjects the correlation between the CMT and the D-48 is .44 ($N = 770$), and there is some evidence that differential performance on these tests may be related to interests (Welsh 1967, 1971). That is, those with high verbal interests as measured by scales on the SVIB may perform relatively better on the verbal CMT than on the nonverbal D-48.

Assessment of Personal Adjustment

Scales of the Minnesota Multiphasic Personality Inventory (MMPI) were used to assess patterns of adjustment in the gifted subjects. A dimensional approach that was used with this test and correlations between the intelligence tests and the art scale as well as ORIG and INT are shown in table 9.3.[4]

The first three scales are designated "validity" scales and reflect test-taking attitude as well as having personological implications. The L scale, "lie," measures a naive tendency to cover up minor personal faults or

[4]The rationale for correlating the MMPI scales with intellectence and origence can be found in Welsh (1975, pp. 81–85). In addition, Dahlstrom, Welsh, and Dahlstrom (1972) discuss in length the concept of artifactuality as it pertains to scales with item overlap.

Table 9.2. Distributions of cases on origence (ORIG) and intellectence (INT) scores in terms of frequencies and percentages with novant designation

Boys

	Low INT	Medium INT	High INT	
High ORIG	(1) 61 11.64%	(1–2) 37 7.06%	(2) 57 10.88%	155 29.58%
Medium ORIG	(1–3) 58 11.07%	(0) 75 14.31%	(2–4) 59 11.26%	192 36.64%
Low ORIG	(3) 59 11.26%	(3–4) 68 12.98%	(4) 50 9.54%	177 33.78%
	178 33.97%	180 34.35%	166 31.68%	524 100.00%

$r = .08$

Girls

	Low INT	Medium INT	High INT	
High ORIG	(1) 68 11.02%	(1–2) 63 10.21%	(2) 67 10.86%	198 32.09%
Medium ORIG	(1–3) 69 11.19%	(0) 73 11.83%	(2–4) 65 10.53%	207 33.55%
Low ORIG	(3) 74 11.99%	(3–4) 85 13.78%	(4) 53 8.59%	212 34.36%
	211 34.20%	221 35.82%	185 29.98%	617 100.00%

$r = .08$

social shortcomings. The K scale, "correction," is a more sophisticated and psychometrically complicated measure of the defensiveness inherent in high L scores but has other implications.[5] That is, high K scores may reflect ego strength and prudence as well as defensiveness, while low K scores may indicate psychological fragility and personal vulnerability. The F scale, "infrequency," comprises items very infrequently answered in the scored direction, so a high F score indicates lack of agreement with the normative group and hence implies atypicality in responding. It is often associated with carelessness and nonconformity.

Correlations with the L scale are attenuated because of the skew distribution of scores that the nature of the scale induces and also because the gifted adolescents answered very few items in the "lie" direction. There was a good range of scores on F and K, however, and a meaningful correlational pattern is apparent. That is, F is negatively correlated with the intelligence tests and INT but positively correlated with the art scale and ORIG; the correlational pattern is reversed for K. The implications are that subjects earning lower intelligence scores and falling lower on INT are likely to manifest the carelessness and nonconformity of the F scale and the lack of ego strength reflected by low K scores. Those low on the art scale and ORIG, on the other hand, will seem more careful, cautious, conforming, and circumspect.

The next ten scales, Hs through Si, comprise the "clinical" sector of the MMPI profile, although the masculinity–femininity (Mf) interest scale does not necessarily carry the psychiatric implications of the other scales. A consistent pattern of correlations, stronger for some scales than others, is found in which these scales are negatively correlated with intelligence and INT but positively correlated with the art scale and ORIG. This pattern is consistent with the interpretation offered above for the F and K scales, and may seem to imply a greater likelihood of psychopathology for those low on intellectence and high on origence. It is possible, however, to interpret scores on the clinical scales in an obverse manner. That is, instead of an admission of psychiatric symptomatology, the elevated scores may reflect greater insight, personal sensitivity, and introspective candor. This view would be consistent with reports of elevated profiles in creative adults (MacKinnon 1961) and offers a positive explanation of the correlational pattern.

The last two scales, A and R, were especially developed to measure two basic dimensions of the MMPI discovered in factor-analytic studies (Welsh 1956, 1965) and are often employed as marker variables in statistical analyses of this test. The first factor, "anxiety" (A), reflects the

---

[5]It should be noted that the correlational analysis of the clinical scales in the present research was based on raw scores alone without the so-called K correction.

Table 9.3. Correlations of MMPI scales with intelligence tests (CMT, D-48), intellectence (INT), art scale (RA), and origence (ORIG)[a]

MMPI scales	Boys					Girls				
	$N=527$ CMT	$N=350$ D-48	$N=524$ INT	$N=526$ RA	$N=524$ ORIG	$N=622$ CMT	$N=419$ D-48	$N=616$ INT	$N=621$ RA	$N=616$ ORIG
L: "lie"	(.02)	(-.02)	.16	(-.03)	-.20	-.08	(-.07)	(.02)	(-.04)	-.30
F: "infrequency"	-.11	-.23	-.15	.13	.51	-.12	-.17	-.11	.12	.46
K: "correction"	.09	.11	.16	-.13	-.42	(.04)	(.08)	.17	-.11	-.42
Hs: hypochondriasis	-.09	-.19	-.18	(.06)	.32	-.15	-.11	-.21	(.03)	.30
D: depression	(.05)	-.11	.10	(.06)	.32	(-.02)	(-.07)	(-.02)	(-.01)	.23
Hy: hysteria	(.06)	(-.01)	(.03)	(.04)	.13	(-.05)	(.00)	(-.08)	(-.01)	.13
Pd: psychopathic deviate	-.13	-.19	-.17	.14	.51	-.18	-.19	-.23	.08	.47
Mf: masculinity–femininity	.17	(.05)	.14	.15	.39	.12	(.06)	(.04)	(-.04)	(.02)
Pa: paranoia	(-.01)	(-.07)	(-.04)	.10	.31	.10	(.00)	(.03)	(.06)	.28
Pt: psychasthenia	-.13	-.20	-.25	.13	.46	(-.06)	(-.08)	-.23	(.03)	.41
Sc: schizophrenia	-.10	-.23	-.20	.13	.54	-.09	-.18	-.23	.08	.51
Ma: hypomania	-.20	-.22	-.33	.10	.47	-.19	-.13	-.31	.16	.48
Si: social introversion	.15	(-.02)	.21	(.03)	.15	.16	(.02)	.17	(-.04)	.13
A: "anxiety"	-.13	-.17	-.24	.13	.43	(-.05)	(-.09)	-.22	(.03)	.40
R: "repression"	.21	(.07)	.36	(-.01)	-.13	.08	(-.01)	.22	(-.03)	-.11

[a](r) signifies correlation not significantly different from zero at the .05 level of confidence.

kind of general maladjustment found in the clinical scales and is positively correlated with them in normal as well as psychiatric populations. The second factor, "repression" (R), has been interpreted as an index of inhibition or control and is generally found to be statistically independent of the first factor.

For the present subjects A is negatively correlated with intelligence and INT but is positively correlated with ORIG, while R shows a reversed pattern of relationship. Thus, the MMPI factor scales are consistent with the interpretation offered above for the validity and clinical scales. It seems likely that subjects high on R and low on A may have the kind of control needed for efficient performance on intellectual tasks but may not have the freedom and lack of inhibition required for spontaneous and original performance in situations that are less conventional.

Assessment of Values

The Allport–Vernon–Lindzey Study of Values (AVL) (Allport, Vernon, and Lindzey 1970) was administered to the Governor's School students in two of the three sessions when research data were collected. Correlations of the six AVL values with the five research variables are given in table 9.4.

Of particular interest are the AVL theoretical (T) and aesthetic (A) scales, since their relationship to creativity in adults has been demonstrated (MacKinnon 1962). Although the correlational patterns are not completely consistent, the general trend is for T values to be positively correlated with intelligence and intellectence and negatively correlated with the art scale and origence. Aesthetic values are positively correlated with intellectence, the art scale, and origence, but with somewhat mixed results for the intelligence tests. A pattern of generally negative correlation is found for economic (E), social (S), and religious (R) values, and a mixed pattern of relatively low correlations for political (P) values.

One of the implications of the origence/intellectence personality model is that characteristics at the high ends of both dimensions are related to creativity. Evidence has been adduced that this is true for creative architects and possibly for scientists (Welsh 1975, chap. 8). To the extent that gifted adolescents from the Governor's School with the greatest potential for creative achievement are found to be high on both of these dimensions, it might be expected that they would share the values found in creative adults and should score high on both T and A values. To test this hypothesis an analysis was made of subjects in novant 2, high ORIG/high INT. The results are shown in table 9.5. It is clear that most of the subjects had peak scores on the expected scales, with boys about

Table 9.4. Correlation of AVL values with intelligence tests (CMT, D-48), intellectence (INT), art scale (RA), and origence (ORIG)[a]

	Boys					Girls				
AVL values	$N=349$ CMT	$N=170$ D-48	$N=344$ INT	$N=349$ RA	$N=344$ ORIG	$N=406$ CMT	$N=193$ D-48	$N=391$ INT	$N=402$ RA	$N=391$ ORIG
Theoretical	.23	(.13)	.34	-.15	-.13	.14	.14	.29	(.03)	-.10
Economic	-.18	(.00)	-.24	-.12	-.19	-.17	(-.05)	-.20	(-.07)	-.12
Aesthetic	(.05)	(-.02)	.10	.31	.54	.19	(-.04)	.25	.18	.43
Social	(-.07)	(-.12)	-.09	(.01)	(-.02)	-.11	(-.04)	-.18	-.12	-.16
Political	.10	(.09)	.13	(-.06)	(-.08)	(-.02)	(-.03)	(.01)	.14	.21
Religious	-.14	(-.09)	-.25	(-.08)	-.26	(-.07)	(.02)	-.20	-.14	-.25

[a] (r) signifies correlation not significantly different from zero at the .05 level of confidence.

Table 9.5. Peak scores on AVL value scales for subjects in novant 2, high origence/high intellectence

AVL scales	Boys	Girls	Total	Percentage
Theoretical	15	10	25	30.9
Economic	1	0	1	1.2
Aesthetic	16	22[a]	38	46.9
Social	1	2	3	3.7
Political	1	3	4	4.9
Religious	4	6[a]	10	12.3
Total	38	43	81	99.9

[a]Two girls tied on A and R counted as .5 for each scale.

equally divided between the two but with girls showing twice as many peaks on aesthetic as on theoretical.

A count was also made of the second highest value score. For boys, of the four cases with peaks on R, two were next highest on A and one on T. For girls aesthetic was next highest for one of the two cases with a peak on S, for two of the three P peaks, and for three of the R peaks. Adding these second-highest cases to those with peak scores gives a total of thirty-four boys and thirty-eight girls who have either T or A values of the first or second highest value in the AVL profile. That is, seventy-two out of eighty-one subjects high on origence and intellectence—88.9 percent —were high on theoretical or aesthetic values.

Finally, a count of those high on both values was made. There were three boys and four girls with theoretical first and aesthetic second, and six boys and four girls had A/T patterns. Thus, while these patterns may be infrequent in gifted adolescents groups,[6] 21.0 percent of the Governor's School subjects who were high on origence and intellectence were also high on both theoretical and aesthetic values. By contrast, only 3.4 percent of eighty-seven students low on both dimensions showed this value pattern, with one additional subject having a tie score on the economic value.

Assessment of Vocational Interests

Vocational interests of gifted students at the Governor's School were studied by using scores from the Strong Vocational Interest Blank.[7] A

[6]See Fox and Denham (1974), Fox (1976), George and Denham (1976), and Keating (1976a).

[7]Data are based on scales from the earlier 400-item form of the test (Strong 1959) since the current revised Strong–Campbell Interest Inventory form was not generally available during the Governor's School testing program.

brief summary of dimensional relationships will be given here, since an extended report has been previously made giving correlations of both intelligence tests with the fifty-five SVIB scales (Welsh 1971). Correlations of these vocational scales with origence and intellectence have also been presented in detail (Welsh 1975, chap. 7).

Intelligence is positively related to professional and scientific interests such as those represented by SVIB scales for physician, psychologist, mathematician, physicist, and chemist. A negative relation to intelligence is indicated for business and sales occupations, which include mortician, pharmacist, banker, and sales manager. The pattern of correlation for the personality dimension of intellectence is quite similar.

Origence is positively related to occupations that stress individual initiative and allow relative freedom for the practitioner; these include SVIB scales for advertising man, author–journalist, artist, lawyer, musician, real estate salesman, and architect. Negative correlations are found for occupational scales related to business detail and those emphasizing routine application of rules and regulations, such as accountant, math-science teacher, production manager, office worker, banker, and pharmacist.

Comparison with Holland's Vocational Theory

John L. Holland has developed a theory which relates vocational choice to personality characteristics in terms of a typology based on six basic categories of occupations: enterprising, social, artistic, conventional, realistic, and investigative (Holland 1966). The present writer has carried out a rational and logical analysis of Holland's sixfold typology in comparison with the implications of the personality dimensions of origence and intellectence (Welsh 1975, pp. 187–91). In brief, the analysis suggests that Holland's enterprising category has many characteristics of the high origent/low intellectent type, the artistic seems similar to the high origent/high intellectent type, the conventional to the low origent/low intellectent type, and the investigative to the low origent/high intellectent type. The two remaining categories do not seem to differ on intellectence and might lie in the middle of this dimension; on origence, however, social and realistic seem to fall at opposite ends of the dimension with the former lying relatively high and the latter relatively low.

A test of the hypothetical relationship was made using SVIB scores of the present subjects. One scale typical of Holland's classification was selected for each of the six categories, and an analysis of variance was conducted for the scale scores of Governor's School subjects in terms of

Table 9.6. Mean scores on representative Strong Vocational Interest Blank scales for Governor's School subjects grouped by scores on origence and intellectence novants[a]

	Enterprising			Social			Artistic		
	Real Estate Salesman			Social Worker			Artist		
Boys	*43.1*	39.8	32.8	32.2	*36.6*	35.4	33.0	38.0	*43.5*
	39.3	36.8	32.1	30.9	30.7	32.3	27.1	29.2	36.8
	37.4	34.1	31.1	27.9	28.8	25.7	23.0	26.9	29.7
Girls	*43.1*	42.1	37.4	37.9	36.3	39.5	36.6	41.2	*45.3*
	41.9	38.4	35.7	36.6	37.2	39.7	35.0	34.7	39.0
	39.7	34.9	32.1	38.0	37.0	33.3	30.4	33.9	37.9

	Conventional			Realistic			Investigative		
	Banker			Vocational Agriculture Teacher			Physicist		
Boys	29.0	22.4	16.9	16.0	15.2	12.2	11.7	17.6	30.4
	28.6	25.3	19.3	19.2	18.4	14.8	16.9	22.4	33.3
	31.1	27.1	24.4	25.0	21.8	20.5	20.1	27.1	*34.2*
Girls	29.3	24.2	18.6	14.9	9.6	8.4	9.3	12.7	21.2
	31.3	27.1	21.3	14.9	15.7	11.9	10.8	15.3	21.9
	35.0	28.4	25.0	15.9	*16.7*	15.7	11.8	20.6	*28.0*

[a]

(1)	(1–2)	(2)
High origence	High origence	High origence
Low intellectence	Medium intellectence	High intellectence
(1–3)	(0)	(2–4)
Medium origence	Medium origence	Medium origence
Low intellectence	Medium intellectence	High intellectence
(3)	(3–4)	(4)
Low origence	Low origence	Low origence
Low intellectence	Medium intellectence	High intellectence

the novant classification discussed above.[8] A summary of the findings is given in table 9.6. It is clear that there is remarkable agreement between the predicted relationships for the four extreme origence/intellectence types and the corresponding Holland categories. For the enterprising category, represented by the SVIB real estate salesman scale, statistically significantly higher means were obtained for both boys and girls in the high origent/low intellectent novant. Statistical significance was also obtained for artistic and the artist scale, with the highest means for the high origent/high intellectent novant, for conventional and the banker scale with highest means for the low origent/low intellectent novant, and

[8]Complete tables giving the statistics and a summary of the analysis of variance are available from the present writer.

for investigative and the physicist scale with highest means for the low origent/high intellectent novant.

Predictions for the remaining Holland categories were only partially confirmed. For boys, as expected, the social worker scale representing the social category achieved significance for origence, with intellectence being unrelated and the highest mean appearing for the novant high on origence and medium on intellectence. For girls, however, both dimensions were nonsignificant, although there is a trend for an increase along origence. A significant interaction term resulted, and it may be noted in table 9.6 that the highest and lowest means appear for the adjacent novants of medium origence/high intellectence and low origence/high intellectence.

For the realistic category, the vocational agriculture teacher scale showed a significant interaction term for the girls, but the highest mean fell in the predicted novant, low origence/medium intellectence. For boys the scale was negatively related to origence, as predicted, but was also negatively related to intellectence rather than being independent. Thus, the highest mean occurs for low origence/low intellectence.

In sum, results from the previous correlational studies and the present analysis of variance suggest that gifted adolescents scoring lower on intelligence tests and intellectence may have vocational interests typical of Holland's enterprising and conventional categories, such as sales, business, and service occupations. Those scoring higher on intelligence and intellectence may be more interested in artistic and investigative vocations represented by artistic, humanistic, and scientific occupations and professions.[9]

Implications for creativity may be inferred from the conjoint relationship of origence and intellectence as discussed above. That is, the present students who fall into novant 2, high origence/high intellectence, resemble creative adults in their personality characteristics. Further evidence for this inferred relationship may be adduced by comparing correlations of SVIB scales with rated creativity in architects (Hall and MacKinnon 1969). If the correlations reported by these workers for the six scales utilized above in testing Holland's theory are arranged in the same configuration followed in table 9.6, the sequence of correlations is:

Real Estate Salesman	Social Worker	Artist
−.31	.17	.59
Banker	Vocational Agriculture Teacher	Physicist
−.66	−.28	.37

Thus, the relationship of SVIB scale scores to rated creativity for the architects shifts from negative to postive for the scales postulated to be

---

[9]An extended discussion of Holland's theory and its application in studies of mathematically precocious youths may be found in Stanley, Keating, and Fox (1974).

higher on origence and intellectence and shows the highest negative value for banker and the highest postive for artist. This correlational pattern obtained with adults is congruent with the findings of the present research with gifted adolescents, and may be interpreted as further evidence for the importance of both origence and intellectence for creative achievement.

EVALUATION BY TEACHERS

Students at the Governor's School did not receive formal grades in their classes, and no academic credits were granted. For purposes of research, however, it was necessary to have some measure of academic performance, so the cooperation of teachers was obtained in making systematic evaluations. At the close of each summer session every teacher was asked to rank each student in his or her class from highest to lowest on five categories of behavior. These traits as defined for the teachers are:

Intellectual competence. Effective utilization of the capacity to think, to reason, to comprehend, and to know.
Originality. Sensitivity, flexibility, openness, ability to set aside established conventions when appropriate, and/or evolve novel solutions.
Sustained endeavor. The strength of the need to do serious work as shown by persistent effort.
Progress. Gain in proficiency as determined by your (the teacher's) objectives.
Likeability. Your own personal subjective reaction to the student.

Since the size of classes ranged from eleven to twenty-seven, there were unequal numbers of ranks for them. To make the ranks comparable so that they could be collated for analysis, each rank within a class was converted to a normalized standard score with a mean of 50 and a standard deviation of 10. Although the classes contained both boys and girls, separate distributions were not made; combined distributions were used so that an absolute comparison between the sexes could be made on each of the five traits. As it turned out, boys were consistently ranked higher. Correlations of these traits with other variables and novant analyses, however, were conducted separately for each sex so that comparisons within, as well as between, sexes could be made.

Correlations of these traits with the variables of the present report are shown in table 9.7. Intelligence and intellectence are systematically and significantly correlated with all five teacher rankings for the boys in a hierarchal pattern. That is, the two traits most closely related to aptitude and ability, intellectual competence (IC) and originality (OR), show the highest degree of correlation with the research variables; the motivational traits of sustained endeavor (SE) and progress (PR) are next in magnitude; correlations with likeability (LK) are the lowest in value. Girls also

Table 9.7. Correlation of teacher ratings with intelligence tests (CMT, D-48), intellectence (INT), art scale (RA), and origence (ORIG)[a]

| | Boys | | | | | Girls | | | | |
Teacher ratings	$N=480$ CMT	$N=305$ D-48	$N=448$ INT	$N=451$ RA	$N=448$ ORIG	$N=564$ CMT	$N=345$ D-48	$N=523$ INT	$N=529$ RA	$N=523$ ORIG
IC: intellectual competence	.41	.23	.35	(−.01)	.14	.27	.14	.25	(.01)	(.04)
OR: originality	.33	.30	.33	(.01)	.13	.23	.11	.25	(.02)	(.05)
SE: capacity for sustained endeavor	.26	.17	.23	(−.06)	(−.01)	.17	(.10)	.17	(−.01)	(−.07)
PR: progress made	.24	.16	.18	(−.05)	(.03)	.12	(.09)	.14	(−.03)	(−.07)
LK: likeability	.16	.12	.11	(−.03)	(.00)	(.08)	(.06)	.15	(−.02)	(−.07)

[a] (r) signifies correlation not significantly different from zero at the .05 level of confidence.

show this ordered pattern, although the absolute magnitude of correlations are lower in every case except that for LK and INT.

Teacher rankings are not significantly correlated with the art scale or with origence except in two instances for boys, IC and OR with ORIG. Evidently, the teachers did not recognize or react to behaviors in their students related to this dimension of personality. Since evidence has already accrued which reflects the role of origence in creativity, the failure of any systematic correlation here has important implications that will be discussed below.

Pattern of Teacher Rankings

In order to look at teacher rankings in a combined format rather than separately as was done in the correlational analysis, the novant schema was employed. Mean scores for each of the five traits were calculated for the novants separately for each sex. These means are presented in graphic form as a five-point profile for each novant. Figure 9.1 shows the mean ranks of the extreme-corner novants, and figure 9.2 gives the profiles of the medium novants.

Particularly striking in figure 9.1 is the superiority in rankings for novant 2, high origence/high intellectence, for the boys. It is also clear

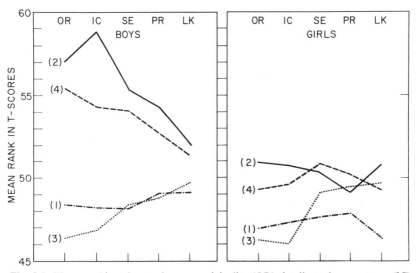

Fig. 9.1. Mean rankings by teachers on originality (OR), intellectual competence (IC), sustained endeavor (SE), progress (PR), and likeability (LK) for Governor's School students in extreme origence/intellectence novants

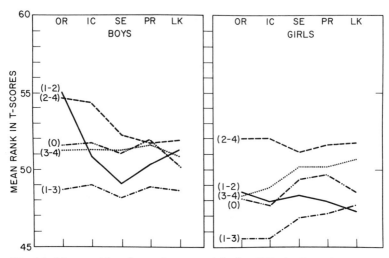

Fig. 9.2. Mean rankings by teachers on originality (OR), intellectual competence (IC), sustained endeavor (SE), progress (PR), and likeability (LK) for Governor's School students in medium origence/intellectence novants

that the first two traits, OR and IC, show wider separations between novants than SE and PR, while the profiles converge on LK. This is consistent with the ordering disclosed in the correlational analysis discussed above. Both of the novants for boys high on intellectence, 2 and 4, are similar in profile pattern and quite different from the novants low on this dimension, 1 and 3.

Profiles for the girls do not manifest the same pattern of relationships, although there is a similar tendency for greater differentiation on OR and IC between the high and low intellectence novants. It may also be seen that novant 1, high origence/low intellectence, does not show convergence on LK but is as consistently low on this trait as on the other four. Apparently, teachers viewed girls in this novant in a generally unfavorable way.

The medium novants in figure 9.2 do not exhibit such clearcut patterns for the boys, although there are some interesting features to be found. Boys in the high origent/medium intellectent novant, 1-2, are notably lower on IC and SE than on OR, which is relatively high. This pattern implies that although teachers view these students as capable of original work, they may not have the necessary ability and strength of motivation for successful achievement. Novant 1-3 is lower on all of the traits than the other medium novants but is quite similar to the other low intellectent novants, 1 and 3, seen in figure 9.1.

For girls, the most obvious pattern is the relatively flat profile of the medium origent/high intellectent novant, 2-4, showing consistently higher rankings on all five traits. These means are higher than those of the extreme novants shown in figure 9.1 and implies a favorable view by teachers.

Finally, it may be pointed out that boys are ranked higher than girls for all traits in eight of the nine novants. Only in novant 3 for SE and PR are the girls higher than their counterparts in origence/intellectence configuration. Thus in forty-three of forty-five mean rankings boys exceed girls; this event certainly cannot be considered fortuitous from a statistical viewpoint. Similarly, the superiority of novant 2 for the boys and novant 2-4 for the girls in all five traits seems remarkable. It may be concluded, then, that the high origent/high intellectent boys and the medium origent/high intellectent girls are ranked highest by their teachers, but that there is a sex difference in these rankings in favor of the boys.[10]

TEACHER NOMINATIONS IN CREATIVITY STUDIES

A common method of identifying creative or potentially creative subjects of school age is to ask teachers to nominate subjects either on the basis of their general knowledge of the student or in terms of some specified characteristics ostensibly related to creative performance. While this is a feasible and a practical procedure in many situations, results are often equivocal, since there is no single criterion variable of "creativity" agreed upon by workers in this area against which the judgments of different nominators can be compared and contrasted. The use of objective personality tests in studying creative subjects has a primary advantage, since subjective and personal biases that may affect nominations or ratings of individual teachers (or other judges) are not inherent in a standard psychometric instrument. This kind of objective advantage is claimed for the personality dimensions of origence and intellectence, which have the added convenience that scales for these dimensions can be scored on widely used instruments such as the MMPI, ACL, and SVIB.[11]

It was pointed out above in discussing teacher ratings at the Governor's School that correlations with conventional kinds of intelligence tests and with intellectence showed systematic relationships as expected. With origence, however, most of the correlations were essentially zero. To the

---

[10]Initially, analyses were made separately controlling the sex of the teacher and the sex of the rated student. There was no apparent bias in rankings related to these factors.

[11]Counterpart origence/intellectence scales for the California Psychological Inventory (CPI) are now available. Dimensional scales for the WFPT to measure directly origence and intellectence have also been developed. All of these scales may be obtained from the present writer. For use of the CPI with mathematically precocious youths see Weiss, Haier, and Keating (1974) and Haier and Denham (1976).

extent that this dimension represents an important personality characteristic in creativity, the present findings suggest that teachers may not be incorporating into their ratings the personality traits associated with origence and to some extent may overlook potentially creative subjects or estimate inexactly their creativity. Further research on this problem is needed, of course, but it is recommended that objective personality tests be used to supplement teacher judgments in research designs requiring nominations, rankings, or ratings in studies of creativity.

CONCLUSIONS

Gifted adolescents may be expected to score higher than unselected groups of adolescents on conventional intelligence tests such as the verbal Concept Mastery Test and the nonverbal D-48. In addition, they may be expected to fall relatively higher on a theoretical dimension of personality, intellectence. The more intellectent subjects in the gifted group may appear better adjusted in terms of clinical scales on the MMPI, but in terms of validity and factor scales seem to manifest a higher degree of control and efficiency. On the AVL, intelligence and intellectence seem to be associated primarily with theoretical values, although there is some relation to aesthetic values. Vocational interests tend toward occupations and professions of a scientific, humanistic, or artistic nature rather than those of commerce and business. Teachers generally gave more favorable ratings to high intellectent students, especially when rating traits related to ability and motivation.

Creativity is conceptualized in terms of a conjoint elevation on another theoretical personality dimension, origence, in addition to intellectence. Gifted adolescents falling high on both dimensions are seen as similar in many characteristics to adults of demonstrated creativity. These gifted subjects may seem to be less well adjusted in terms of MMPI clinical scales, but this was interpreted as an index of candor and insight rather than maladjustment per se because their responses are more unusual and nonconforming. On the AVL a pattern of aesthetic/theoretical or theoretical/aesthetic values was found for many of these subjects. Vocational interests are most like those of Holland's artistic category and least like those of his conventional category. A sex difference was found in teacher ratings, with boys consistently being ranked higher than girls. Boys with a high origent/high intellectent pattern were highest in ratings, and those in the opposite low origent/low intellectent position were rated lowest by teachers. For girls, however, the medium origent/high intellectent pattern was associated with higher ratings by teachers and the high origent/low intellectent pattern with lower ratings by them.

REFERENCES

Adair, F. L. 1969. An analysis of intelligence test scores and WFPT scales for two groups of subjects. Unpublished study, Franklin and Marshall College, Lancaster, Pa.

Allport, G. W., Vernon, P. E., and Lindzey, G. 1970. *Manual for the study of values: A scale for measuring the dominant interests in personality.* Boston: Houghton Mifflin.

Barron, F. 1955. The disposition toward originality. *Journal of Abnormal and Social Psychology* 51: 478–85.

––––––. 1961. Creative vision and expression in writing and painting. In D. W. MacKinnon (ed.), *The creative person.* Berkeley, Calif.: University of California Extension, pp. 1–19.

––––––, and Welsh, G. S. 1952. Artistic perception as a possible factor in personality style: Its measurement by a figure preference test. *Journal of Psychology* 33: 199–203.

Bayley, N., and Oden, M. H. 1955. The maintenance of intellectual ability in gifted adults. *Journal of Gerontology* 10: 91–107.

Black, J. D. 1963. *The D-48 Test preliminary manual.* Palo Alto, Calif.: Consulting Psychologists Press.

Boyd, M. E., and Ward, G. 1966. A factor analysis of the D-48. *Proceedings of the West Virginia Academy of Science* 38: 201–04.

Dahlstrom, W. G., Welsh, G. S., and Dahlstrom, L. E. 1972. *An MMPI handbook: Clinical interpretation,* vol. I. Minneapolis, Minn.: University of Minnesota Press.

––––––. 1975. *An MMPI handbook: Research applications,* vol. II. Minneapolis, Minn.: University of Minnesota Press.

Fox, L. H. 1976. The values of gifted youth. In D. P. Keating (ed.), *Intellectual talent: Research and development.* Baltimore, Md.: The Johns Hopkins University Press, pp. 273–84.

––––––, and Denham, S. A. 1974. Values and career interests of mathematically and scientifically precocious youth. In J. C. Stanley, D. P. Keating, and L. H. Fox (eds.), *Mathematical talent: Discovery, description, and development.* Baltimore, Md.: The Johns Hopkins University Press, pp. 140–75.

George, W. C., and Denham, S. A. 1976. Curriculum experimentation for the mathematically talented. In D. P. Keating (ed.), *Intellectual talent: Research and development.* Baltimore, Md.: The Johns Hopkins University Press, pp. 103–31.

Getzels, J. W., and Jackson, P. W. 1962. *Creativity and intelligence.* New York: Wiley.

Gough, H. G. 1961. Techniques for identifying the creative research scientist. In D. W. MacKinnon (ed.), *The creative person.* Berkeley, Calif.: University of California Extension, pp. 1–27.

––––––, and Heilbrun, A. B. 1965. *The Adjective Check List manual.* Palo Alto, Calif.: Consulting Psychologists Press.

Haier, R. J., and Denham, S. A. 1976. A summary profile of the nonintellectual correlates of mathematical precocity in boys and girls. In D. P. Keating (ed.),

Intellectual talent: Research and development. Baltimore, Md.: The Johns Hopkins University Press, pp. 225–41.

Hall, W. B., and MacKinnon, D. W. 1969. Personality inventory correlates of creativity among architects. *Journal of Applied Psychology.* 53: 322–26.

Helson, R. 1961. Creativity, sex, and mathematics. In D. W. MacKinnon (ed.), *The creative person.* Berkeley, Calif.: University of California Extension, pp. 1–12.

Holland, J. L. 1966. *The psychology of vocational choice: A theory of personality types and model environments.* Waltham, Mass.: Blaisdell.

Horn, J. L., and Bramble, W. J. 1967. Second-order ability structure revealed in rights and wrongs scores. *Journal of Educational Psychology* 58: 115–22.

Keating, D. P. 1976a. Creative potential of mathematically precocious boys. In D. P. Keating (ed.), *Intellectual talent: Research and development.* Baltimore, Md.: The Johns Hopkins University Press, pp. 262–72.

———. (ed.). 1976b. *Intellectual talent: Research and development.* Baltimore, Md.: The Johns Hopkins University Press.

Lewis, H. M. 1969. *Open windows onto the future: Theory of the Governor's School of North Carolina.* Winston-Salem, N.C.: Governor's School (Drawer H, Salem Station).

MacKinnon, D. W. 1961. Creativity in architects. In D. W. MacKinnon (ed.), *The creative person.* Berkeley, Calif.: University of California Extension.

———. 1962. The nature and nurture of creative talent. *American Psychologist* 17: 484–95.

Raychaudhuri, M. 1966. *Studies in artistic creativity: Personality structure of the musician.* Calcutta: Rabindra Bharati University.

Rosen, J. C. 1955. The Barron–Welsh Art Scale as a predictor of originality and level of ability among artists. *Journal of Applied Psychology* 39: 366–67

Saunders, M. M. 1968. *A cross-validation of the Welsh origence–intellectence keys for the Strong Vocational Interest Blank.* Greensboro, N.C.: Creativity Research Institute of the Richardson Foundation.

Stanley, J. C., Keating, D. P., and Fox, L. H. (eds.), 1974. *Mathematical talent: Discovery, description, and development.* Baltimore, Md.: The Johns Hopkins University Press.

Strong, Jr., E. K. 1959. *Manual for the Strong Vocational Interest Blanks for Men and Women—Revised Blanks (Forms M and W).* Palo Alto, Calif.: Consulting Psychologists Press.

Terman, L. M. 1954. The discovery and encouragement of exceptional talent. *American Psychologist* 9: 221–30.

———. 1956. *The Concept Mastery Test manual—Form T.* New York: Psychological Corporation.

Weiss, D. S., Haier, R. J., and Keating, D. P. 1974. Personality characteristics of mathematically precocious youth. In J. C. Stanley, D. P. Keating, and L. H. Fox (eds.), *Mathematical talent: Discovery, description, and development.* Baltimore, Md.: The Johns Hopkins University Press, pp. 126–39.

Welsh, G. S. 1956. Factor dimensions A and R. In G. S. Welsh and W. G. Dahlstrom (eds.), *Basic readings on the MMPI in psychology and medicine.* Minneapolis, Minn.: University of Minnesota Press.

————. 1959. *The Welsh Figure Preference Test, preliminary manual.* Palo Alto, Calif.: Consulting Psychologists Press.

————. 1965. MMPI profiles and factor scales A and R. *Journal of Clinical Psychology* 21: 43–47.

————. 1966. Comparison of D-48, Terman CMT, and Art Scale scores of gifted adolescents. *Journal of Consulting Psychology* 30: 88.

————. 1967. Verbal interests and intelligence: Comparison of Strong VIB, Terman CMT, and D-48 scores of gifted adolescents. *Educational and Psychological Measurement* 27: 349–52.

————. 1969. *Gifted adolescents: A handbook of test results.* Greensboro, N.C.: Prediction Press (distributed by Consulting Psychologists Press, Palo Alto, Calif.).

————. 1971. Vocational interests and intelligence in gifted adolescents. *Educational and Psychological Measurement* 31: 155–64.

————. 1975. *Creativity and intelligence: A personality approach.* Chapel Hill, N.C.: Institute for Research in Social Science.

IV
GENERAL DISCUSSION
FOLLOWING THE
SYMPOSIUM

10
GENERAL DISCUSSION IMMEDIATELY AFTER THE TERMAN MEMORIAL SYMPOSIUM

Edited by J. W. Getzels

This discussion was conducted on Friday afternoon, November 7, 1975, from about 2:00 P.M. until 5:00 P.M., immediately following the presentation of the papers at the symposium. It was chaired by Professor Getzels and participated in actively by the thirty-one persons whose remarks appear in the following edited transcript. Another twenty or so persons listened but did not make comments. Names, affiliations, and addresses of the discussants are as follows:

Dr. Robert S. Albert, Professor of Psychology, Pitzer College, 1050 N. Mills Avenue, Claremont, California 91711.

Dr. Anne Anastasi, Professor of Psychology, Fordham University, Bronx, New York 10458.

Ms. Ann H. Barbee, Research Assistant, Terman Study of the Gifted, Stanford University, Stanford, California 94305.

Ms. Jane S. Brockie, Curriculum Specialist, Gifted Program, Pasadena Unified School District, 351 S. Hudson Avenue, Pasadena, California 91109.

Dr. Gwendolyn J. Cooke, Coordinator, Gifted and Talented Programs, Baltimore City Public Schools, 3 E. 25th Street, Baltimore, Maryland 21218.

Dr. James L. Fisher, Consultant, Gifted and Talented, Division of Instruction, Maryland State Department of Education, P.O. Box 8717, Baltimore–Washington International Airport, Baltimore, Maryland 21240.

Dr. Lynn H. Fox, Assistant Professor of Education and Coordinator of the Intellectually Gifted Child Study Group (IGCSG), Evening College and Summer Session, The Johns Hopkins University, Baltimore, Maryland 21218.

Mr. William C. George, Associate Director, Study of Mathematically Precocious Youth (SMPY), The Johns Hopkins University, Baltimore, Maryland 21218.

Dr. J. W. Getzels, R. Wendell Harrison Distinguished Service Professor in the Departments of Education and of Behavioral Sciences, University of Chicago, 5835 Kimbark Avenue, Chicago, Illinois 60637.

Ms. Gina Ginsberg, Executive Director, The Gifted Child Society, Inc., 59 Glen Gray Road, Oakland, New Jersey 07436.

Dr. Richard J. Haier, Laboratory of Psychology and Psychopathology, National Institute of Mental Health, 9000 Rockville Pike, Bethesda, Maryland 20014.

Ms. Elise A. Hancock, Editor, *Johns Hopkins Magazine*, The Johns Hopkins University, Baltimore, Maryland 21218.

Dr. James R. Hobson, retired Coordinator of Pupil Personnel Services, Public Schools of Brookline, Massachusetts, 463 Boylston Street, Newton Centre, Massachusetts 02159.

Dr. Ellen Hocking, Coordinator of Secondary Mathematics, Montgomery County Public Schools, 850 Hungerford Drive, Rockville, Maryland 20850.

Dr. David M. Jackson, Co-Director, National Institute on Gifted and Talented, 11539 Maple Ridge Road, Reston, Virginia 22090.

Dr. Elizabeth I. Kearney, Curriculum Specialist, Gifted Program, Pasadena Unified School District, 351 S. Hudson Avenue, Pasadena, California 91109.

Dr. Albert K. Kurtz, State Consultant and former Professor of Psychology, 300 N. Knowles Avenue, Apt. 418, Winter Park, Florida 32789.

Mr. Leon L. Lerner, Counselor, Roland Park Junior High School, and Director of the B'nai B'rith Career and Counseling Services, 5207 Roland Avenue, Baltimore, Maryland 21210.

Dr. Richard F. McCoart, Professor and Chairperson, Department of Mathematics, Loyola College, 4501 N. Charles Street, Baltimore, Maryland 21210.

Dr. William B. Michael, Professor of Education and Psychology, University of Southern California, Los Angeles, California 90007.

Dr. Ellis B. Page, Professor of Educational Psychology, U-64, University of Connecticut, Storrs, Connecticut 06268.

Ms. Margaret Parker, Executive Director, Kootenay Centre for Gifted Children International, Box 805, Kaslo, British Columbia, Canada.

Dr. Kamla Patel, Institute for Behavior Research, 624 Graduate Studies Research Center, University of Georgia, Athens, Georgia 30602.

Dr. Marshall P. Sanborn, Professor of Education, University of Wisconsin, Madison, Wisconsin 53706.

Dr. Pauline S. Sears, Professor of Education, *Emerita*, Stanford University, Stanford, California 94305.

Dr. Robert R. Sears, Professor of Psychology and Education, *Emeritus*, Stanford University, Stanford, California 94305.

Dr. Julian C. Stanley, Professor of Psychology and Director of the Study of Mathematically Precocious Youth (SMPY), The Johns Hopkins University, Baltimore, Maryland 21218.

Dr. Virgil S. Ward, Professor of Education, University of Virginia, Charlottesville, Virginia 22903.

Dr. George S. Welsh, Professor of Psychology, University of North Carolina, Chapel Hill, North Carolina 27514.

Mr. Joseph R. Wolfson, fast-paced mathematics teacher, Montgomery County Public Schools, 850 Hungerford Drive, Rockville, Maryland 20850.

Dr. Dean A. Worcester, Professor of Educational Psychology, *Emeritus*, University of Nebraska, 1050 Arapahoe, Boulder, Colorado 80302.

DISCUSSION

GETZELS: There are a number of ways of proceeding with the free discussion. One way is to keep in mind several major topics that should be covered. This does not mean that we need to proceed in a rigid topical way; rather, here are four topics that I hope would be covered.

First, some rather more general remarks regarding the papers themselves—remarks that did not lend themselves to expression in the brief question–answer periods in the paper-reading sessions themselves.

Second is the kind of pertinent research being done either by those present here but who were not speakers or by others about whom we should know. That is, reports of studies which are relevant to what was said so that we have information beyond the information given at the symposium itself.

Third, along with that, additional practices. What is being done elsewhere in schools, classrooms, experimental programs, and such?

And fourth, suppose that money were to become available from foundations or government for work with the gifted, what should be done? What are the priorities? And with that, what should *not* be done?

ANASTASI: I had a few associations to Lynn Fox's paper, especially with regard to your reference to global versus analytical approaches in connection with sex differences. At another point you talked about the preference for social classroom learning versus solitary learning. I am reminded in that connection of the distinction between what Jerry Kagan calls "reflective" and "impulsive" cognitive styles. Quite apart from sex differences, is there any relation between an individual's preference for solitary versus social learning and his/her performance in mathematics? I would like to get your reaction to this idea. Isn't it the case that mathematics, probably more than any other subject, requires the kind of cognitive style characterized by highly focused and sustained attention? This certainly corresponds to an analytic rather than a global style and implies a preference for solitary rather than social learning. Do you have any information, from the literature or from your own research, that would support the hypothesis that this kind of style is particularly required in mathematics?

FOX: I personally think that the sex per se is not as important as some of the authorities claim. There is no research evidence with which I am familiar that has clearly defined it. But I think that what you are suggesting is an entirely different approach to determine this. We do find boys who have some of these social interests, who don't seem to be as analytic, who show some of the same reactions as girls, not wanting to be in special classes, not wanting to go to college early—things like this that don't show the high interest in math, even though they have the aptitude. Do you know of something more specific?

ANASTASI: No. I was thinking if you didn't know of such a study that it might be worth following up. You may want to look into these cognitive styles as they relate particularly to mathematics.

FOX: I was trying to think in the Helson studies of the female mathematician, if she actually said anything about cognitive style per se.

WELSH: Yes, she did. She talked about the patriarchal and matriarchal unconsciousness in the Jungian sense, general personality characteristics that she applied to the work of the mathematicians, and showed differences between the males and the females in this regard. I can't remember all the details. The patriarchal I think is a more incisive, analytic way of dealing with the problems, whereas the matriarchal is a more flexible, adaptable, somewhat more open kind of style. So I don't know whether this fits in exactly with what you were thinking in terms of cognitive style. I think that she is speaking here more in terms of personality characteristics.

ALBERT: I want to follow up on that. It seems to me that for a long time we have regretted that no one ever followed up Leta S. Hollingworth's brilliant youths, but I think that in a way this project [SMPY] is the follow-up to that and much more. I wonder if with this group we could make some distinction between highly competent people and people who might be potentially creative. One of the things that struck me is that these boys and girls, really adolescents, have a lot of the characteristics that you find in describing competent people. They don't, as far as we can tell, have many of the characteristics that would result in creativity later on. It came to my mind, along the same line, that you might want to find out something about convergence and divergence.

Something that struck me in the literature about people who are really fine researchers is that they tend to either have both styles in very high quantity or they pair up with somebody who complements them very well. The Watson and Crick "double-helix" pair is a good example. They really are twins. But they phase in beautifully. I remember that Einstein had a mathematician assigned to him. Sometimes his math gave out. That is true.

GETZELS: I would hope it should happen to me.

ALBERT: It should happen to all of us. The fact is, we have a group of people who really are on the threshold of potential great achievement. I don't know if we know yet if many of them will achieve it, have the kinds of background, personality, and cognitive style that might determine this.

STANLEY: I wanted to ask you a sort of rhetorical question. Suppose that you had Einstein on the panel last night at age thirteen, fourteen, or fifteen. Do you think you would have been impressed by him as a prospective great scientist, as the greatest scientist of the century? That is speculation. According to reports we read, Einstein was not an impressive youth; he was a stubborn person who wouldn't learn languages in the German gymnasium, and therefore couldn't pass the exams for the Technical University of Zurich. In answering questions last night, would he have seemed potentially creative in the sense we are talking about?

ALBERT: On that basis, just looking at them, no, although there were a couple of persons up there who really struck me. One was Eric. He had an edge to him which the others didn't and in a way, while he is far more verbal than perhaps Einstein would have been, Einstein had his quality of doing his own thing and setting his own pace. The only thing, you couldn't do it from the distance last night. But many of these people will have a predominant interest, one that forces them to work rather than one they are good at and will work at. I thought Eric did. I thought the boy at the very end [Joe B.] who was at Cornell was suggesting that not only they like to do their work but also they enjoy their work. That is what was in Einstein very early.

R. SEARS: An obsession.

ALBERT: It is not obsessionally neurotic but a person passionately in love with something.

LERNER: I would like to pull this out of the laboratory into a kind of empirical framework. I guess I am looking at this from about 2,000 character and interest tests I have done in the last ten years or so working with high school kids, kids interested in math, and so on. I had the good fortune of sitting next to Eric's mother yesterday and talking at length with her. I wonder to what degree all of these cognitive items we are dealing with also involve interpersonal and social–domestic factors, and so on—other factors, which in turn touch on what kids do with all of these items that Dr. Anastasi mentioned.

Take Eric. Maybe because inherently I have been a couselor all my life, his mother immediately started telling me the whole story. What would have happened if Eric's mother were not the kind of vigorously assertive woman she seems to be? She said to her son, "This is what we do. This is what we are going to do," and wasn't cowed by the educators. What would Eric have been? I know Julian places very heavy emphasis upon what parents do with kids, don't you?

STANLEY: We in SMPY place heavy emphasis on what the youth is *eager* to do. That is quite different. Sometimes the student's real desires are difficult to discern. As I was arguing with an overpowering mother this morning before the first session, it is very difficult for her son to find out what he wants to do, because the mother won't even let him talk. I had to shut her up and say, "Let him talk."

I would like to make that clearer. We never are eager to find out what the parents primarily want to do, but instead what the youngster, considering all possibilities, is eager to do.

LERNER: I will set up another hypothesis and that is the child in relation to the parents. What can the child then do? David, one of my protégés, who did not participate in the panel simply because his parents think he is being pushed too hard, should have. So I am suggesting some kind of a relationship factor other than the cognitive style. There is a need for more research. I have seen some Einsteins remain in the womb, so to speak, simply because other factors impinged on the cognitive factors. Others were strong enough to say to their mothers: I will do what I want to do. This is an empirical kind of a problem.

KURTZ: I want to answer Stanley's question. I think I would have been very much impressed by Einstein for the simple reason that I was very much impressed by all those kids.

SANBORN [to Fox]: I had a number of thoughts running through my mind connected with your statements and Anne's. All of our work has been with young people one at a time, and with their parents one at a time. I think we have come to the conclusion that we are not willing to subscribe to very many sweeping generalizations. For example, what is cognitive or what we talk about as that might not be entirely cognitive.

What we found, for example, are things like this: that boys may differ from girls on whether they want to be identified as gifted, and furthermore they differ dramatically, depending on what kind of community they live in. Where they live, what the social context is, all these kinds of things have a lot to do with what we are likely to see them doing, what their performances show, and what kind of style they develop. To me, style is enormously important, but it is not cognitive, strictly.

ANASTASI: I want to follow up on that point and also on something Dr. Stanley said. I used the term "cognitive style" because it is common in the literature. I completely agree that the term may be misleading; I think this response style is probably more than 50 percent noncognitive.

To follow up the question about Einstein, I think one point that we might lose track of—and this fits in with Dr. Sanborn's point about the importance of the individual and his situational context—is that perhaps we would not have been impressed with Einstein as a child. Perhaps the thing that determined whether he eventually became so successful or not was something that happened between the time when he was twelve and the time when he was twenty. In other words, you cannot predict with 100 percent certainty from what you see in the child, because there is going to be an effect of what happens to him in the intervening years; and his final success is a product of all that happens to him. It is not just something that you can predict with 100 percent accuracy when a person is twelve years old.

P. SEARS: I would like to suggest that we have heard that mathematicians often like to be solitary and have few friends. We have also heard that the gifted child needs a warm relationship with people within the school. I will just suggest, because no one can prove me wrong, that Einstein would not have liked, as a boy, a warm relationship.

WARD: As a matter of fact, if I remember correctly from his autobiographical sketches, Einstein indicated just this preference for individual absorption. His phrasing was about like this: "I am a horse for single harness, built neither for tandem nor team work." And, he did *not* want "warm" relationships.

P. SEARS: He did the abstract.

WARD: Yes. I believe his observations indicated exactly what you were suggesting—that despite the extraordinarily warm compassion he felt for all mankind (reminiscent of Erikson's "my kind—mankind"), he did not want warm relationships even with members of his own family. I trust that I am recalling his sentiments faithfully, and if so, both observations are important.

PARKER: I want to speak to the point of something happening between 12 or 15 or so. I am thoroughly convinced, and maybe I will be proved wrong in the course of time, that it is what happens very much earlier to these kids that makes the difference between the survivors and the nonsurvivors. I happen to be a parent of two brilliant children. I can look at them and see the difference between what has happened to our brilliant children versus the learning-disabled child. Maybe I am jumping the gun on this. I think we very seriously need research. Stanley in his papers has told us over and over about kids from the sixth grade onward, but I feel we have to go back. Our knowledge of learning and development is very shaky. We have to go back and do some vigorous, statistically based studies, and get samples, controls, and everything to find out whether or not there can be something very early in life to help us predict. Maybe if this child is helped, he can survive instead of going under, and he may be the one who gets through. I don't feel that we can start with age twelve.

ALBERT: What happened to Einstein between twelve and sixteen is that he had been thinking about relativity and had sort of met a dead-end and then had a tutor—which makes it very relevant to our program—who presented him with books dealing with relativity in the early stage. That was really the breakthrough.

The other thing which happened to him quite early was that his father gave him a compass. After that, he was fascinated by the interdependence of physical laws. This went on in his head to the point where relativity became a concept. He said at one point that he had the concept without the word, and he had the word after he had the tutor. I think there is a lot of relevance to what you are doing with these potentials.

GINSBERG: I want to react rather emotionally, I guess, to the concept of the child being killed in the womb by a pushy parent, and I would like to say two things.

Number one, the parent is the child's first teacher, and therefore has great impact. And number two, all parents love their children first and are pushy second. What we probably need as well as a lot of research is increased parent awareness and training. We need to take the emphasis out of the school and at least keep it in the home for those years when the children are still at home and the school is secondary in their lives. That happens much later.

PAGE: I would like to pick up on the comment made by Gowan when we began, which is related to what we are saying here. He wanted to classify the investigators of the gifted under a category called humanistic psychologists. I wish he were here to defend himself, because I still am not clear on his categories. The definitions seemed circular.

However, I do want to argue against the view that science should not dehumanize. It seems exactly the process of dehumanizing something rather than humanizing it. It is a matter of observing things in a global kind of way and abstracting from that and ultimately, we hope, moving toward not just a verbal abstraction, but a symbolic abstraction of it, and this is what we think of as scientific law.

This seems to be true on two levels. One, in studying creativity itself, it seems to me we are missing the point badly if we mush it up with words like "humanistic." We are closer to the mark if we follow the research talked about and described by Michael and others and look at the personalities of the people. Virgil Ward's comments about Einstein are certainly relevant.

Persons such as Einstein are, so far as science is concerned, rather queer birds, and I think we are missing the point if we don't acknowledge that. I would take exception with the idea that the first thing we notice about the gifted is that they are human beings. I would say that is the last thing that really differentiates them from other people.

It seems to me that the second level at which we must dehumanize is the level of the creative activities. That is to say, if we are interested in science, we need to take this process and look for the mechanism in it, look exactly for the inhuman aspect of it—that is, what goes on inside this gap of what is called incubation or the other "black boxes" which we have talked about, and later we can consider some processes toward that.

SANBORN: I have one reaction. I agree very strongly with the notion that, especially in our attempts to do formative studies, we often lose sight of the individuals about whom we are talking. We deal with abstractions. I nevertheless believe the human quality of the gifted child is enormously important as a major means of understanding gifted children as well as others.

At Wisconsin we have dealt entirely with adolescents. It is interesting to me to notice how often they give us almost textbook descriptions of things that are supposedly going on during adolescence. If you read adolescent psychology textbooks, the delightful thing about the youngsters we have worked with is that they are able to articulate and talk about issues in their lives which are what I would call adolescent issues. Maybe one of the ways that they differ from other children their own age is that they can talk so lucidly about what is going on inside themselves, but I don't think what is going on inside is all that much different from many other people their age and in their situation.

PAGE: I think we can agree that they are human beings. I think we can also agree that what distinguishes them from other human beings is not their humanness but rather strange qualities. I will quote from the Michael quote of the Taylor and Barron summary, and I will just pick out those things which make them seem obviously less than warm.

One, "manipulations involving things rather than people." Two, "a distant or detached attitude in interpersonal relations," and a "preference for intellectually challenging situations rather than socially challenging ones. . . ."

"A liking for method, precision, exactness, a preference for, among other things, isolation in dealing with a fact . . . a dislike of personally toned controversy . . . a control of impulse amounting almost to overcontrol. . . . Relatively little talkativeness, gregariousness, impulsiveness . . . a lack of abstract thinking . . . rejection of group pressures . . . elegance in explanation. . . ."

I submit that none of those are traits which make them just folks.

STANLEY: We had the youth panel in front of us last night and it was interesting. I know a great deal about those youngsters. For some we have a folder two inches thick, and for others at least an inch thick. We have such things as personality scores for the group. The boys in our study, including those on the panel, tend (particularly on Eysenck's personality inventory) to be low on extroversion and low on neuroticism.

There were perhaps only one or two boys on the panel who probably don't fit that stereotype of the scientist fairly well. Last night, Mike, a sixteen-year-old physics major junior at Johns Hopkins who entered when he was fourteen, responded only once or twice, and then only when called on. Now, Mike is not bashful, timid, or shy, he is just not voluble. So because Gene didn't know the panel well enough to ask Mike points, Mike said nothing more. Even in that group, an especially personable and effective group, you have pretty much the stereotype of the achieving scientist—somewhat introverted but stable.

GETZELS: We keep thinking of the gifted as somehow the "quiz kids" who are "queer kids." They are not queer; they are human in a unique sense. In this sense I suspect they are the very best kind of human beings. It is appropriate for them to be that way. It is appropriate, for example, for an artist to spend eighteen or twenty hours by himself in a studio; he is not prepared to do other more gregarious things. It is no more queer for him to be that way than it is, say, for dentists to be stoop-shouldered.

Having stooped shoulders does not make him, how shall I say, inhuman. The artist's being alone and really finding his expression that way rather than in some other way does not make him queer. It makes him unique. It doesn't make him bizarre. It certainly does not, I hope, make him inhuman.

SANBORN: You know, my reaction to that list of adjectives is that for one small segment of the people whom we call gifted, maybe it fits. I don't know who the norm group was that these adjectives were meant to describe, but they don't describe the 3,500 kids we have been working with in any general way at all. Our research shows that as a group, these kids are highly active socially, they are highly active physically. Two-thirds of the boys and about one-third of the girls are on varsity athletic teams, which far exceeds the varsity participation of kids in general in school. They are cheerleaders, they are social leaders, they are elected as class presidents. They are involved in Sunday School teaching and just a whole great variety of activities.

Now within the group there are going to be some youngsters for whom those adjectives would fit, but my concept of the gifted and talented child does not lead me to think that that is in any way adequate as a general description.

P. SEARS: There is some confusion here between scientists and gifted.

SANBORN: I mean even scientists.

P. SEARS: You are talking about a large group of gifted, talented children, I presume selected on a verbal intelligence test or artistic criteria.

SANBORN: There are a variety of criteria.

P. SEARS: You have got all of this variety, and I think this relates to Ellis Page's point, scientists and mathematicians are a little different in their modes of thought and their modes of reaction from a highly verbal kid—from Winston Churchill, who incidentally was not highly verbal as a child, but became so. But this is very different, and I think you are overgeneralizing and also over-individualizing at the same time by saying that there is a wide, wide variety. There are certain requirements in the personalities for a scientist or a mathematician that other highly talented people may not share whatsoever.

PATEL: There are several things that have been said I so much wanted to react to. It seems that personality characteristics are constantly being used as the criteria for describing the gifted, but some of us here are agreed that more than personality characteristics makes up what a person is.

I would prefer to think of it in terms of life style, not just cognitive style, but life style which is made up of many, many more components, and that successful people who are not scientists will not display one life style. I would like to suggest that that will take care of individual differences and different patterns of success. Success, I would like to submit, is not a composite factor. It is a profile. It can be seen as a profile of several factors, and if we look at it that way, we can look at it as several subsets of profiles. If we begin to think of success in terms of subsets of profiles, trying to match these together, I think we may be able to get a clearer picture of development from the point of view of integration.

LERNER: I want to pull together what Dr. Patel and Mrs. Ginsberg said. It suggests two things: the first being a need for research. I think we need research that above and beyond the personality and the internal aspects also gets at these external aspects. It isn't all inside, it is outside as well, which suggests the need for research. The technique for research needs to get out into the community, into the living space, into where these life styles are happening and the pulling together of what is being seen, especially in 1975. Maybe we might not think that this guy who sits alone is queer, but I bet his peers would, you see. We need to find this out, which gets us into a footnote here. This is to what degree, for instance, ethnicity, the whole factor of ethnicity, bears on gifted and talented people. We have ideas. I don't know how much research we have. Here we will probably touch on why there are so few talented and gifted black children. We have them, certainly, but in comparison to other ethnic groups—Chinese, Jewish people, Greeks, etc.—we just don't know the answers. We may have our prejudices and ideas. I think we need to get out of the laboratories and into where the life styles are taking place, so I suggest a need for research and a possible technique for research.

WELSH: You said not to make any speeches, but may I use the blackboard?

STANLEY: Go ahead.

WELSH: It seems to me that what we need is a paradigm [see figure 10.1]. Whether with empirical research it turns out to be adequate or not, I think we have a way of organizing some of the concepts, personality, style, interest, personal characteristics, traits of behavior, ways of dealing with the world, etc. What I have proposed at some length, and I will simply profile it here, is two basic general personality dimensions that I think are more akin to the concept of style or temperament than anything else. One, a horizontal dimension that I call *intellectence*, differentiates the people at one end who are interested in concrete, literal, pragmatic ways of dealing with the world. At the other end of this dimension are those who are interested in abstractions, conceptual, and symbolic ways of dealing with the world. The other dimension, the vertical dimension, which I call *origence*, differentiates those who are more at home in and like a structured kind of situation from those at the other end, who want it unstructured, if we can use that word, as an open end. You can see where the situation enters and mathematicians fall. They fall here in the lower right quadrant of the figure. There are all kinds of evidence from the IPAR group and others. [For details, see chapter 9 in this volume.]

I think this is where we get the problem that somehow they are not human. I think they are impersonal in the sense that, say, psychologists are, who tend to fall around here (between upper and lower right quadrants). They deal with people as objects when they are dealing with psychology. It doesn't mean that we are then talking about their relations with their friends—that they are some kind of inhuman people who would exploit them. As a matter of fact, the exploiters fall up in this corner (upper left quadrant). At any rate, in terms of the style I have used an alliteration to refer to this type as the imaginative (upper left quadrant), this as the intuitive (upper right), this as the industrious (lower left), and this as the intellective (lower right).

The industrious person can get a great deal done by hard work and application; the intuitive one by letting his mind go and not being bound by restraints; the imaginative one, well, it comes from the unconscious

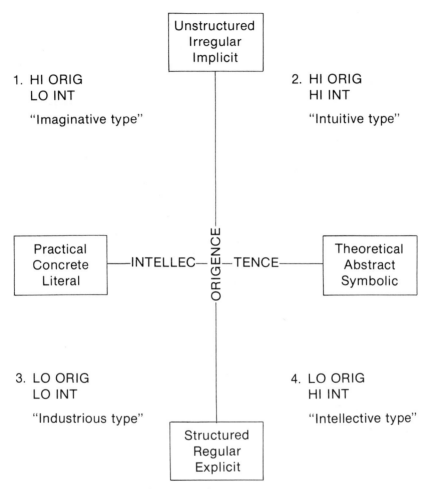

Fig. 10.1. Welsh's two-dimensional model for personality study

and there it is; and the intellective one by cognizing in a symbolic and orderly way, and this is where the mathematicians fall, here.

One final thing, and I will stop. The problem I think is that people keep thinking of creativity as a single dimension. They think of it as a continuum, in which the more the better. What I argue is, depending on what you do, what you want to do, and the situation in which you find yourself, the person who is relatively higher on these two dimensions will be the more creative, more original. If he is a banker, he falls here (lower left). The creative banker will be relatively higher than the rest of the bankers, but he won't be as high in his dimensions as an artist.

GETZELS: This is very pretty. I am struck by the applicability of the model to the longitudinal study of artists I have been doing. The use that different types of art students make of their similar technical talents depends very much on their personality and values. That is, students who have a need for structure tend to go into commercial art and those who prefer to work in unstructured situations go into fine art, so that although one cannot differentiate commercial art students and fine art students by technical skill—they are equally fine draftsmen—they can be differentiated on a structured–unstructured dimension like origence.

PAGE: What is the spine of that? You said—

WELSH: I use the term "origence" because some of my early work was done on originality with Frank Barron and uses the Barron–Welsh art scale for the origence axis.

PAGE: O-r-i-g-e-n-c-e?

WELSH: Yes, that implies an on-going activity. The horizontal axis was the scores on Terman's Concept Mastery Test. Then I got personality characteristics for the four types generated by these two independent dimensions, analyzing the adjective check list, the Minnesota Multiphasic Personality Inventory, and the Strong Vocational Interest Blank.

PAGE: Do I understand that origence is the same dimension as structured–unstructured?

WELSH: Yes, the low of origence refers to interest in structure, regularity, rules, system, etc., and it opens up at the high end of origence.

LERNER: There is something to that from this point of view. If you move into the structure area, again thinking of thousands of kids and thousands of tests, why are kids structured? Are you moving into some organic basis or parental influence? I think of some of the art institutes in Maryland or the Rhode Island School of Design, which are unstructured. I will bet you two to one if you look into the case records of the kids you will find something in the behavioral aspect that wants them to beat the traces and become unstructured.

All I am suggesting again is that this seems to impinge on a life-style aspect, which suggests another item. Do we not therefore need to move in a sociological direction? I am not knowledgeable enough to know in terms of the research. Are we suggesting a need now to move into a kind of marriage with a sociological framework whereby we begin to understand this? For instance, medical sociology is a relatively new field and the sociologists are getting into the medical area and are finding they can help medicine by some kind of a sociological approach. How much can we find out if we move in this direction?

WARD: If I may add—the concept of the *sociology of knowledge* seems scarcely to be understood among educators. Some kind of generalization, of abstraction upon the *epistemological base* in all this paralleling what the child is and needs, it seems to me, is an essential consideration here also.

ANASTASI: I like the two-dimensional pattern very much, but I would still add a third dimension to it.

WELSH: I am working on that.

ANASTASI: I would say the third dimension is what others might call cognitive style but I prefer to call work habits; or what others call reflective versus impulsive, and I would like to call superficial versus subtle. Reflective persons delve deeply into something, stay with it, narrow their focus. The impulsives respond quickly, superficially, over a wider area. I think we can describe it better by calling it thorough (or deep, or subtle) versus superficial; but there is a very important dimension there.

WELSH: I can't develop it in all details, but my model delves in terms of the global to the surface, to the depth, and so on. If you take the upper corner, the imaginative corner up there is a global, diffused kind of way of dealing with things. As you move across the top, you go into a depth where you have a synthesis of what seems to be an open-ended kind of thing. Einstein, for example, brought order into what had before been diffuse. The unrelated detailed is at the lower left-hand corner; these are arranged in pattern relationships in the other corner. You can deal with cognitive style that way in terms of transition from one to the other.

PARKER: I am getting uncomfortable because there are so many categories that kids can be divided into. Our experience is that they are whole persons. Now, you know in the disciplines we are finding people who are wanting to bring things together. We have a person in Arcadia who I think is interested in universal studies. He set up a whole department where kids can take courses in math, science, history, bring them all together, and try to synthesize, because we need universal people in this world. Our problems are no longer simple enough to be dealt with by one person who is specializing in the tree or the leaf. He doesn't know enough about the world around him.

We have here a small group of kids who might be capable of the kind of universality. If we look back into their origins, one of the things we know about little kids is they don't split up until they are a little older. When you look at little kids, our information tells us little kids are not differentiated by math or science or verbal and nonverbal.

KEARNEY: I wanted to relate a comment that Dr. Gell-Mann of Cal Tech made when speaking to a parent group in our district one time. One of the parents asked him what he felt had been most beneficial to him, and he said, having parents and teachers who knew when to lend support and when to get out of the way. In reaction to your comment about values, Texas Institute devised a value test a short while back. They used it in placing personnel with managerial groups so they don't clash.

I tested 150 of the gifted high school students and 150 of the students at the other end of the scale, the students who were in the remedial classes. I found that the gifted were almost always in the manipulative category —where they like to control the world, not necessarily Machiavellianly, but tried to control the situation they were in.

At the other end of the scale, I found ghetto leaders in exactly the same categories. They had the same responses. I thought it was very interesting that we had practically no gifted children who fell in the highly structured end of the scale where they really wanted to end up being controlled, where they wanted to go into a fundamentalistic situation. Our alternative school is about one-third gifted. I think they try to control their world. I don't know what its validity is, but it was an interesting attempt to see what would happen.

STANLEY: I don't want to choke off this discussion, but getting back for a moment to Mrs. Parker's real concern for some kind of wholeness in the child, all of us remember over the years the big argument about whether early general ability differentiated into special abilities at a later age. Betty Hagen did a study of this around 1949. Jerry Doppelt did one, also. Henry Garrett made this the topic of his presidential address to the American Psychological Association. But it doesn't seem to me with the limited experience I have had with mathematically talented youth who are quite young that this necessarily applies to these gifted youngsters. They do seem to be pretty strongly differentiated fairly early. I think Thurstone found that for samples of preschoolers. What we don't know is the form of development of each of the various abilities of the primary mental abilities or Wechsler intelligence test sort. Some develop quite differently from one individual to another. Nancy Bayley's work seems appropriate, showing that we don't have very good prediction of general intelligence from age two to age eight, but we do from (for example) age two to age two and one-half. By the time one gets to age six or seven, intelligence sort of settles down and becomes predictable. I won't feel comfortable in the gifted area with any concept of an undifferentiated child six or eight years old.

PARKER: I agree with you. It is the little kids I refer to. The reason I brought this up is that I have a very great concern if we are somehow socializing into bright-kid differentiations. I am only asking the question, and I appreciate what you said. I don't mean it in the sense of a single thing at all, but I mean it more in the sense of a breadth and a depth that has not yet been channeled by some of the things we find in the literature, when we ask the people what happened to you to make you a physicist, mathematician, and so on. If there were some way we could preserve—we are going to get back into general words, global, universal, or wide-coverage aspect—a brilliant child is what I am talking about now. If we could preserve that, we might bring a more Renaissance-type man to attack the kinds of interdisciplinary problems we have in the world today, with a kind of mind that we are no longer producing. We really are getting the tree thinned out.

STANLEY: You may be implying the possibility of having an Erasmus instead of an Einstein and I don't—I just don't know. It doesn't seem, certainly in the scientific field, that this much breadth and depth both are any longer usable. Obviously, a person can attack a particular problem from all vantage points with an interdisciplinary team. But to create in one cortex all of the qualities that are needed seems to be, you know, unprofitable, an unlikely way to go about things. You may have unique synthesizers, politicians, and so on, but the idea that we should try to make a universal man out of one person isn't appealing to me, somehow.

HANCOCK: I have no professional expertise at all, but I have always understood that mathematical and musical talents often go together. Isn't the extreme musical talent obvious at one and one-half or two, some of them composing at three, this sort of thing? [This question did not get an answer. The answer seems to be "Yes," even though there may never have been a single individual who was both a musical and a mathematical *genius*. Among Dr. Stanley's talented youth there are several who could be excellent performers in either area. One at age sixteen was the top high school composer of classical music in the nation.]

ALBERT: Eric was very differentiated at six. I think we have a living model there. I have a question for you, Dr. Getzels, and that is, where would you put the fact that most creative people seem to have a capacity to be alone and work alone more than others and that they show this early? I don't find it in any of the quadrants. I find it as a common denominator. You were speaking of that earlier.

GETZELS: It puzzles me. The question is the chicken or the egg. That is, are the creative artists and scientists personalistically first loners, and therefore they immediately disregard certain kinds of occupations, vocations, whatever their talents are? That is, because they have to be alone, they are not therefore going to be salespersons, for example. Or, the other way around, since they have this talent that they want to express which requires being alone, therefore they must be alone; if they don't want to be alone, they cannot express their talent and therefore must slight it. I have no way of knowing that, because by the time the art students have come to art school to present a portfolio of stuff, they are already in fact alone and not in the queer sense alone. There is no great painting, anymore than a great poem, that has ever been done by a committee. In this sense it is hard to say that if they are going to do this, going to be a poet, or a pure scientist, or something of that sort, they can be anything except loners.

ALBERT: I know of only one paper, by a British psychiatrist, that has dealt with this point.

R. SEARS: I just wanted to add one little item to support your art argument and Albert's comment. In the last few years I have been working rather extensively with modern novelists from a biographical standpoint, and the one thing that stands out so terribly characteristic of them is that they have been alone, and alone almost from birth. None of them, not one that I know of who is a nineteenth- or twentieth-century novelist, has ever grown up even in a large family. It is small families or else isolated within the family.

GETZELS: If I may make one more comment about the small family or isolation in the family, this is true also of the fine arts students. What is interesting also—we have heard this several times from several sources, a thing that puzzles me a great deal since I have no theoretical view in which to encompass the observation—is the gifted oldest son or oldest child phenomenon. It may very well be, to go back to Mrs. Parker's comment, that there is a period in which the gifted child grows up alone. At a very important early period of his life, he is either with adults or alone in the family.

ANASTASI: It is my hypothesis that their solitariness is closely linked with the reflective and thorough work style. To me that is a dimension.

May I add a footnote to the question of the differentiation of abilities with age? There is a fair amount of evidence from the factor-analytic literature that differentiation is not associated with age per se. It is associated with any condition that makes for a high level of development in the ability in question. Many conditions have been investigated in this connection, such as socioeconomic level, cultural differences, amount and kind of education, and occupational experience. There are even drug studies showing that, as performance level is depressed, performance becomes more generalized, or dedifferentiated. In general, differentiation in any cognitive domain is associated with a high level of performance in that domain (Anastasi 1970). This would fit in with your gifted children being more differentiated than normals at an early age.

LERNER: This is probably going to be emotional, maybe not on the topic but will hinge on Mrs. Parker's statement. I agree with Dr. Stanley that at this point Erasmus is dead. We can't be Erasmus because knowledge has exploded and you are going to spend a whole lifetime studying the left part of the right side of some triangle. Yet, some place along the line, we have got to do something with our approach to knowledge as we know it. Maybe this is a whole new study, a whole new discipline itself, which pulls together the myopic aspect that we all get locked into. Departments in universities don't talk to each other because they don't understand each other, except that you now have interdisciplinary work.

Well, I would like to see us at least think about moving in that direction, because I think it is the only way we are going to survive. We are going to fall apart if we don't.

WARD: This gentleman [Lerner] has a propensity for exciting me somehow or other, and I want to bring it over again to the sociology of knowledge, and to Professor Stanley's doubts (relating to Mrs. Parker's thought) that the Renaissance man is a viable concept today. I have long been fond of a work which I can scarcely read with understanding, i.e., the two-volume *International Encyclopedia of Unified Science* (Neurath, Carnap, and Morris 1955), which is not exactly a "whole earth cata-logue," but rather a work which in the contemporary period undertakes something of the holistic and integrative view of knowledge, which interested the eighteenth-century Encyclopedists. Another marvelous work is that of Margenau and his colleagues, entitled *Integrative Principles of Modern Thought* (Margenau 1972). There are only about twelve chapters in the Margenau volume, one on mathematics, as I remember; one on the life sciences, the physical sciences, and so on. Now both these extraordinary intellectual attainments suggest to me an epistemological depth and breadth which is entirely proper as an objective in the differential education of gifted youth. And such works may indeed represent a contemporary compromise between the tenuous prospect of knowing everything, to the more realistic curricular potentiality of representing in a useful and manageable way the entire range of human inquiry.

HAIER: I have a theoretical question that might be appropriate. Klaus Riegel at the University of Michigan and others have written about dialectical reasoning. I wonder whether what would distinguish the creative from noncreative within this highly select group might be the fact that although they all are very good at abstract thinking, only some of them will have dialectical reasoning ability. I wonder if anyone who has had experience with a gifted child has noticed a special ability to see inherent contradictions or what is called dialectical thinking, and whether or not that may be related to creativity.

MICHAEL: That is a hypothesis. It seems reasonable on the surface. I don't know of evidence on that. Some of the people who worked on formal operations processes, disjunctive sets, may have something to say on that. Copeland down in Florida was working a bit in that field, at least tangentially. I don't know much more than that. Does anyone know if there are psychometric tests to get what they call—

WELSH: No. Let me respond. I don't mean to dwell on this, although I would like to, but empirically I have found that students who fall in the upper part of the high origence are better able to see things relationally that other people see as distinct and separate. They are able to see ways of bridging them. I don't know of any formal tests. I think we can probably devise one to get at this type of thing. You can observe it in the student, at any rate.

GETZELS: This is a good breaking point for the recess.

[Recess]

GETZELS: Dr. Pauline Sears is leaving shortly, and I think that we ought to take this opportunity to ask her to say something not just about the women in the Terman study but about the status of the study as a whole—how far it has to run, and perhaps both Pat and Bob Sears may respond to any questions.

P. SEARS: I will say something first because I have run into several misconceptions about the men. I told you there have been nine contacts over the fifty years. Every time the men have been surveyed as well as the women, and a lot of this has been published. It has been published up through the '60 survey [See Melita H. Oden's 1968 *Genetic Psychology Monograph*.] It just happens that we haven't had time to analyze the data on the men yet. Dr. Robert Hogan from the Psychology Department here at Hopkins, with whom I just talked, made a very interesting suggestion. We have been hearing a lot about men going into a demanding profession or business at a rather early age, competing first with a lot of pressure, and then at age forty-five or fifty deciding that they have lost out in a broad sense in life and going off to a desert island or to build a log cabin or something like this.

On the other hand, for many of our women, it was first marriage and children and then at age thirty-five or so deciding they have lost out on another aspect of life, which is professional work. The suggestion is to chart the men and women throughout these different age periods, changes in occupations, and so on. That is an interesting idea: men and women surveyed at the same age but with different past experiences.

R. SEARS: Just a word as to the present status of the study. Dr. Getzels was saying perhaps people would like to know where we stand. We had this last follow-up, from which Pat derived these three consequent variable measures on life style for the women. We will do essentially the same thing, but of course with different definitions, because they have to be different for the men. It just happens that Lee J. Cronbach and I, who had agreed to do the study of the men on the general subject of retirement, have been tied up with other things and are only just now getting free. Pat had more time available, so she went to work on the women and did the study that was reported here. We hope to get started sometime later this year on the work with the men (Sears 1977).

The present status of the data is such that it can go public eventually, and I think before too long. We are now coding everything that was coded from 1921 on. I don't know how many variables there will turn out to be. I would guess somewhere around 2,000 to 3,000. This will all go on to a tape—anonymously, of course—with case numbers, and will be available for responsible investigators. We will have to have some kind of local committee to determine who is a responsible investigator. In the meantime, if people do have the kind of interesting ideas that Dr. Hogan has just expressed to Mrs. Sears and want to write to us and propose investigations, we will be more than happy to be responsive to this.

I don't think this tape is going to be ready much before spring, but—

BARBEE: Dr. Sears, I just fainted; 2,000 variables, 1,528 cases!

R. SEARS: Actually, the problem is not quite as serious as that. As many as 80 percent of the variables don't have to be recoded. They are on cards at an appropriate place. They will be put on the tape. The study started in 1921. The only kind of machinery available then was the old hand-type machine. A lot of stuff was put on cards. You can imagine what a madhouse these files actually are, but fear not, they will be ready within the next year, I hope.

GETZELS: Thank you both, very, very much.

[Professors Pauline and Robert Sears depart.]

MICHAEL: Did I interpret them to say they are looking for people to help?

STANLEY: There seem to be two points. One was that they would welcome suggestions about what they might do themselves in terms of studying certain areas. For instance, Pat Sears said that she will take Bob Hogan's idea and do something with it.

The other point is that they would welcome proposals from persons like us to do studies of our own. They would screen such requesters and give the acceptable ones permission and lend them the tape. Is that correct?

GETZELS: I think that's correct.

STANLEY: Very, very good. It is the first time I am aware of, except for limited use by Schneidman (1971) of data about suicides in the Terman group, that they have ever let anybody have any of this information. I may be wrong. I have never heard or seen anything of that sort before, in terms of opening up the data.

MICHAEL: It would seem to me that you would need to know what variables they had and which ones they had access to, which ones they weren't going to report. I know you could get some of this by reading the past volumes.

STANLEY: They will probably have a list of some kind.

MICHAEL: I suspect if you went up and talked to them for an hour or two you could get a pretty good idea.

GETZELS: The examination of their information blanks would give you some ideas of the kinds of data they have in the files.

Are there any other comments regarding the Terman project? May we then return to where we were just before we stopped. The issue was being raised that thinking is not just convergent–divergent but some other kind of thing which you called—

HAIER: Dialectical.

GETZELS: I think Dr. Michael was responding to it.

MICHAEL: I think all I said was that the hypothesis seemed to be a reasonable one and I was beginning to wonder whether people who had worked in the study of cognition haven't treated this problem. I was thinking there is a man named Copeland at one of the Florida universities, the one in Boca Raton—

STANLEY: Florida Atlantic?

MICHAEL: Florida Atlantic, who has endeavored to translate many concepts into methods and teaching in mathematics. It seems to me he touched on related topics, so I am sure work of this nature has been going on. But I am not well informed on it.

ALBERT: I was going to say I think Dr. Getzels has done a study that relates to problem spotting in creative people. I wonder if you could describe it. It seems to me we are talking about seeing a gap and following it up.

GETZELS: That is what Ellis Page and I were talking about during the break, so perhaps he will comment.

MICHAEL: There is sensitivity to problems, about being able to spot problems?

PAGE: In a way. It has to do—Dr. Getzels was talking about it—with asking the right question instead of giving the right answer, and I was discussing with him some work which is going on now, of which psychologists seem relatively unaware. This work is in the field of artificial intelligence (AI).

Now, at MIT, there has been for some time a laboratory of artificial intelligence. Marvin Minsky is the head of it and if you wish to bone up in this area you can look at his works, largely ones he has edited. For instance, he has one about semantic information processing, which is marvelous. It is a collection of doctoral dissertations in artificial intelligence, where people have been representing the world in certain ways.

Another source you can look for is the work of our fellow psychologist, Herbert Simon, and his colleagues at the Carnegie–Mellon University in Pittsburgh. You are aware that he has studied game playing at length in simulation, and simulation and AI have a lot to do with each other. It seems to me that these two areas are places in which there has been real attention to what we tend to treat as a "black box" in discussing the gifted. That is, what happens when one is presented with a problem and what the period of "incubation" could mean.

One of the characteristics of the solutions from AI or from a related field of operations research is that they tend to, they wish to, optimize some dimension of value.

Curiously enough, psychologists can talk forever about problem solving without realizing that what they are doing is optimizing a dimension of value. They are coming out for a solution that will satisfy certain needs or desires. This can be expressed, and has been expressed in the work in AI, operations research, and computer simulation of game playing as a dimension of value. Therefore, I think we need to pay attention to what values are being optimized, what the criteria of good solutions are, and then how these may be achieved.

It is rather astonishing that there is this field of operations research, for instance, which has concentrated on exactly a set of well-developed mathematical models for optimizing such things, and that these have not been applied yet to research on the gifted, at least in any great degree. For example, as I look over the Rossman model, which struck me as very desirable, they start out with some observation of a met difficulty, and the AI people start out with a statement of a verbal problem. Their models are so well developed that they actually print out on a computer. They are not just verbal circularities. You start with, say, a verbal problem. This verbal problem is parsed into deep structure, parsed into a symbolic, logical representation sometimes in the predicate calculus.

There is then an algebraic transformation of this problem, a statement of the desired solution. Then the question is raised, Is the solution available? and there is a consultation of some problem-solution matrix. You can imagine the problems to be the rows and the solutions to be the columns. If the answer is yes, a solution is available, you will go to a later step, seven. If it is no, you go to the next step. The next step is: Can you divide the problem into subproblems? If the answer is yes, you do so, divide it. If the answer is no, you examine it with failure; the problem is unsolvable. If the answer is yes and you have divided it into subproblems, then you take the first subproblem, is the solution available? You consult the problem-solving matrix. If yes, you go to seven, we will say; if no, you go back to five. Seven is the last step, are you finished with the problem?

Yes, examine it with success; if no, go back to step four, the solution available to the problem it presents.

One thing they use is something called a push-down store, where you put the major problems. The top problem is in first. If that is solvable, you solve it, your stack is empty, you have success. If not, you divide that into subproblems, put the subproblems in the stack. You solve those one at a time. As those are solved, the first one lifts and you get that. If not, you keep adding, dividing the problems until finally you reach an impasse, in which case you can't empty the stack and you are out. There are models available from these nonpsychologists, extremely bright people who are in this field of artificial intelligence. And, of course, I don't mean to be so parochial as to suggest MIT as the only home of such things; AI is being studied all over the country now.

MICHAEL: Also in Wales and Scotland.

PAGE: Yes, there has been a marked amount of work in it in Edinburgh.

GETZELS: If I might add to this from a somewhat different point of view. I don't know of any model of either creative work or problem solving that does not begin with a problem that is already given. In the Rossman, Wallas, or Dewey models, there is always a situation in which a problem is presented, is formulated. Then begins the real work of solving it, and the steps are clear.

There are hundreds of papers and experiments on problem solving, but I know almost no empirical paper or experiment on problem finding, on how one goes from a dilemma or indeterminate situation, to use a Dewey term, to a stated problem. And to quote Einstein, the formulation of a problem is often more essential than its solution, since once the problem is formulated, the solution, and I quote him, may be merely a matter of mathematical or technical skill. It is this part of the thinking process—the formulation of problems—that we know very little about.

Let me give an instance of the relation between how a problem is formulated and the quality of the solution that is reached. A car is traveling on a lonely rural road and blows a tire. The people look in the trunk and discover there is no jack. They pose the problem: Where can we get a jack? They remember that five miles back they had passed a gasoline station and they begin walking back to get a jack. Seems a reasonable thing to do. While they are gone, a car coming the other way also blows a tire, and its people also discover they don't have a jack. They look around, see a deserted barn at the side of the road with a pulley for lifting bales of hay. They move the car to the barn, lift the car on the pulley, change the tire, and drive off.

We are likely to say: What a clever solution. We should say: What a clever problem. The first ones formulated their dilemma into the problem:

Where can we get a jack? The second ones formulated the same dilemma into the problem: How can we lift the car? In the formulation of the problem is all the difference as to the kind of solution that will be reached (Getzels 1975). It is about this aspect of thinking and creativity that we know very little.

PAGE: Could I relate that as we did before? In the structure that I was talking about, if you start with an overall goal, such as I want to drive the car, can I drive it? No. Then I divide it into a subproblem, the wheel is bad, and so on. You keep dividing it. When a solution is impractical to solve at a low level, then one goes to a higher level, and, in fact, you do reach automatically the more important overreaching question: Can I lift the car?

GETZELS: That is what I came to also if I worked with most scientists. But this issue came to me when I was working with artists. You watch them put things together in their studio and ask them what they are doing, and they say they are creating a still-life problem. The difference between the commercial artist and the fine artist is that when the commercial artist walks into his studio he is given a problem. Some one says, would you draw an attractive corncob for a cereal box so that people will buy it? Note that the problem is presented to him, and then he goes through the steps you suggested with the presented problem as a beginning.

The fine artist does not begin that way. The fine artist walks into his studio, and all that is there is a blank canvas. No one presents him with a problem. He himself must formulate, create, the problem he will work on. Some artists run out of problems and turn to canned problems—problems that are not original with them. Their work may be technically proficient but not original or creative, like the copyist who makes a perfect copy but cannot conceive an original problem to work on. And that is the mystery: How are original problems found and formulated?

STANLEY: We know we use analysis a great deal, trying to reason about how the artists and others work. But in reading Eric Temple Bell's *Men of Mathematics* (Bell 1937), a fascinating volume about eminent mathematicians who of course had a great deal of insight, it is obvious that though many mathematicians created their own problems, a lot of them were simply solving very difficult problems that equally good or inferior mathematicians had formulated and that had resisted solution for many years.

So, although the art example is partly applicable, it would probably be a bit simplistic to generalize from a humanistic framework, an art framework or literature framework, to a mathematics framework, without entertaining the possibility that the solution, the creative solution, the original pioneering of the whole area often is in the process of solving problems. The point is that some literary-oriented people thinking about mathematics—I am not talking about you, Jack, at all—will think, well, solving the problem is only a technical skill.

GETZELS: It is like the discussion of creativity and intelligence. People say they are different, which they obviously are not. They are related. Problem finding and problem solving are also obviously related. They are not dichotomous. To go back to Dr. Michael's paper, there is in all models he presents—Rossman's, Wallas's, Dewey's—the crucial step —as if by magic the formulation of a problem. We study thinking through problem solving by giving the person the problem he is to solve, when really the more creative thing might very well have been the thinking up of the problem rather than the solution afterward.

MICHAEL: We have this in doctoral statements. I try to say to students, if you could actually create a problem, that in itself would be a dissertation.

GETZELS: You bet. That is why the most popular degree, although people start for the Ph.D., is the A.B.D. All But Dissertation. No one really fails courses any more in graduate school. They take eight or ten hours of preliminary examinations in which we pose the problems. If they don't pass the first time, they do the second. They pass French, German. They have been solving problems right since the first grade. Now we say, you are ready, go out and formulate a problem, write a proposal on your own problem. It is at this point that there is the greatest attrition, or sometimes it takes them how long?

ANASTASI: Ten years.

STANLEY: May I at this point in the symposium, because our time is running out, make a soft pitch for a little more practical approach for the rest of the time? I see some very practical people here, three of our speakers and others. We professors like to act as academicians, as basic researchers. But one of the things that Terman did not do in his study, at least half of the ones here have tried to do. That is intervene on behalf of the intellectually gifted with techniques we already know to be useful to understand some rather practical things about how to set up programs that facilitate the development of the gifted. And maybe that would be worth some of the rest of the symposium's time.

MICHAEL: I am not quite satisfied to let this go yet—almost. I wish you would put down, not today obviously, but in writing the distinction here that you are trying to make. It almost seems to me as if we have possibly convergent production versus divergent production of problem formulation. I think this is something you and I might work on or think about.

GETZELS: I would be glad to. If you know something, you say it succinctly. If you don't, you go on and circle the problem.

MICHAEL: I alluded partly to this very concern this morning and I got partly the idea from Julian in the note he wrote on the side of the manuscript or in a letter, what about the elegant solution in the process of arriving at convergent production. That is the heart of it. I would like to follow this up, not today but in the future.

GETZELS: Fine. May we turn, then, as Julian suggested, to the more practical aspects, and why don't you pose the problem in this sense?

STANLEY: The problem is not so much to get practical as to focus on intervention on behalf of the intellectually gifted to help them in ways that are now known but seldom used.

HOCKING: I have an Ed.D. degree, which makes me feel out of it as far as everybody here is concerned. My Ed.D and dissertation happen to be chiefly in the field of mathematics teacher education, and for my dissertation research I did experimentation with student teachers on cognitive style. Along with that I am now in a position of supervising a program in which teachers are teaching the gifted, and I am very much concerned with what kind of teaching the gifted students need. I am wondering has any research been done. Has anything been done to say what these students need? We have talked about what they are and how to identify them, and what to do with them. But has anybody done it from the viewpoint of need, that they need this to succeed in the world, not just to be defined to be creative in one little narrow thing?

KEARNEY: There have been some studies, at least pieces of which I have seen that indicate some of the needs of the gifted. One of these at the secondary level is that the teacher is not only actually an expert in the field but has the characteristics that will allow him to put this information across successfully. The expert who is brilliant in his field and cannot communicate, does not have a good sense of humor, does not have a willingness to step aside, does not have a willingness to allow experimentation or open-ended questioning, probably isn't going to succeed with this group, at least not at the secondary level.

I think that, certainly at the elementary level, many characteristics of the teachers have been identified. I am interpreting your question to be the teacher talent because the needs are going to be academic needs that vary from child to child. I think it is a characteristic of personality frequently that is important in conveying information. There is a pa-per—by May Seagoe?—that sets forth the particular characteristics that she feels are very important. There is also a questionnaire for teachers to let them have a self-check to see whether or not they are the type of person that will succeed in this program. I think one thing that stands out over and over again is sense of humor and ability not to be threatened. The children last night made this comment several times, that they can't get along in a classroom where the teacher feels threatened by them.

FOX: I think Dr. Kearney covered all of the major points that I would have made. The expertise of the teacher is important, but so also is the openness to respond to students' questions. We have seen this a lot where in the course of teaching a fast-paced kind of mathematics program, the students pose questions that at that point in time are not in the teacher's lesson plans and are not in the textbook. The teacher responds to what they are asking. I think a master teacher is here.

STANLEY: Two of them.

FOX: Yes, Joe Wolfson and Dick McCoart, who have been very successful with gifted mathematics students. I think they could tell us what they do. There is probably a similarity.

McCOART: I think the best way to succeed with fast-paced students is to have a class that has just finished having Mr. Wolfson as a teacher. I found that no matter what I did, it was going to be a great success. The students did very well in the course.

I think the main thing I did for them, which their high school teachers couldn't possibly do, is that I went at a pace it would be impossible to keep up in a high school, at least in an average type of calculus class in high school. I was able to go deeply into groups, in proofs, in fact in some cases slightly more deeply than I go in my regular college course. Of course, one reason for this is that I would be asked questions about certain details that I wouldn't even be asked by some college students. As a matter of fact, I found myself doing a little bit of research on a couple of topics to get prepared to finish answering the question the next week. But I think of myself mainly as having been a pacesetter, and I think that for the students, just being together and working with other brilliant students, helped a lot.

For instance, this year I have a student who is taking a calculus course in independent study in high school, and being all alone, there is nothing except the book to challenge him. I could easily see a situation whereby no matter what the student did, the teacher would think that he was doing splendidly, whereas in this class, he is not the number one student. He has got to—even though on the aptitude scores he is very high—he has got to put forth the work. I tell the students they are not in competition with each other. They are there to enrich themselves, to see how well they can do on the Advanced Placement Program higher-level calculus exam next May, but certainly the spirit of competition is there and it helps them.

KEARNEY: I think there is another factor and it is very important. It was brought out by one of the students last night: Colin, I believe. The way the teacher poses the question is crucial to the learning process. Not what did Plato say and what did he mean in the cave allegory, but perhaps evaluate some aspect of Plato from the point of view of Machiavelli.

Then, even though you may not have covered this and that, you have caused them to take off in a new direction and synthesize their own information.

WOLFSON: I think a lot of this goes back to the point of not being threatened. You have to be willing to not come in with a lesson plan, because personally, I can't do that with any class that I teach. I don't particularly find in working with the gifted kids that I do anything in substance really different, except that they move at a much different pace. I have open-ended discussions in all of my classes.

LERNER: There is another ingredient. I have had the pleasure of working with Dr. McCoart and agree with him. Now, after the children have been to master teachers like Wolfson and McCoart, and had this lovely acceptance and warmth, and the pace that Dr. McCoart sets, the school has got to provide them with one more thing if they are going to survive, and that is freedom. This is contrary to what happens in many schools, namely, you don't have freedom to conceptualize, to be creative with what Dr. McCoart or Mr. Wolfson has just given you. For instance, we found after the kids left Dr. McCoart's class in an eighth-grade level, I was able to give them ten study periods a week. They could do what they wanted. They could go to the library, go across to the Enoch Pratt Library, go out onto the lawn if they wanted, but we found them gathering in groups and doing some peer teaching. This doesn't happen, for instance, in a lot of private schools which are supposedly better than public. The kids get a lot of busy work. I think the answer is a degree of freedom in which they can summon their soul. This is not new, read the poets. Whitman said summon your soul on a lonely beach and you will be creative. I think we can do some aspect of this administratively within the school setting.

We have the three ingredients, acceptance, nonthreatening, a degree of intellectual drive and freedom. I think that Dr. Stanley begins to put it on a practical level in the school setting. The question is: How do you sell all of this to administrators? I haven't found the answer.

STANLEY: Just one little clarification. I have known Joe Wolfson for several years, and he and Dick McCoart are about the best math teachers I have ever heard of since starting to teach math myself in 1937. I have never run across better ones. I don't think of Joe in his teaching as being especially warm. He is a great teacher, but not a sentimental-type teacher. He is a splendid stimulator and pacer who works closely and enthusiastically with the students. He accepts their questions, their answers. He is friendly with them, but there is no great deal of extra sentimentality and warmth. I don't mean that derogatorily at all. I have known a number of great teachers who have been like that. I would like to suggest that, for the fast-paced math classes in particular, the teacher does not have to be an unusually warm, feeling, sympathetic, empathizing person to do the job well.

MICHAEL: Slow learners in statistics need that.

GEORGE: I would like to comment, bringing up what the kids said last night. There are a couple of things I think we have found, Joe and Dr. McCoart will agree. First is the learning style of the students. It tends somewhat toward a particular orientation. Some students are more socially oriented, and they get along better in a certain type of classroom atmosphere. Other students are much more theoretical, investigative; they move much quicker if that type of environment is maintained.

Second is that the students themselves want to do it. This is a big factor. They have made the decision themselves on the program or on the process by which they want to learn. In other words, it is their choice, if they want to go into a math class or into another area. I think a student has got to be able to make that decision, not the counselor, not the teacher, not mom, not dad, but the student. I think that too often we get teacher, counselor, and parents advising. There is a need for guidance and stimulation, of course, but it comes back to finding out what the student himself or herself really wants to do. Sometimes we lose that when everybody is trying to be helpful.

I think Terri pointed out she was glad to have parental support, but at the same time it wasn't you *have* to do it. If she had really wanted to stop, she could have.

The other important area is homework. It is a matter of self-pacing, learning not to do homework at the last minute. Terri commented that she waited until the last minute because she didn't think she could do it. Toward the end, she spread her homework out some. Much has to do with self-pacing. There are a lot of other factors you have to consider. The ones I have mentioned are three of them.

PATEL: My work with students in India has continuously brought up the factor of communication. The students feel that the teachers must not communicate downward to them and the students must not communicate upward, but they must communicate horizontally. They must communicate on the same level. The teachers must be accepting, and both must work together. The fact is the teachers learn many things and are not ashamed to learn something from a student or say they are unable to answer questions. These are some of the aspects of communicating horizontally, as I call it. I feel that this, of all my studies, is one of the most important factors in making a successful teacher for an intelligent student.

COOKE: I wanted to pick up on Dr. McCoart and Mr. Wolfson's comments about the teacher of the gifted. I am willing to bet that in the dynamics that take place in your classes with those boys and girls, although it might not be especially warm and sympathetic—it is teacher-directed as well as student-initiated—there is interaction between the students as a result of a question posed by you, as well as students responding to you.

Also, you are accepting of the solutions or postulates that they might pose to a given problem. But some teachers aren't able to deal with this. It is this that makes the difference in terms of a good teacher of the gifted and one who is not successful with them. It goes back to Ned A. Flanders' interaction scales; I think it is a model that teachers of the gifted can use in order to allow gifted students to feel free to be creative, feel free to take risks, feel free to resolve problems or come to various kinds of solutions.

FOX: The study that was done by Casserly [see chapter 6 in this volume] of the girls in the advanced placement courses noted that the teacher of these classes demanded that everyone in the class had to participate. He would ask them questions and he helped bring his girls to the point where they weren't shy about being wrong. So often girls are allowed to sit passively in a class and are afraid. It is a risk-taking thing, I think, and these teachers encourage the girls. We are not negative about people's having wrong ideas. You know, you put forth your ideas and the rest of us will help you modify and we will pose the point to you, but it is not in a critical way. We are not attacking you. We are all working toward solving the problem.

GETZELS: Over and over there is the issue of risk taking. The classroom must be a place where one may take a risk because expressing something new or dealing with something you don't already know is risky. You think of a group of us here who have to say something. It is threatening, and I think the big achievement is to create a situation in which the student and the teacher both are able to take a risk without feeling that they will be derogated if they happen to be wrong.

STANLEY: There is one other thing both of these persons said that is fundamental to our whole concept of fast-math classes, and particularly for the benefit of the public school persons I would like to bring this out clearly. That is, attending a fast-math class on Saturdays or after school hours is a privilege, not a right. Failure of certain students, failure to keep up is bound to occur, and therefore dropping out is expected of some of the youngsters. Quite a few will not work hard enough. They do the homework hurriedly on the last night before class, or they are not able to stand being lower in the group, or some of them will prove not to be able enough. There is a certain amount of dropout expected. The corollary of this is that neither Mr. Wolfson or Dr. McCoart feel terribly threatened by losing a few students.

Dr. McCoart, for instance, is heroic with his willingness to come to class early and stay late. We provide an assistant, Mike, who was on the stage last evening, as his assistant. Mike tutors all who seek his help or who drop behind. If the student won't use that and drops down so far he cannot keep up with the class any longer, that student is expected to quit. We even have them, in this case, taking calculus in high school for credit and taking Dr. McCoart's supplemental course without credit. The attitude the typical public school teacher must have is that being in a class is a right and the teacher must work a lot with the slow ones to the detriment, often, of the average and above-average; that cannot be tolerated in fast-paced classes for the mathematically highly able. The teacher must work with the faster ones and say to the others, you are able enough to learn much of the material through homework. If you don't, it is too bad. Sounds like a hardhearted prescription, but it can't work well otherwise.

McCOART: One interesting thing that I have run into is that when I ask a question in a fast-paced class, and the person starts to answer, I am not too quick in calling that person wrong until I see exactly what it is going to develop into, because quite often it will turn out to be a different way of looking at it from the way I looked at it. If I will just give the student a chance to speak, it often turns out that he has got quite a good way of doing the problem his way.

HANCOCK: There is a man at Hopkins [Professor Robert Pond], head of the materials sciences department, who taught a course last spring on creativity, which sounds nutty but he is himself an adventurer. His theory was that what he needed to teach is what he calls the forgettery, which is a capacity to tackle the problem without having presolutions in mind. It was his idea that he could teach this ability, and eight of his nine students have come up with stuff that was patentable; I think there are five patents, some having already gone into production. Some of you might care to ask him how he is doing this. It is what you were saying about posing the problem. Incidentally, he himself also avoided the Ph.D. mill. This may have something to do with it.

PARKER: The same question that I put to the brilliant kids last night, with respect to what they want in a different class, also asked them what they like in a teacher. Two of the recurring themes are first, that the teacher be well prepared; you assign to brilliant youths a teacher who doesn't know his subject, and they are embarrassed. Another one is that he be fair, that he wait until the kid is finished and evaluate his idea first before saying no, you are wrong. This is what they ask for but hardly expect. When they tell you what they want in a teacher, this is the kind of answer that comes up most frequently.

KEARNEY: I have two comments that I think tie in with this. One, I think the teacher has to have enthusiasm for his subject. The other thing is that I think we can kill the risk-taking urge so that school kids won't take risks.

Last year we had an opportunity to test a number of private school students who entered our school. They came from a very structured private school, and our psychologist came back and said, "I think there is something wrong with me. I am getting a strange pattern of responses. Every time I ask a question and they answer, they say, is that right? In the section where they are assembling pictures or puzzles, many of the children, not just one, took the puzzle, and when they had a piece left over handed it back." These were straight A students, did very well in academic subjects, but there was a tremendous tension about taking a risk. I think somewhere along the line they had been discouraged. I am not certain that willingness to take risks is killed permanently, but I certainly think that it is hampered and maybe stifled for a long time.

MICHAEL: There's a point I would like to make on that. In reading as I was getting ready for the paper, and I am not knocking anybody's religion, it appears that the Catholics as a group have made very few contributions in science or mathematics. I have worked with Catholic students and Sisters, and all exhibited the same behavior: May I do this? Is it okay if I proceed this way? They cannot feel free to go on their own. I am not trying to condemn their religion or their faith, or anything like that. But I think there is a certain rigidity there, at least up to a few years ago, in the way they were taught that prevented freedom of risk taking.

GETZELS: There is a paper by David McClelland on risk taking and creativity. [See chapter 7 in this volume.] I think that is part of it.

WARD: Are you going to come to the money question before we leave?

GETZELS: Yes. It is really not a money question but a general practical question. And we have, if I may put it this way, our man from Washington here. We will call on him.

WARD: May I take a risk, since that appears (thankfully) to be appropriate in this conference? I have been prompted a half-dozen times to make at least a minispeech on a certain idea, and I'd like very much to get it in at this point—watching time closely.

GETZELS: Please.

WARD: Can we any longer afford in society, in human culture, that old cultural lag, in which I believe some fifty years were observed to transpire between the origination of a good idea and its implementation? Could we not, rather, say once a decade or so—a kind of academic or scientific generation in this era of knowledge explosions—deliberately calculate, or recalculate our gains in given bodies of information, and use the firmest residual generalizations within that field of endeavor as ground upon which to advance toward next-higher levels of inquiry? There have been, as this conference of course remarks, some fifty years of inquiry into the nature of giftedness or talent since the launching of Terman's studies; and I believe that there is from this great volume of inquiry, scattered and discrete though it is, a sufficient body of reliable information to warrant an effort toward the formulation of at least a rudimentary order, or science of Differential Education for the Gifted. I have been calling for this kind of effort for some fifteen years, and my confidence in our need for it has grown stronger with time.

Now I would like to tie this notion to the money question. As we know, federal monies are now—the proposal deadline being November 14, some six and three-quarter days from this afternoon—being given categorically for the special education of gifted and talented youth for the first time in the history of federal aid to education. Two-hundred and fifty thousand dollars is small money as things go these days, and the very wisest stewardship of this sum is indicated. Thus I would greatly like to see some portion of this sum go to a nonempirical research activity, possibly centering on a training effort as well, through which this search for order and reliable principle within a massive and loose volume of information would take place. Even a moderately successful effort of this intellectual nature would be greatly consequential. The study and direct utilization of reliably established constructs and generalizations could, and should, replace uselessly repetitious inquiry into the simpler problems; and essential research could, and should, take place above the level of primitive induction. And, most importantly, of course, youth who qualify for differentiated developmental experience would receive the benefits of what is our most discerning effort in their behalf.

Finally, lest this minispeech extend beyond intent and propriety, may I urge even in this assembly of proven researchers, and even in the tall shadow of the empirical scientist whose work is memorialized on this occasion, that the quest I am urging is a philosophic one, best mounted by persons qualified for philosophic analysis and reconstruction, as distinct from experimental. We should continually remind ourselves that Terman himself spoke of his research as being a "prolegomenon" to education; and that science is advanced by alternating transactions between controlled investigation and reflective imagination. May we paraphrase: "Terman, like Galileo, is dead; but long live Terman!" Despite the educator's apparent dread of imagination and of "theory," the man himself would, I respectfully submit, favor our breaking occasionally, and deliberately, from the perennially empirical in favor of the rational quest after order within the masses of information that have accumulated through our interest in gifted and talented youth.

WELSH: Amen.

GETZELS: Perhaps this is the time, Dave, Dr. David Jackson, he is from an organization near Washington dealing directly with the gifted. He probably knows more about the funding for the gifted, not only in government but also in the private sector, than anyone else.

JACKSON: I would like to speak first to Virgil's last statement. I am afraid that what we know about the American government would lead us to believe that the wisdom necessary to go in the direction he has outlined is more likely to be found among scientists than to be found within the political structure.

Turning to the subject of money, I believe the most significant money which is available today is available at the state level in a few states. The federal funding is beginning in a small way and will require tremendous efforts on the part of many people if it is to grow, whereas we find some surprising things at the state level. The largest expenditure at the state level for the education of gifted children is found in Florida, where a recent reformulation of the basic state-aid formula gave a factor of three to one to the gifted. However, this money is not found so much at the local level, because the money comes to the county level, where it doesn't all reach local school gifted programs. Yet Florida, Pennsylvania, Illinois, and California make multimillion dollar appropriations annually for the gifted.

There is another group of states, perhaps half a dozen, that also make substantial allocations. Yet the total number of states that make funding available to every school district in the state is today probably only about nine or ten.

The thing I would feel most strongly about, that I would like to convey to this group, is that not much is going to happen in terms of funding for the gifted until we change public consciousness in this country. We must reach the general public, and of course professional educators are part of the general public.

BROCKIE: We have had extensive experience in going to electors and trying to raise their consciousness. We have been successful in the last two years. Two bills related to improving the funding for gifted students in California have gone through the legislature with very little resistance, and in both cases they were vetoed by two different governors.

KEARNEY: Republican and Democratic.

BROCKIE: One Ronald Reagan and the other Jerry Ford [she meant Jerry Brown].

KEARNEY: What?

BROCKIE: I know why I made that slip.

GETZELS: So do the rest of us.

BROCKIE: He made the statements when he vetoed the bill and other bills in education that he intended not to sign any education bills. He wanted the education program in California to be totally reorganized. But we learned something else, incidentally, in talking with one of his advisors. He said, "Where are the parents? We don't want to listen to you. The people who want it should be the parents. They are the ones who got the funding in the first place in California." One of the women with us said, "I am a parent here. I represent several parent groups, including several hundred families." He said, "But you are with them."

KEARNEY: He also does not want to hear from students. He feels that we have used them as pawns if he hears from them, and therefore support must come from the parents themselves. I think that, in addition, another factor must be involved. That is to indicate why gifted programs will end up profiting, making all schools more profitable for all students. If it is seed money that is being used to expand educational opportunities for all children by exploring new fields, I think you will find a more ready acceptance on the part of the legislative bodies.

STANLEY: What about the possibility that you could show definite savings through, for example, the kinds of things that SMPY has tried?

KEARNEY: We have done that.

STANLEY: In other words, there could be cost-accounting efficiency. It would be very difficult to take the kind of things we do and show that they apply to all students because they clearly don't in the same degree.

KEARNEY: We use placement to make savings. We have used programs that started new directions and saved money in the sense of time and energy. We have done a number of these things. What it really boils down to is that old feeling that the gifted are going to make it in spite of us, so put the money where it is needed at the other end. We really have trouble breaking through.

BROCKIE: When you start with students already at the top, how do you show growth?

STANLEY: You get a higher ceiling for the curricula they use.

JACKSON: I would like to comment on an example of poor legislative draftsmanship in the federal program, because the section of Public Law 93383, Section 404, supporting the gifted, says that money for research shall be transferred by the Commissioner of Education to the National Institute of Education. This law was passed at a time when the climate was such that the Commissioner would in no wise make any such transfer for any purpose to the National Institute of Education.

Yes, sir, we had a little chat with one of the administrative aides to a senator, another man and I, about how we could somehow get an appropriation for research, get this actually accomplished, because one of the most severe problems we have in demonstrating the utility of programs for the gifted is that we don't have the technology available to really do a good job of finding racial and ethnic minority group children who are gifted.

Three examples of work in this area are hung up at the moment because validity studies have not been conducted. We badly need this kind of thing and we are trying to think of ways that we could get a federal appropriation to support research in this field and other fields which are badly needed.

I feel that this whole program of trying to help gifted children will gradually fall apart if we don't get some fundamental research done in the next few years.

STANLEY: And yet, Dave, we in our own efforts have studiously avoided the word research. We do some research of a sort, but we do not say the word. The word frightens teachers, parents, and legislators. Can you not somehow use other words to get around that problem?

BROCKIE: Evaluation, or is that scary?

STANLEY: Helping youngsters, developing and evaluating curricula, and so on, but leave off the "research" side as an emphasis. I don't think it will be popular. It will be the expendable part of the budget, particularly for the U.S. Commissioner of Education.

JACKSON: But there is a new popularity of honesty in this country, and I think one reason we haven't gotten too far in recent decades on the gifted is we have tried to proceed euphemistically. We have talked about the more able learners, and so on, and we have not confronted the hard question of educating the public as to what the actual needs of these students are and how it will benefit society. I think we have got to turn honest and take the longer-range point of view and do the job.

KEARNEY: California demands that we use the term gifted in any materials that go out that have to do with a legal program. It must have the term "gifted" in it. All euphemisms we are told to cross out. We are told to rephrase them. I think this is one move in that direction.

COOKE: Dr. Jackson, was not the legislation drafted so that indeed it did speak to five or six areas where universities could do research? The problem is that it was not funded at a level whereby the different kinds of things recommended by the persons who were instrumental in getting that legislation passed could take place.

FISHER: That is, I think, a very valid statement, because if there had been $10 or $15 million instead of $2.56 million, then perhaps such a transfer would have taken place. Research would have been supported.

COOKE: And to respond to Dr. Kearney here, I am surprised, if I heard you correctly this morning, when you say that you received $67 per pupil in excess costs for the gifted. We in Baltimore City spend that much in excess costs for the handicapped, and yet we had a senator from Montgomery County to pose the position that we were padding and that those funds were not needed. I applaud California for using those kinds of funds in that fashion.

KEARNEY: There is $1,800 per pupil for the handicapped in California, so it is the same percentage approach.

GETZELS: Dave, just one more. I think we would appreciate the kind of data that the rest of us do not easily come by, the ratio of funds for gifted as against, in the same bureau, the handicapped and others.

JACKSON: The gifted get about 1 percent of what the handicapped get in the Bureau for Education of the Handicapped.

KEARNEY: If we could convince the public, and I am using the word loosely, that certain children are severely handicapped by being gifted, we would end up having sympathy on our side.

PARKER: Someone spoke yesterday or this morning—maybe it was one of the youngsters last night. They took the words that you have used so beautifully so many times: Who has looked at what happens to the gifted kids who are not taken care of? I got started on that years ago, and the thing that I have found most successful when I am talking to boards of trustees, radio, television, parents, meetings, anyplace where I am talking with the public, is that I know my facts from the public health people. I bring out the child, demonstrated by the correctional agency, who is very high level, off all the tests, but who is not communicating and needs psychiatric care costing hundreds of dollars a week to the state because he was not served adequately as a gifted child when his parents went and beat on the door and got turned away. If you want to get something done, get yourself half a dozen case histories, go to your public health man, find out if he understands your ways—you have to know how to do it—and take the statements that Stanley made years ago about what happens to the kids who aren't helped. Take this to the public and say, you want to save money? Look at what is going on in your correctional institutions, what juvenile delinquency is doing in the world today. Where are our best criminals coming from? Our bright kids that get turned off; our bright kids that aren't helped. It is one thing that nobody has a comeback for. I am talking in public and to anybody from public health, corrections, mental health. You get a good psychologist or psychiatrist who counsels with kids in trouble; he can give you case after case of a kid who busts the test but is asocial. That is the kind of help that gets the parents on our side who don't have a bright kid themselves, but who see the social cost of not helping a gifted kid.

STANLEY: Dr. Hobson, who is sitting back here—

HOBSON: I have been itching, yes. I have been itching and now I am going to risk. One thing we have not addressed ourselves to is what a school system can do for itself to help solve this problem. There are two or three very practical things that can be done. I would like to say first, it is awfully hard to arouse the gifted to put on a big show to a school committee. What is the percentage of gifted? Well, even in the most favored communities you won't call it more than five percent. How much noise can five percent of the parents make against the taxpayers and the other people who don't want to spend that money? But there are things the school system can do.

In the first place, you can practice early admission. You can admit a whole flock of children, not just the gifted, but the bright, the ones who could profit by entering school a year early. All you need to do is look. Look at physiology. I don't remember the figures. As I recall, a child's brain is 90 percent grown at age six. The things that happen after he learns language, say between three and six, are much more important than what may happen to him in any other three years of his life. What you have to do, you need grist worthy of the mill. You need it for all children, but especially for gifted children.

If they differ in school, they differ before they go to school, at least a year or two before. Let's practice early admissions. [See Hobson 1963.]

There is another little strategy we can use. If you have a high school organized with department heads, it is awfully difficult to take care of individual children who show precocity in various areas down in the junior high school or in elementary school. But if you have directors of instruction, it also helps the curriculum, I might add. If you have a unified curriculum from kindergarten through grade twelve, the director of instruction has a very great say. He can arrange for the child to take some work in high school. That is not the same as picking out these children who are talented in one specific direction. I think that universities and contacts with schools around them are better fitted to do something about that.

You are better fitted in your own school system if you have a director all the way through from kindergarten to grade twelve. He can move the children up. He can make an excuse for them to go to high school and take certain things. You can do those things. Then after you prove the value of this, perhaps you can get a little money. You have to have somebody who wants to do this. It takes a lot of work. You have got to commit your superintendent. You have got to have an enlightened electorate who will elect school people who will go for something like this. If you have those things, it can be done.

It has been mentioned that teachers are not comfortable. They don't like to have people taken out of their class. I would like to suggest in closing that if you had a few Erics to put in a few classes that teachers would be very glad to have these children out.

GETZELS: Dean Worcester, perhaps you might like to comment, sir?

WORCESTER: I would like to say something. They say that pride is the worst of the deadly sins, in which case I am a grievous sinner, but my guilt has to be shared a good deal with Dr. Stanley, who has nurtured my pride so much by inviting me to come here to these meetings.

I have talked with some people who have been more or less discouraged about the outlook of the programs for the gifted. But during the time that I have vaulted into middle age, maybe I have seen a good many changes, but I think the spiral is always upward.

In the '20s we had the age of what some people call the common man. Margaret Mead called it, I believe, the age of mediocrity, when the idea was to have everybody just as near alike as they could be. We developed standardized tests, and administrators had as their ideal to bring everybody to the standard, but they had no interest in carrying anybody beyond the standard. The ideal of the typical administrator was to have a curve of distribution which would be a straight vertical line.

Then regardless of the major law passers, in Cleveland and various places we could cite over the country, we began to have quite an interest in gifted children. I took a half year to travel over the country and found they were appointing committees widely. They hadn't gotten very far, but there were a lot of individuals who were busy, and we gained something very definitely over the '20s.

Then we came into the '60s with the demand that everybody should be admitted to college, whether he was competent or not. Once he was there, there should be no grades, everybody should pass, regardless. And we had, again, a tendency to level off in our affirmative action groups. Again, I think there was a tendency more and more to have us all alike. For every place we had to find somebody who was, if not highly qualified, at least not totally incompetent from some other group to fill it.

I think I see now very definitely a swing again, another curve on the spiral, and I think it is a spiral upward. With such programs as we have here and others we could cite, I think we can see with a good deal of hope a development for some little time now, at least encouraging development, in our total interest for the gifted.

At least, that is my feeling as an optimist, and for me it is just as easy to be an optimist as a pessimist and a lot more fun.

[Applause]

GETZELS: This would be a happy note on which to stop. Yet there is still a little time until scheduled adjournment for further consideration of the last topic we mentioned at the beginning. That is the policy question of what needs to be done. Assume that California does well by gifted children and Washington does well and foundations do well, what are the kinds of ideas that they ought to entertain both in research and practice, and in other activities as well?

PAGE: Being incorrigibly an abstractor, I would like to try to put the policy question about where the money should be spent in an abstract formulation. Operations research has ways of considering such matters, once the dimension of value is specified.

Now, if we think of an outcome of an educational program as being a set of scores from tests, then one can design a program with a number of possible outcomes in mind. One of them is to maximize the sum of the scores. That has an obvious appeal, but it does mean that the resources may be spent more on the gifted than on the dull because the gifted will grow more in their scores.

Another outcome possible is to minimize the variance of the scores. This is the egalitarian approach. We want everybody to be equal, a straight vertical line of distribution. The only way you can do this is to pound the gifted on the head.

Another is to maximize the sum of scores, keeping the variance of scores no greater than before, so that we are not too offended by increased differences among people. This seems to me impossible, again without drastically handicapping the able.

Another is to maximize the sum of scores, keeping the expenses for the bright no greater than before, no greater than they would be for the rest of the distribution. This implies the kind of policy formulation that was described here, what the district can do for itself.

Well, practically, in a climate which is anti-elitist and unrealistically environmentalist, maybe this last is the necessary kind of solution. This requires a definition, an accounting of the performance and a demonstration to decision makers that you really are maximizing the score without too great an increase in the variance.

I think that can be shown. I think it can be shown in traditional research terms using objective measures, which of course is one of the brilliancies of the present SMPY.

KEARNEY: I have a concern that I would love to have someone —there are quite a few psychologists here—do something with. This is a group of gifted that we know have neurological handicaps, not enough to ever put them in our mental health programs or our programs for special education. They survive in our schools. They are certainly adequate students, but their potential has a lid on it. I know there is research done by Kephart and Cruickshank and a number of other people in the field of learning disability. I would love to see someone take on these students, work with them, and try to do something to at least relieve to some extent the problems that are causing them to perform at a level lower than their potential.

I understand it is a very expensive process. I naively suggested that if we could find $25,000, we would try to do something. I was told by our special education division that if I could find $200,000, I could probably do something. Would any of you like the project?

FOX: I think one of the problems I see with the suggestions for what the local system can do for itself is that local school systems are not good risk takers. It is very easy for them to set entrance requirements that don't have to be defended; it is very easy for them to say, your child has to be five before a certain date in order to enter kindergarten in the fall. It is very easy for them to have straight promotions: no one is accelerated, no one is held back. I think the problem is: What incentive can parents offer to the school system to make them willing to take the risk to use other criteria for entrance, more realistic criteria for entrance? That is, to make them say we believe that scores on a test indicate readiness for reading better than chronological age itself does. Therefore, we are going to let children into school earlier who exhibit this readiness. We believe that readiness for algebra is not determined well by chronological age, but has other components.

One of the problems I see is how to get the school system to be willing to put itself out on the line to make these decisions about children and then to take the responsibility. Also, the fact that some gifted children may, when challenged, fail.

I hope that maybe Dr. Kearney will respond to this. You have come the closest to describing what might be an ideal school program for the gifted. You are closer, from what we can gather, than elsewhere in the country in having risk-taking operations for students. But the state in your situation has already said you use the school board to determine these things.

KEARNEY: You need school board support. It is a permissive program in California. It does exist only with the permission of the school board. They may withdraw their support and decide you won't have a program. We have a pet line and actually we stole it from Dr. Barbour, who was the assistant superintendent in San Diego, that parents own the schools; whether they realize it or not, they own the schools because they pay the taxes that support them. If the parents really want the program and they organize and are logical and present their case persuasively and strongly, as you were talking about presenting it, I think most school districts will respond.

We happen to be involved, and I think I will pass the buck to Jane at this point, with a district that abuts ours. The parents at San Gabriel wanted a gifted program. They came to visit us.

BROCKIE: The parents felt they weren't having the services they wanted. They had a paper program that wasn't really definite. A PTA president pushed it all the way to the board and got no response. Finally, she was told, well, prove it. She got a committee of parents, and came and visited our program. They were interested in the elementary level particularly. They went back and said, this is the kind of program we want, invited us to come and show their school board. And they made their point. They were assigned a consultant who came and said, "I have got to have a program, I have got to do it similar to yours. Where do you get your teachers? May I have teachers referred to me who decided not to work for you? Will you come and in-service my teachers?" As a result of this parent pressure, they evolved the program. This happened in more than one district. We had a district closer to us than San Gabriel. I was invited to attend a meeting of parents. We went with our slide projector and handouts, thinking we would sit around in a group about like this. We arrived at the junior high school auditorium. It was overflowing. There must have been 500 parents there. We explained our program, much as we have done today, but we had more time. We went into a little more depth and showed some photographs, things children do. We were just swamped. Those parents organized a newsletter. They started charging for membership. They turned that entire school district around. It was not a diverse population; it was a homogeneous population and really an upper-middle-class community. They have a "swinging" program now, and it was totally done by the parents. They said they met resistance at the administrative level. They shopped around. Then they brought what they wanted back to their district.

PARKER: May I get on the record that childhood research is a must? I would also like to state this—that if parents and people like us let the school district get away with things that are not law but custom, it is our fault. The first thing we need to know is what the school law is in our state for our kids, and you would be surprised what is not in school law.

If you go to the principal and say it is law, and he says show me in the law, read it. He won't know what to do. Parents should take the trouble, at least one of you in your group, to read the law and tell the others what it is, what is in it. You can be polite but you can know your facts, get your information before you go, and this is what your group probably did. They came to you and got the information and they went ahead.

KEARNEY: That's right.

PARKER: If you know what is available to you, you can go and ask for it. The principal can't, but you can go down and say, the law says. You can say, show me. And about research, I want to emphasize that there is a great need for infant research as a foundation for our other research.

COOKE: In terms of research, I would like to see two areas touched, longitudinal studies with the culturally different in addition to peer identification.

PATEL: I was thinking in terms of this nation at the present going through this economic crisis which this nation has not known for many, many years. I would like to see studies on career change and studies of people capable of changing from one pattern of doing something in their lives to something else and adjusting easily. I think perhaps the gifted have this capacity, which people have not looked at. [E.g., see Sears' chapter in this volume.]

Another, I would look at the teacher in the world community. A lot of work that is done here is copied elsewhere; I would like to see a lot of cross-national, cross-cultural validity type of work done, initiated by leadership here.

WARD: In addition to all these, please, a philosophic reordering of our information and our obligation.

STANLEY: I don't want to sound overly proud, but just today I received a notice of the award of a grant from the Robert Sterling Clark Foundation, congratulating me on the symposium. They had held it up a week in order to coincide with these meetings. SMPY has a twenty-month grant to package some of the ideas that we have developed. I have been invited by the Director of the Office of Gifted and Talented of the United States Office of Education to disseminate them nationwide through his office. Within twenty months or so we should have at least three distinct packages available for implementation in various parts of the country. These will probably be about identifying mathematically highly talented youths, studying their characteristics, and setting up special fast-math classes for them.

These will be detailed programmatic packages. If we are successful for the first twenty months, we may get further support from the Clark Foundation to develop another five or six packages to disseminate.

PAGE: That is marvelous news and thoroughly deserved.

GETZELS: On this happy note again, thank you all very, very much, and unless the organizer [Dr. Stanley] wishes to say another word, we stand adjourned.

PAGE: I would like to compliment our chairman for the splendid way in which he has moderated this long, productive discussion.

GETZELS: Thank you.

[Thereupon, at 5:00 P.M., the discussion was concluded.]

REFERENCES

Anastasi, A. 1970. On the formation of psychological traits. *American Psychologist* 25(10): 899–910.

Bell, E. T. 1937. *Men of mathematics*. New York: Simon and Schuster.

Getzels, J. W. 1975. Problem-finding and the inventiveness of solutions. *Journal of Creative Behavior* 9(1): 12–18.

Hobson, J. R. 1963. High school performance of underage pupils initially admitted to kindergarten on the basis of physical and psychological examinations. *Educational and Psychological Measurement* 23(1): 159–70.

Margenau, H. (ed.). 1972. *Integrative principles of modern thought.* New York: Gordon and Breach, Science Publishers.

Neurath, O., Carnap, R., and Morris, C. (eds.). 1955. *International encyclopedia of unified science* (2 vols.). Chicago: University of Chicago Press. (Original edition, 1938.)

Schneidman E. S. 1971. Perturbation and lethality as precursors of suicide in a gifted group. *Life-Threatening Behavior* 1(1): 23–45.

Sears, R. R. 1977. Sources of life satisfactions of the Terman gifted men. *American Psychologist* 32(2): 119–28.

NAME INDEX

SUBJECT INDEX

Library of Congress Cataloging in Publication Data

Hyman Blumberg Symposium on Research in Early Childhood
    Education, 7th, Johns Hopkins University, 1975.
    The gifted and the creative.

    (Studies of intellectual precocity; no. 3)
    Includes indexes.
    1. Gifted children—Education—Congresses.
I. Stanley, Julian C. II. George, William C.
III. Solano, Cecilia H. IV. Title. V. Series.
LC3992.H95 1975   371.9'5   77-4790
ISBN 0-8018-1974-1
ISBN 0-8018-1975-X pbk.